S0-BAV-735

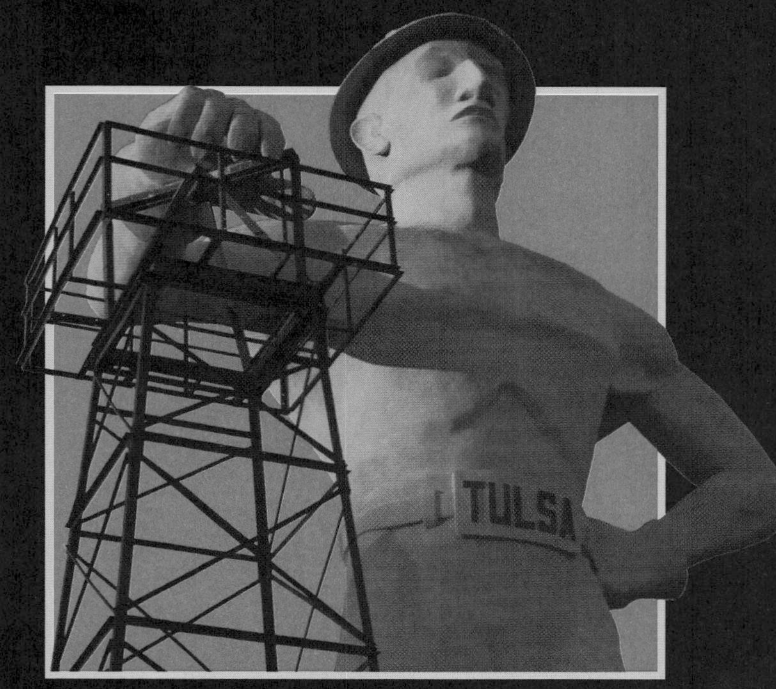

WEIRD OKLAHOMA

Weird Oklahoma

Your Travel Guide to Oklahoma's Local Legends and Best Kept Secrets

By Wesley Treat

Mark Sceurman and Mark Moran, Executive Editors

STERLING

New York / London

www.sterlingpublishing.com

WEIRD OKLAHOMA

STERLING and the distinctive Sterling logo are registered trademarks of Sterling Publishing Co., Inc.

Published by Sterling Publishing Co., Inc.
387 Park Avenue South, New York, NY 10016

Distributed in Canada by Sterling Publishing
c/o Canadian Manda Group, 165 Dufferin Street
Toronto, Ontario, Canada M6K 3H6
Distributed in the United Kingdom by GMC Distribution Services,
Castle Place, 166 High Street, Lewes, East Sussex,
England BN7 1XU
Distributed in Australia by Capricorn Link (Australia) Pty. Ltd.
P. O. Box 704, Windsor, NSW 2756, Australia

10 9 8 7 6 5

Manufactured in China.

Photography and illustration credits are found on page 239 and constitute an extension of this copyright page.

Layout and production by bobsteimle.com

Sterling ISBN: 978-1-4027-5436-4

For information about custom editions, special sales, premium and corporate purchases, please contact Sterling Special Sales Department at 800-805-5489 or specialsales@sterlingpublishing.com.

DEDICATION

Dedicated to Mary Treat, one of the four most wonderful and caring grandparents anyone could ask for, and Leon Sanders, an Oklahoman who embodied the best of the state's humor and compassion

Contents

A Note from the Marks

Our weird journey began a long, long time ago in a far-off land called New Jersey. Once a year or so we'd compile a homespun newsletter to hand out to our friends called *Weird NJ*. The pamphlet was a collection of odd news clippings, bizarre facts, little-known historical anecdotes, and anomalous encounters from our home state. The newsletter also focused on the kind of very localized legends that were often whispered around a particular town but seldom heard outside the boundaries of the community where they first originated.

We had started the publication with the simple theory that every town in the state had at least one good tale to tell. *Weird NJ* soon become a full-fledged magazine and we made the decision to actually do all of our own investigating and see if we couldn't track down just where all of these seemingly unbelievable stories were coming from. Was there, we wondered, any factual basis for these fantastic local legends that people were telling us? Armed with not much more than a camera and notepad we set off on a mystical journey of discovery. Much to our surprise and amazement, much of what we had initially presumed to be nothing more than urban legend actually turned out to be real, or at least contained a grain of truth that had original sparked the lore.

After about a dozen years of documenting the bizarre we were asked to write a book about our adventures, and so *Weird NJ: Your Travel Guide to New Jersey's Local Legends and Best Kept Secrets* was published in 2003. Soon people from all over the country began writing to us, telling us strange tales from their home states. As it turned out, what we had first perceived to be a very local-interest genre was actually just a small part of a much larger and more universal phenomenon. People from all over the United States had strange tales to tell that they believed to be true, and they all wanted somebody to tell them to.

When the publishers of the book, asked us what we wanted to do next, for us the choice was simple: "We'd like to do a book called *Weird U.S.*, in which we could document the local legends and strangest stories from all over the entire country," we told them. So for the next twelve months we set out in search of weirdness wherever it might be found in these fifty states.

In 2004, after *Weird U.S.* was published, our publisher asked us once more where we wanted to go next. In the year that it had taken us to put together *Weird U.S.* we came to the conclusion that this country had more great tales waiting to be told than could be contained in just one book. We had discovered, somewhat to our surprise, that every state we researched seemed to have more fascinating stories to offer than we actually had pages to accommodate. Everywhere we looked we found unwritten folklore, creepy cemeteries, cursed locations, and outlandish roadside oddities. With this in mind we told our publishers that we wanted to document it all, and to do it in a series of books, each focusing on the peculiarities of a particular state.

One of the first states we set out to document the weirdness of was Texas, and in Wesley Treat we found the perfect person to act as our eyes and ears in the field. We enjoyed our literary road trip with Wesley so much that as soon as he had finished his travels throughout the Lone Star State we sent him off to new weird frontiers in Arizona to write another book for us. Wesley has been traveling around the highways, byways, and back roads of America for years now, chronicling all of the out-of-the-way roadside spectacles and odd goings-on. As soon as we invited him along on our Weird ride we knew we had found a kindred spirit in strangeness. With his talent for seeking out unusual sites, his whimsical storytelling style, and his dynamic photographic technique, Wesley's appetite for unusual adventures would be immediately apparent to anyone who shares a similar wanderlust for offbeat attractions.

With a couple of Weird books under his belt and several thousand miles added to his odometer, Wesley has proven beyond a doubt that he possessed what we refer to as the "Weird Eye." The Weird Eye is what is needed to search out the sort of stories we were looking for. It requires one to see the world in a different way, with a renewed sense of wonder. And once you have it, there is no going back—you'll never see things the same way again. All of a sudden you begin to reexamine your own environs, noticing your everyday surroundings as if for the first time. And you begin to ask yourself questions like, "What the heck is that thing all about, anyway?" and "Doesn't anybody else think that's kind of weird?"

So come with us now and let Wesley take you on a tour of a state that he has come to know and love over the past couple of years. We're pretty sure that there are some stories in this book that will come as a surprise even to many native Oklahomans. With all of its haunted history, ancient mysteries, colorful characters, and eye-catching roadside oddities, it's a place we like to call Weird Oklahoma.

—Mark Sceurman and Mark Moran

Introduction

All right, we may as well get this out of the way before going any further: I'm not from Oklahoma. I'm a Texan.

Now, don't slip the book back onto the shelf just yet! Yes, yes, I'm fully aware there's a long-lived animosity that's lobbed across the border from both sides, but personally I like to think that it's all in fun. Sure, there are those who like to make scathing remarks about the other side's tendency for inbreeding or invent new and obscene gestures to flash at the opposing flag, but in all the time I've spent in Oklahoma, the worst I've gotten when admitting where I'm from is a chuckle and a "Well, we won't hold that against ya!"

Which brings me to one of the reasons I opted to write this book. Having finished two other contributions to the Weird series—one for Arizona and one, of course, for Texas—creators Mark Moran and Mark Sceurman gave me the option of which state I'd like to tackle next. It would be Oklahoma, for sure. I wanted to do my part to show there was no genuine ill will between our states and that both Okies and Texans could work together to create something fantastic.

Besides, there seemed to be a feeling on both sides of the state line that Oklahoma was more than just a little bit . . . how should we put it . . . boring? Except for a couple of casinos and a few run-of-the-mill museums, there apparently just isn't much to do there, even according to friends living north of the Red River.

It couldn't be true, I insisted. There's plenty out there to see, all across this great country. You just have to look for it. And so my journey began, combing the big cities and small towns of Oklahoma for the unusual, the exceptional, and the downright bizarre. I'll admit, it was sometimes a challenge, and I had to do a fair amount of digging in some areas to discover something truly unique, but in the end I believe I've uncovered more than enough material to prove once and for all that beneath the Sooner State's conventional facade lies a character as exciting and uncanny as any other.

So, let's save the Red River Rivalry for the Cotton Bowl and make I-35 a channel for sharing our mutual eccentricities. After all, there's nothing that brings people together like a reciprocal love of the weird. —*Wesley Treat*

CAVANAL
"WORLD'S HIGHEST HILL"

Local Legends

No matter the region, no matter the town, everywhere you go there are stories that skirt the boundaries of believability. Tales of bizarre murders, cursed locales, and demented reclusives: These are the narratives that we pass down from generation to generation, sharing them like rites of passage.

Some consider such myths and urban legends as something merely to be debunked. These stories, rather, should be cherished, recorded, and passed on. They're an important part of our culture. They're our folklore. They're as much a part of our lives as art and music.

Besides, if you dig deep enough, sometimes you just might find more truth to them than you think.

The Hex House

The spookiest parking lot on record, according to the thousands of curious looky-loos who've visited over the years, has to be the quarter block of asphalt at the corner of East Twenty-first Street and South Main Street in Tulsa.

What's so spooky about a parking lot, you ask? Good question. On the surface it looks like any other parking lot. Story is, though, that it's cursed. When the Akdar Shriners' temple held this spot before it was moved a few years ago, patrons reported strange happenings on the property, which included cars starting themselves and even spontaneously changing parking spots. The cause, apparently, was a lingering hoodoo from the ivy-covered home that once stood at 10 E. Twenty-first Street known as the Hex House. The woman who lived within was said to possess hypnotic powers, which she used in keeping two young women captive in her basement and under her control.

Admittedly, autonomous automobiles are probably just the fabrications of a few mischievous Shriners having fun with the kids who used to gather at the corner every Halloween. As hard as it may be to believe, though, the rest of the story is true—witchy woman, hex, captives, and all. It's just another case of Oklahoma's truth being stranger than fiction.

The story surfaced in 1944, when the apparently mystic inhabitant of the Hex House, who gave her name

as Carolann Smith, applied for World War II ration books at Lee Elementary down the street. She gave the names of her dogs as her two children. A few of the students, who recognized Smith from the neighborhood and knew the dogs' names, overheard the fib and tattled on her. They also informed the woman in charge that Smith and two other women had recently been seen burying a coffin in Smith's backyard late at night.

When the police were called to investigate, they discovered that the casket wasn't just the invention of some imaginative kids, although they found that it simply contained one of Smith's dogs, recently deceased. Upon searching the house, however, authorities turned up two women sleeping in Smith's cold, unheated basement with scant clothing and no blankets. They had obviously been mistreated and had been living there for a long time (in fact, several years).

Carolann Smith's real name turned out to be Fay H. Smith, though the women knew her as Mrs. Fontane. She had convinced thirty-year-old Nell Willetta Horner and thirty-one-year-old Virginia Evans to live with her, do her bidding and turn over their paychecks to her for seven years. Just months before the investigation, Smith had also taken in an eleven-year-old boy, whom she falsely presented as her nephew.

Smith had taken out life-insurance policies on all three of her tenants, an unsettling revelation considering what the police discovered next. Smith had previously issued a $25,000 policy for her maid, who was promptly and mysteriously killed by a car. A month before that, she also received a $31,000 insurance payout after her husband died. He supposedly killed himself with a shotgun, at Carolann's instigation. It seemed likely that the two women and the boy would meet their ends, too.

Meanwhile, Smith had been collecting funds from the government, under various aliases, as well as money from the father of one of the women, alleged by Smith as mentally ill and requiring the care of a nurse. These payments enabled Smith to live a luxurious life in a houseful of fine clothes, shoes, and jewelry.

Meanwhile, she regularly starved Horner and Evans, denied them all but the most basic garments, and forced them to sleep on wooden crates. Smith abused them both physically and mentally, and set the two against each other.

Yet, by their own admission, they were devoted to Smith. They severed ties with their own families and professed a loyalty to her that was described as obsessive. Smith had them convinced, through some strange, quasi-religious programming, that their piety and service would earn them a huge reward in heaven that she referred to as "the big payoff." Even after the women were released and resumed normal lives, they still couldn't explain what had happened to them. Evans later admitted in an interview, "I'll never understand the control she had over us."

The Hex House was torn down in 1975, though it's believed the basement may still exist a few feet belowground. Otherwise, the only thing left of the estate looks to be the stone retaining wall adjacent to the street and the old steps that divide it, which appear to be the same ones that once led up to the property.

As for Fay Smith, she received little more than a slap on the wrist. She was never implicated in her maid's or her husband's suspicious death, nor was she punished for the abuse of Evans and Horner. Instead, she received three years' probation and a year in prison for mail fraud, for persuading the women to lie in court during an earlier, unrelated case involving a neighbor, and for providing false information to obtain ration books.

Wintersmith Dam

The city of Ada, an hour and a half southeast of Oklahoma City, provides 150 acres of wholesome fun and outdoor activities in the form of Wintersmith Park. Officially known as the Wintersmith Park Historic District, it was developed as a collaboration between the Civilian Conservation Corps and the National Park Service in the 1930s as part of President Roosevelt's New Deal program.

It resulted in a man-made lake, an outdoor amphitheater, beautiful stone bridges, and wooded trails. Today, the park also boasts a swimming pool, ball courts, a playground, and even a small amusement park and zoo—a lovely place for a family outing.

When most of the park has shut down and night has fallen, however, it feels more like a good place for a family massacre. Though the mile and a half of paved trails are lighted, the bulbs do little to cut through the darkness and chilling quiet. The bridges look like something the Brothers Grimm might have dreamed up, and the amphitheater, spacious and welcoming in the light of day, feels like some sort of satanic arena.

If you listen to some of the locals, though, the real terror lies at the bottom of the dam that holds back Wintersmith Lake. Like some goat eating troll, an irritable man—or the spirit of an irritable man—bides his time in the spillway below, waiting for young passersby to harass. A few will disagree on the old guy's temperament, insisting he's not so quick to cause trouble, but they'll still warn you not to bother him. Otherwise, he might just dash up the embankment to the wooden overpass and assail you with flailing arms and incomprehensible threats.

No one's reported any injuries as yet, although that hasn't been much consolation to those who've suffered sudden frights and the ensuing inconvenience to undergarments.

Lake Jed Johnson

In the earlier part of the twentieth century, Lake Jed Johnson was one of the Southwest's more happening recreational spots. People flocked to the site just northwest of Lawton to grab some sun, enjoy the wildlife, and splash in the cool waters covering nearly sixty acres of Oklahoma's scenic Wichita Mountains.

These days, however, its shores are much quieter. Blame it on more modern attractions like go-cart tracks and waterslide parks if you want to, but you might also pin it on the two allegedly misfortunate spots that bookend the reservoir.

The first is a dam located at the south end of the lake. Built in the mid-1930s as an addition to the Wichita Mountains National Wildlife Refuge, it's far from a paragon of architectural design. But if you've never seen a dam up close, you might want to follow the stairs down to the water's surface, which are accessible to all visitors. On the other hand, there are those who would avoid it altogether, aware that some have experienced incidents they might describe as unearthly. According to a handful of paranormal enthusiasts, a woman died some years ago at the dam, having fallen to her death on one side or drowned on the other, depending on whom you ask.

On the other side of the reservoir a stone tower overlooks the calm waters below. Built in 1941, it was constructed with surplus money and materials left over from the erection of the dam. Sometimes mistakenly referred to as a fire-lookout tower or a lighthouse, it's actually a visitor's observation tower, though it's been closed now for a number of years.

Its closure, according to folks at the visitors' center, is supposedly due to its unusual popularity as a site for suicide attempts. The tower's sixty-foot-high veranda apparently made a spectacular jumping-off point for a final exit, and at least one person has taken his life near the tower with a gun.

Visitors today, especially those brave enough to hike to the summit after dark, will tell you that they've heard footsteps climbing the structure's spiral staircase, even though there's no way for anyone to access it these days. More common are the screams of a woman that emanate from the observation deck and echo across the lake.

Perhaps more frightening, though, is the extraordinary behavior of the local wildlife as reported by one of the site's staff. Around midnight, many of the park's bison, longhorn, and elk allegedly gather at the tower and form a circle of livestock, along with a parliament of screech owls that alight atop the tower's parapet, the animals' eyes all glowing eerily in the moonlight.

Black Magick House

Just southwest of Oklahoma City lies Kitchen Lake, a reservoir of modest size, located off South Sooner Road at Southwest 119th Street. The area has only begun to urbanize, so it's still popular with the weekend hook-and-worm crowd looking for a quiet getaway.

It's also popular with the enthusiastic paranormal research crowd, as it's purported to be the former stomping ground of the so-called Kitchen Lake Witch. About a mile down 119th, across from South Air Depot Boulevard's dead end, is where her home was once located, now little more than a concrete scar on a seemingly peaceful, grassy field. Long gone are the walls, the roof, the fixtures, and whatever implements of sorcery the inhabitant may have valued, leaving only the foundation and the remains of a brick chimney.

The house, it's said, burned many years ago, the result of arson by a terrified mob or else the witch's own misdeeds. Either way, the woman burned along with her home. Her remains, some believe, are buried nearby, which may explain the unusual phenomena witnessed here. The chimney, which remained standing until just a few years ago, is said to produce smoke as though it were still being used. Some say it's fairly common to find dead, sometimes headless, animals scattered about. Nighttime visitors are often vexed by the sound of disembodied footsteps following directly behind them. Oddly, all the trees in the immediate vicinity are dead, dying, fallen, or somehow violently split in two.

For those who care to hike another mile or so east to the nearby creek, that's where an old, neglected bridge can be found, where even further activity has been said to occur. There, people report having seen animals or other objects hanging from the trees and a strange red light darting among the surrounding branches. Piles of toys or discarded junk have been found there too, all charred by fire, the supposed actions of a vengeful sorceress looking to give back what she got.

Spare Ribs at Kitchen Lake

There's a lake in Oklahoma City called Kitchen Lake, and there's a legend there about a witch who once lived alongside of it. When her home burned to the ground, she died in the fire. There's a small area of what appears to be stone in a field that allegedly was her house, and it's been said that sometimes smoke can be seen there.

I came across a concrete slab with a rib cage on it . . .

I've been out there several times with friends and heard footsteps behind me. I didn't see headless animals hanging from trees, but my friends and I came across a concrete slab with a rib cage on it. There was a spray-painted symbol on the side of the slab, and some kind of box was laying in the grass with something like "end-o-world" written on it. I had my video camera with me and took footage of the area.

Because of the ribcage, I went to an Oklahoma City Police station on Santa Fe to report what was there. The cops were skeptical and thought it was us playing a joke, but they followed us to the site. I surrendered my camera's memory card to them and they said they'd call the medical examiner. Later that night, a police officer informed me that the medical examiner thought it might be an animal rib cage and not human.

Kitchen Lake is a drinking spot for a lot of people and I think the whole thing was a joke left by some teenagers to spook someone. *—Brian Hill, via e-mail*

The Hatchet House

Within the Gatewood Historic District of Oklahoma City lies Carey Place, a quiet block of Mediterranean- and Spanish-style homes dating to the 1930s. The somewhat narrow road, a 160-foot-wide plot once reserved for a streetcar line, skews incongruously from the otherwise parallel grid of the surrounding neighborhood.

Its layout, however, is not the only thing that sets Carey Place apart. On one particular street corner stands what the local kids all refer to as the Hatchet House, the sinister setting known for a gruesome murder that occurred several years ago. The name derives from the unusual and ominous-looking shutters that frame the house's windows, each of which features a cutout of a medieval-style ax.

Hatchet House, the sinister setting for a gruesome murder . . .

Two doors to the north, at a home with a decidedly non-concrete-colored driveway, neighbors say a little girl was brutally killed, her body dragged to the porch of the Hatchet House. The driveway on which her blood was spilled, as well as the porch on which she was dumped, were both painted red to disguise the bloodstains.

Unlike the unusual details cited in many other urban legends, both the crimson pavement and the hatchet-shaped shutters exist right where they're said to, making the location a popular destination for scare seekers at Halloween.

The Parallel Forest

Trees inside a nature preserve aren't anything surprising, but it's fair to say that one particular grove of conifers inside the Wichita Mountains National Wildlife Refuge would almost definitely arrest your attention. Situated right along SR 115, about a mile north of S.R. 49, you might not notice it at first, but hop out of the car and take the trail that leads beneath the forest's dark canopy and you'll quickly notice something pretty irregular: The trees are oddly not irregular. To the contrary, this thicket of cedar has grown in eerily tidy rows, all evenly spaced as if on a grid. Seen from the air, it forms an almost perfect rectangle of evergreen.

Truth is, this Parallel Forest, as visitors have come to call it, was planted in 1912 to grow specifically in this manner. The trees were planned as stock for fence posts and other projects, but were never harvested. Still, the uniform spacing and nearly perfect congruence makes for an environment that's unusually surreal, like some enchanted wood where you might run into creatures dreamed up by J.R.R. Tolkien.

Some seem to think the harmonious nature of the planting may, perhaps, influence some sort of spiritual balance, like a sort of supernatural tuning fork. If so, that might explain why so many people reportedly experience strange, sometimes ominous, sensations amid the trees. Some visitors find themselves unable to walk more than a few feet into the grove before having to turn around and leave. Others say they hear the sounds of ethereal voices or the beats of incorporeal Native American drummers.

Still others insist there are dubious activities going on in the Parallel Forest. Presumably up to no good, unknown visitors have erected unusual wooden structures among the trees, which look like some sort of ritual placements. Better known is the conspicuous stone circle located about two hundred yards from the forest's northeast corner, near Cedar Creek. The arrastra, a drag-stone mill used for grinding ore from local mines, was retired decades ago. There are those, however, that insist the stone circle has since been co-opted by pagan ritualists for the evocation of spirits, or even for sacrificial ceremonies.

Of course, it's hard to know for sure unless you're either in on these activities yourself or you just happen to be visiting the Parallel Forest and stumble across them at the wrong time, in which case you probably won't be talking either way.

If you want get an aerial view, the coordinates are 34.75011, –98.57894.

Dead Woman's Crossing

Look at a map between Weatherford and Hydro, about two miles north of Interstate 40, and you'll probably spot a location marked with the curious name Dead Woman's Crossing. Some maps even label the through street as Dead Woman's Road. Such titles—Dead Man's Curve, Hell's Gate, Ghost Hill—are certainly not uncommon, but they're usually known only to the locals and don't typically appear as formal designations on charted maps. Why, then, is this site so special?

The spot itself is pretty unremarkable, just a basic concrete bridge over a fairly ordinary creek. There aren't any dark roads or foreboding willows here, just a smattering of cows grazing a pretty featureless countryside. A few people might be able to tell you that a woman was once found dead here, said to have fallen, broken her neck, drowned, or was discovered hanged, but no one is ever really sure about the details or even the veracity of the story. It's customarily regarded as an old urban legend. Odd, then, that any authority would officially recognize the spot's given name.

Truth is, a woman really was found dead here, murdered more than a century ago, and her tale yet remains a mystery. Her name was Katy DeWitt James and her remains were discovered on the morning of August 31, 1905. She was found near what would become the bridge, which was at the time a simple, low-water ford used by travelers to cross Deer Creek. A man by the name of G. W. Cornell was taking his sons on a fishing trip when he stepped down from his buggy and spotted a skull lying next to his foot. The rest of James's body, nothing more than a clothed skeleton, lay a couple of feet away. By the condition of the brush, it was evident that a wagon had passed nearby not too long ago. Cornell also discovered a .38-caliber revolver with one spent casing and one unused bullet. The skull had a bullet hole behind the

right ear. The fatal bullet was found rattling around inside the skull.

Katy James had been missing for almost two months. Her father, Henry DeWitt, had dropped off Katy and her fourteen-month-old daughter, Lulu, at the train station in Custer City on July 7. Just the day before, she had filed for divorce from her husband, Martin James, and was on her way to visit her cousin in Ripley. James was an avid letter writer, so when Henry DeWitt hadn't heard from her for about three weeks after her departure, he hired a private investigator to try to find out what might have happened.

DeWitt and his detective-for-hire, Sam Bartell, traced what would have been James's route, discovering their first clues in Weatherford. Apparently, James had met a woman named Fannie Norton while on the train from Clinton, and Norton offered to put her and Lulu up for the night at her brother-in-law's place in Weatherford. Having evidently convinced James to travel with her to Hydro, Norton hired a horse and buggy, and the three set out the next morning. A little over two hours later, Norton returned alone and left for Clinton.

Upon further investigation, Bartell discovered that the two women had been seen riding near Deer Creek, at which point, they turned off into a field and disappeared. About forty-five minutes later, Norton rode out alone and stopped at a farmhouse, where she dropped off young Lulu, asking the residents to care for the tot till she returned, though she never did.

The police tracked down Fannie Norton in Shawnee and brought her in for questioning. Norton, acting very suspicious, told a shaky story in which she and Katy James had encountered a man in a covered wagon outside Weatherford, at which point James left with him. Although James's body had yet to be found, Bartell told Norton she was lying and accused her of murder. Norton denied it passionately. Yet, while no one was looking, Norton ingested a dose of poison and committed suicide right there in the police station.

This unexpected response seems to secure Norton's guilt. Not to mention the fact that the gun later found by G. W. Cornell was eventually identified as Norton's by a lawyer who had defended her after she'd used it to kill a bartender. However, certain questions remain unanswered.

First, what was Fannie Norton's motive? Some have suggested robbery, but there's little evidence, at least in the newspaper accounts of the incident, to support the theory. It was known that James was carrying $23 with her at the time, but the money was never accounted for, neither with Norton nor the body. Besides, Norton was reportedly doing all right for herself, and it seems an awful lot to go through to con James into traveling with her, put her up at a relative's for the night, rent a buggy, and ditch a valuable gun just for that little bit of cash.

Second, why did it take so long to discover Katy James's body? Two separate searches were conducted following Norton's suicide. Both were well organized, included twenty-five to fifty men, and lasted several days each. And despite the fact that the men knew which field Norton and James had disappeared into, and that the supposed murder site was next to a well-traveled crossing, no one found the body until G. W. Cornell came across it by accident after the searches were called off.

Third, why exactly did Fannie Norton commit suicide? The answer seems obvious, but you have to remember this is a woman who had killed before and had survived the subsequent murder trial unscathed. Why would the situation seem so dire this time? Plus, she was apparently hardened enough to plan out and calmly execute a premeditated murder, and sufficiently composed to gain Katy James's confidence well enough to convince her to abandon her normal travel plans and join a virtual stranger on the road. Besides, the police still had no body and no evidence against her, so imprisonment was certainly not a forgone conclusion.

As speculated in Sue Woolf Brenner's account in *The Chronicles of Oklahoma*, vol. LX, Norton may have feared retribution by an accomplice. If she had been hired to, or perhaps was threatened into, murdering James, her capture by the police may have meant a grim fate for her or her four children living in Guthrie, making suicide a preferred alternative. An accomplice might also explain the sudden appearance of James's body where it should have already been easily found by the search parties. Someone may have been concealing the corpse, but with all the blame fully on Norton, there would have been no reason to continue hiding it. In such a situation, the best thing to do would be to dump the body where it would quickly be discovered, bringing all inquiries to a close.

The obvious suspect would be James's soon-to-be-ex-husband, Martin James, who was in danger of losing all claim to the James homestead from the impending divorce. As suggested by newspaper reports, Mr. James seemed wholly unconcerned about his wife's disappearance and never participated in any search to find her. However, he was questioned during the investigation and was able to account for his whereabouts during the time of the murder. Of course, this doesn't preclude his having arranged for someone else to commit the crime. Still, he was never implicated, and he went on to remarry, sell the farm, apparently gain custody of Lulu, and leave the state.

Sadly, the uncertainties of the case will almost surely never be resolved. But at least we have answered one question, and that is why an unassuming bridge at the edge of Custer County bears the name Dead Woman's Crossing.

George Smith's Lament

It's hard to say just what caused the accident that took Robina Smith's life in 1936, but one might presume it was due in part to freezing weather conditions. Traveling on Highway 183 in western Oklahoma, Robina's car collided with a creamery truck, killing the young woman instantly.

When police arrived, they discovered several victims who, although having survived the impact, had frozen to death lying on the icy roadway waiting for help. More gruesome, Robina herself perished when the floor-mounted gearshift skewered her head. She was nineteen.

Yet what bothered her father George the most about the accident was that Robina had not received salvation before she died. Though her headstone reads ASLEEP IN JESUS, Robina had apparently not yet accepted the Lord into her heart as George had hoped, and thus would not reach that great stratocumulus playground in the sky. It was a tragedy that would haunt the man for nearly four decades, up until his own death in 1972—then, perhaps, even into the afterlife.

Near the Smiths' gravesite, visitors to the Arapaho Cemetery continue to hear George's grief-stricken cries. According to those who've heard it, the disembodied voice calls out, "Oh no! Oh my God! Robina has not been saved!" The first report came in 1979 from a minister who was performing a nearby funeral service. This was followed a few months later by a couple leaving flowers at the grave of a loved one. Some of those who've been startled by the voice hadn't even heard the story of George and Robina Smith, yet could clearly understand what was being said.

Several victims . . . had frozen to death . . . waiting for help.

Due to the scarcity of reports, it seems that the phenomenon is fairly rare, although some say your chances of hearing the voice are better if you go to the cemetery at night. Taunting George with inappropriate comments about his daughter, though, doesn't seem to help.

The Smith plot can be found near the center of the circular drive running through Arapaho Cemetery, located at E1000 Road and N2270 Road, southwest of Arapaho.

Vivia Thomas

Within the barracks and other log buildings that make up the remains of Fort Gibson, a restlessness persists. The sounds of footsteps, of doors opening and closing, and of disembodied voices echo through the otherwise quiet buildings. And among them, on occasion, resonates the weeping of a former soldier, an easily recognizable inhabitant who cries with an oddly feminine voice.

The voice, they say, is that of a woman in disguise, a woman named Vivia Thomas, whose tragic story of lost love has been told around these parts for well over a century. Sometimes credited as the first woman to enlist in the U.S. Army, she donned the uniform of a soldier to seek revenge against a man who had scorned her.

Vivia's tale began in Boston, where she was a wealthy young society woman living the good life among the city's upper crust. She had everything she wanted, even the love of a dashing young fellow who had asked for her hand in marriage. Yet, sadly, her dream didn't last. On the day she was to be wed, her fiancé disappeared, leaving young Vivia at the altar, crying and brokenhearted.

Though she marched on as best she could for months thereafter, Vivia never fully recovered. And when she learned that her former lover had absconded to Oklahoma Territory, she sought him out to set things straight.

The man who broke her heart, she discovered, had made his way to Fort Gibson, where he joined up with the army and quickly rose to the rank of lieutenant. What's more, he was now seeing an Indian woman. Angered by what he had done to her, Vivia hatched a plan of revenge. She hacked off her hair, disguised herself as a young man, and joined the army herself.

Now able to keep tabs on the lieutenant, she waited until he rode out to meet his new lover one evening, then snuck away to intercept him. Finding him alone on horseback, Vivia confronted the man who had betrayed her love and shot him dead. When a patrol discovered his body the next day, they assumed he had been killed by Indians.

The guilt of his murder tore at her. Despite what the young man had done to her, Vivia realized she still loved him. Night after night, Vivia braved the cold of winter to visit his grave, weeping and begging for forgiveness, until one morning she was discovered covered in snow, frozen to death.

Her disguise uncovered, the fort's chaplain stepped forward, to whom Vivia had confessed just before her death, to reveal her story. She was then buried in one of the fort's three cemeteries beneath a simple sandstone marker bearing the name VIVIA.

Since then, all three graveyards have been consolidated into the Fort Gibson National Cemetery, where you can still find Vivia's gravesite near its original location, though today it lies within the esteemed Officers Circle and is marked by a white marble stone bearing her full name and the date of her death, January 7, 1870.

The April Fool's Day Deaths of Frank and Susan Labadie

Only a handful of headstones in Copan's lonesome Labadie Cemetery, located on C.R. 3011 a mile south of SR 10, reveal the names of those who lie beneath them. Most, which lie outside the protection of the iron fence, are simple, native stones that could easily be mistaken for incidental rubble if it weren't for the more carefully tended markers nearby.

The reason most visitors come here is to see the graves of Frank Labadie Jr. and his wife, Samantha, marked by the largest of the stones. As revealed by the inscription, they both died on April Fool's Day, 1935.

Some believe the Labadies' simultaneous deaths were the result of a bizarre murder-suicide. Many insist that Frank, for reasons that are numerous and diverse, went crazy and tossed his wife and children from the third-story window of their home, then offed himself out of guilt or as the result of one final dose of crazy.

According to legend, Frank and Samantha had trouble conceiving a child. As a result, Frank, whose heart was set on becoming a father, was distraught, and he distanced himself more and more from his wife. In the years that followed, Samantha turned to the couple's slave, a man named Enos Parsons.

When Samantha became pregnant, Frank believed the child was his. In the months leading up to the birth, he was ecstatic, happy that he would finally have a family. Of course, when the child arrived, it was obvious that Frank wasn't the father. Enraged, he grabbed his rifle and unloaded it into Parsons's chest. He then discarded the victim's body, along with the baby, in the Caney River.

It's said that for years thereafter, Frank became increasingly unsettled by the restless spirits of Parsons and the infant. It is impossible to say whether it was simple remorse or unforgiving specters that tormented him. In the end, Frank took a revolver and shot both Samantha and himself, bringing an end to whole the ordeal. Or did he?

Living relatives of the Labadie family will tell you the entire thing is just a legend. When the story reportedly popped up in a local magazine, family members wrote in to report that Frank and Samantha died from carbon-monoxide poisoning from a poorly ventilated gas stove. Moreover, the ruins that locals refer to as the Labadie mansion, a set of crumbling stone walls that stand atop a private hill about a mile from the cemetery, wasn't the home where Frank and Samantha lived, or died. Apparently the house actually belonged to George Labadie, their son. (Yes, they did, in fact, have a son.)

Nevertheless, visitors who know the location of the Labadies' purported mansion say they regularly experience unusual incidents there at night. Red lights are seen among the trees, as well as shadowy animals that aren't afraid of intruders or the smell of burned flesh. Many have said that any sort of electrical or electronic devices, such as cameras, malfunction with annoying frequency. Worse yet, flashlights frequently leave visitors stranded in the dark.

Apparently, whether there's any truth to the Labadies' story or not, something up there doesn't like visitors.

Ancient Mysteries

For as long as man has been around, there's an astonishing amount of information that predates his own knowledge. The human race has forgotten more than it knows. So many experiences have faded into the past, records of their ever taking place either lost or never created. Where "prehistoric" may once have conjured images of dinosaurs and bubbling tar pits, it now encompasses whole chunks of even the most recent generations of humanity.

On occasion, though, we stumble across traces of these lost eras. Be they entire burial chambers or a smattering of inscrutable symbols carved in stone, they stand as evidence that certain limbs in humankind's family tree were swinging in unknown directions. Sun-worshipping Celts, intrepid Vikings, and pre-Columbian gold miners might all have been up to shenanigans unknown, and right here in Oklahoma.

Rock authority says 'natural phenomenon'

Strange dolomitic rock formations found at an excavation site near Edmond are natural phenomenon, according to a statement by noted southwestern archeologist Dr. E. W. Haury, quoted in an Oklahoma City newspaper.

Haury, retired chairman of ... archeology department at ...zona University, was ...t in by the newspaper to ...ontroversy over origin ... range formation. Con... pinions by experts ...er whether the rock ...l under 33 inches of ...psoil, was the site ...ehistoric camp, or ...as in fact a freak ...

...id he had no doubt ...ion was a natural ...n of sedimentary or... said a shallow lake ...ably once covered the ...nd he was familiar with ... formations in Arizona.

Queried about discovery of an apparent tool found at the site, Haury was quoted as saying the object had no relationship to the formation. He said if it was in fact a tool, finding it by the formation was a coincidence.

Haury was quoted as attaching no significance to holes found exactly one rod apart. He explained they could have been caused by seepage.

Art and drama in OCC exhibit

Drama and an art auction will be combined at Oklahoma Christian College Friday and Saturday.

Beginning at 7:45 p.m. each night will be "Animal Farm," a two-act play adapted from George Orwell's book, under the direction of George Mastick, a member of the OCC speech department.

Paintings by Tom Williams, chairman of the OCC art department, will be on sale both nights. Bids on the paintings, which will be hanging in the lobby of Hardeman Auditorium, should be submitted in writing.

Deer Creek student listed on honor roll

Dan Lee Knight, Deer Creek, has been named to the Dean's Honor Roll for the spring semester at Eastern Oklahoma State College for making a B-or-better average in 15 - or- more hours.

Seventeen students made the President's Honor Roll with all A's and another 221 earned a B-or-better average and were listed on the Dean's Honor Roll.

Spiro Mounds

They certainly aren't much to look at today, but the earthen mounds that make up Spiro Mounds Archaeological Park in far eastern Oklahoma remain among the most valuable Native American sites in the United States. Not only is the place an important vestige of the country's history, but also a source of unbelievable treasure.

Of course, "treasure" means different things to different people and, unfortunately, to the men who first realized the mounds' potential, it meant a quick buck in exchange for Indian gewgaws. This led to almost complete destruction of the mounds' most important structure and a potentially huge loss of Native American culture and history. Thankfully, though, it also led to the protection of this and other such sites and a more careful study of their importance.

From about A.D. 950 to 1450, the Spiro Mounds site served as a Native American settlement, ceremonial center, trading point, and mortuary, and it stands as the westernmost outpost for the Mississippians, a culture that grew out of the Mississippi River Valley and spread across much of what is now the eastern United States. Though not the largest settlement of the Mississippian culture, Spiro stands unprecedented in the amount of wealth accumulated by its people.

The site comprises twelve known mounds, nine of which were platforms either for religious structures or for the leaders' homes. Two others served as temple mounds, where important rituals are presumed to have been carried out. The final mound, known as Craig Mound (named for a family that once owned the property), served as a burial ground and quickly became the site's primary attraction.

The earliest recorded landowners were quite protective of the mounds, forbidding any digging. In fact, one of the original owners, Rachel Brown, was rather superstitious about the site. She claimed to have seen strange blue flames, ghosts, and even, oddly, a team of cats pulling a small wagon in circles around the mounds. Unfortunately, such stories didn't deter interest in the site and didn't stop a few trespassers from reportedly putting shovel to mound when no one was looking, though few got away with anything.

In 1933, however, things changed. Aware of the sorts of artifacts found in other such mounds, a group of treasure seekers formed the Pocola Mining Company and struck a deal to allow digging on Craig Mound. Coal miners were hired to do the majority of the digging, which resulted in haphazard tunnels perforating the mound like Swiss cheese. They kept only what they considered most valuable, trampling over countless irreplaceable artifacts and destroying the integrity of the mound.

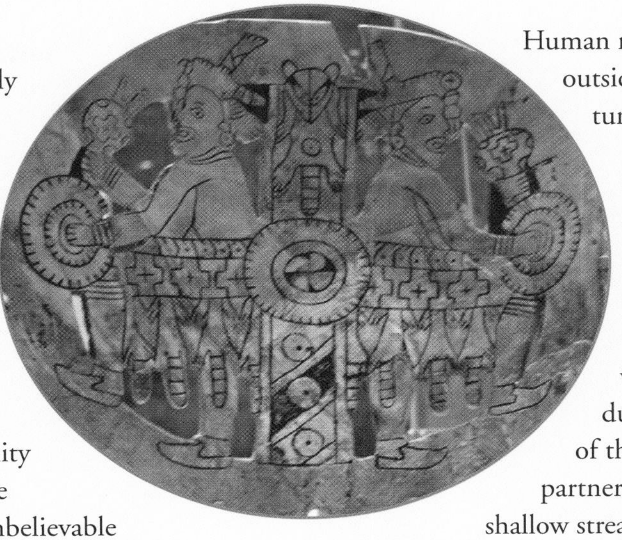

Still, what the men found was astounding. Craig Mound was actually four mounds connected together, measuring 350 feet in length. The northernmost and largest of its cones, which stood approximately thirty-three feet tall, held what became known as the Great Mortuary, topped by a central hollow chamber, protected by a wooden frame and hardened earth. Inside were the skeletons of community leaders—on cedar-pole litters, in cane boxes, and in baskets—along with unbelievable wealth. Excavators found copious amounts of effigy pipes, copper breastplates, stone maces, engraved conch shells, wood carvings, garments, and more. Looters were said to have taken up to two gallon jugs filled with pearls. There was even a copper box containing what appeared to be surgical instruments, though that was soon stolen, never to be recovered. Spears, ear spools, ornamental axes, inlaid masks, statues, scepters, embossed copper, conch pendants, and around 1,200 pounds of shell beads—in fact, more than can be listed here—were all carted out by the wheelbarrow. Spiro proved to be the largest treasure trove of pre-Columbian Indian artifacts ever found north of Mexico.

With so much disappearing so quickly, the state passed an antiquities act in 1935 to further protect the mounds. Unfortunately, the Pocola Mining Company paid little attention. They were forced off the property, but as soon as the police were gone, the diggers returned to dig out as much as they could before their lease ran out. They stripped the central chamber of its artifacts, carelessly strewing beads, arrow points, and pottery across the ground to be crushed underfoot. Structural cedar poles were burned as firewood. Human remains were dumped in a pile outside of camp, where they soon turned to dust.

When the story reached the newspapers, the site was touted as the American version of King Tut's tomb, complete with a similar reputation of being cursed, as it was connected with three deaths that occurred during the dig. R. W. Wall, one of the Pocola Mining Company's partners, drowned in a suspiciously shallow stream; twelve-year-old James Craig, of the family that owned the property, died of tuberculosis "in the shadow of the mound"; and a lawyer who opposed the 1935 antiquities bill died just before it went to a vote.

Still, sightseers, collectors, and relics dealers flocked to what they called the Great Temple Mound (now called Craig Mound) to get a look and to buy up as many items as they could. Sadly, little reached the hands of genuine archaeologists or museum officials. What's more, no one kept any records, and just before the Pocola men abandoned the site, they blasted it with dynamite. The whole ordeal was deemed quite conservatively "an archaeological crime."

By the time the University of Oklahoma arrived to excavate Craig Mound in 1936, the site was an utter disaster. Nevertheless, they did their best to conduct a systematic excavation of what remained and retrieved a surprisingly large number of remaining artifacts. The mound was in such bad shape, though, that it ultimately had to be leveled. Sadly, what sits inside Spiro Mounds Archaeological Park today is a mere re-creation, but its remaining treasures can still be enjoyed by all.

Prehistoric Pavement

For some, the summer of 1969 represents an age of innocence, a recollection of youth and the best days of one's life. For those paying attention to the headlines in Oklahoma City, that summer was about a different sort of controversy: Was the OKC suburb of Edmond the site of a lost, prehistoric civilization or were a pair of otherwise accomplished geologists and story-hungry newspapermen just letting their excitement get the best of them?

Construction crews were grading undeveloped land near the Broadway Extension at 122nd Street and uncovered what appeared to be a section of tiled mosaic flooring three feet beneath the dirt. Workers weren't quite sure what they were looking at, but it was unusual enough to prompt the tilting of a few hardhats and the scratching of heads.

The tiled flooring contained several well-rounded holes across its foundation, suggesting some sort of structural planning. It seemed as though the bulldozers had just uncovered the remnants of a forgotten civilization.

A petroleum geologist from Oklahoma City, Durwood Pate, was called out to investigate. The stones, Pate said, were placed in perfect sets of parallel lines that intersected to form a diamond shape, which pointed to the east. Pate also observed that the distance between the holes measured exactly one rod, a nearly forgotten unit of length equal to five and a half yards. As Pate told reporters at the *Edmond Booster*, "I am sure this is manmade. . . . Everything is too well placed to be a natural formation." The underlying surface of the stone was rough, he noted, but the top was much flatter, as though worn smooth through use, leading him to believe that the floor was an artifact of one or more shelters. "The Mayan Indians of Central America used stone floors," Pate explained. The Plains Indians weren't known for doing the same, he added, "but it is possible they could have."

Robert E. Bell, professor of anthropology at Oklahoma University, did not agree. The floor, in his estimation, was a natural deposit of sandstone and lime, similar to formations he had found elsewhere. He also noted the absence of any mortaring substance. The so-called floor, he said, was geological.

No wood or other such item could be found nearby, however, so carbon dating could not be performed to determine a possible age for the structure.

Unfortunately, the debate was never resolved and the disputed mosaic floor was lost forever to progress.

Rock authority says 'natural phenomenon'

Strange dolomitic rock formations found at an excavation site near Edmond are natural phenomenon, according to a statement by noted southwestern archeologist Dr. E. W. Haury, quoted in an Oklahoma City newspaper.

Haury, retired chairman of the archeology department at Arizona University, was brought in by the newspaper to settle controversy over origin of the strange formation. Conflicting opinions by experts centered over whether the rock layer, found under 33 inches of red clay topsoil, was the site of some prehistoric camp, or whether it was in fact a freak of nature.

Haury said he had no doubt the formation was a natural phenomenon of sedimentary origin. He said a shallow lake had probably once covered the area, and he was familiar with such formations in Arizona.

Queried about discovery of an apparent tool found at the site, Haury was quoted as saying the object had no relationship to the formation. He said if it was in fact a tool, finding it by the formation was a coincidence.

Haury was quoted as attaching no significance to holes found exactly one rod apart. He explained they could have been caused by seepage.

Art and drama in OCC exhibit

Drama and an art auction will be combined at Oklahoma Christian College Friday and Saturday.

Beginning at 7:45 p.m. each night will be "Animal Farm," a two-act play adapted from George Orwell's book, under the direction of George Mastick, a member of the OCC speech department.

Paintings by Tom Williams, chairman of the OCC art department, will be on sale both nights. Bids on the paintings, which will be hanging in the lobby of Hardeman Auditorium, should be submitted in writing.

Deer Creek student listed on honor roll

Dan Lee Knight, Deer Creek, has been named to the Dean's Honor Roll for the spring semester at Eastern Oklahoma State College for making a B-or-better average in 15 - or- more hours.

Seventeen students made the President's Honor Roll with all A's and another 221 earned a B-or-better average and were listed on the Dean's Honor Roll.

The Heavener Runestone

A winding stairway, composed of what seem to be more than a thousand clumsy steps, carry you down into a damp ravine. The noise of civilization quickly fades and gives way to the trickle of water and soft rustle of green foliage. If you're lucky enough to avoid any other visitors, you find yourself in a private world of serene seclusion.

Reaching the bottom, you're confronted with a skylit cabin. Too large to be a utility shed, yet too narrow to make for any kind of livable space, its purpose might be a complete mystery if you hadn't just purchased two souvenir coffee mugs at the top of the stairs. But you know why you're here. You've come to see one of Oklahoma's great enigmas: the Heavener Runestone.

The imposing, twelve-foot-tall slab was discovered around the 1830s by Choctaw Indians. At the time, no underbrush obscured the view atop Poteau Mountain, where the runestone remains, leaving the monolith to stick out conspicuously like a huge broken tortilla chip. The meanings of the eight peculiar symbols carved into its surface were collectively a mystery.

Nevertheless, the stone became somewhat of a local attraction, and for a time the monument was known as Indian Rock.

Then in 1923 a man sent a copy of the symbols to the Smithsonian Institution and received a response stating that the characters were definitely runes (an ancient form of alphabet) and probably Scandinavian in origin. For decades thereafter, specialists studied the inscription, and many agreed that the message had indeed been left by ancient Vikings.

Of course, the thought of horn-helmeted Norsemen trekking across the Sooner State seems absurd. How could explorers from northern Europe have ventured so far inland and have done so hundreds of years before Christopher Columbus claimed the land in the name of Spain? Well, it's been established that Norwegian explorers traveled successfully across the Atlantic Ocean and settled both Iceland and Greenland. Moreover, famed Norse explorer Leif Ericson is regarded as the first European to set foot on North America, which he did five hundred years before Columbus at what is now the Canadian island of Newfoundland. So, according to researchers, it may not be that great a stretch to consider that Vikings followed the North American coast and entered the Gulf of Mexico. There they could have used their wide, shallow-bottomed boats to follow the Mississippi River into the continent's interior. Fantastic? Yes. Impossible? Probably no more so than sailing three ships across more than four thousand miles of unknown open ocean.

The monument at Heavener is not the only runestone in the area. In fact, two other smaller stones have turned up near Heavener, as well as three more near Poteau, Shawnee,

and Turley. Locals have reported the existence of several more over the years, but most have been lost to vandals and treasure hunters.

So the question remains: What does the Heavener Runestone say? Unfortunately, no one quite knows for sure. Epigraphers have argued over translations for decades. Runes, as it turns out, can be rather difficult to interpret. Scholars and cryptographers have proposed names, dates, and warnings as possible transcriptions. However, the most compelling translation so far appears to be a pithy land claim: GLOME WUZ HERE.

Heavener: Rife with Artifacts

In addition to its inscrutable runestone, which has become such a popular attraction that it warranted its very own state park, the city of Heavener appears to have become a kind of vortex for unexplainable anachronistic artifacts.

In 1928, a miner was working a coal deposit a couple of miles north of Heavener when he struck the side of an unusual structure deep underground. The man, Atlas Almon Mathis, was blasting away a section of coal when he uncovered what appeared to be several man-made blocks. Mathis, whose story has been recounted in several publications, reportedly described his discovery thus: "There were several concrete blocks laying in the room. These blocks were 12-inch cubes and were so smooth and polished on the outside that all six sides could serve as mirrors. Yet they were full of gravel, because I chipped one of them open with my pick, and it was plain concrete inside."

Part of the room in which Mathis was working soon collapsed, exposing even more of the apparently ancient structure. When the air cleared, he was able to see "a solid wall" of polished blocks. Mathis also added that about 100 to 150 yards farther down the tunnel, "another miner struck this same wall, or one very similar." Evidently, the subterranean structure extended for quite a distance.

The coal that was being mined, and in which the wall was found embedded, was dated at around 286 million years old. Unfortunately, no further research was conducted to determine how the structure got there. According to Mathis's story, officials at the mining company pulled everyone out, closed that section of the mine, and told everyone not to talk about what they saw. Most interesting is that this story appears to be a repeat of a similar event that took place in Wilburton two years earlier, in which miners found a similar wall, as well as a solid block of silver cast in the shape of a wooden barrel. No further details of this previous incident exist.

Almost fifty years later, author Gloria Farley, who spent much of her life researching the famed Heavener Runestone, stumbled across another object. In September 1976 an acquaintance asked her to identify a coin that he had found while working around Heavener's Hamilton Homes. The man, Wilbert Stewart, obtained the object in a ditch, though he could not identify it as a coin before he spent two hours scrubbing at the patina that had encrusted it. The coin was described as being a little smaller than a quarter with an apparently Roman profile on the front, and an eagle holding a thunderbolt on the back. Both sides were inscribed in what appeared to be Greek.

The coin was offered for study. A coin expert identified it as a bronze piece called a tetradrachm, struck in Antioch, Syria, in A.D. 63. The profile proved to be that of Nero, with the inscription on the front reading NERO CAESAR AUGUSTUS. Though it's not considered a rare coin, how did it get to Oklahoma? No one in the housing unit where it was found knew anything about it. Besides, the thickness of the encrustation suggested that the coin had been mislaid for quite some time.

The Nero Coin, as it came to be called, might have been considered a fluke except that an even older coin was found nearby soon thereafter. It was uncovered by an amateur treasure hunter named Jessie Kelley, who found it just six inches deep in the earth near Cauthron, Arkansas, just nineteen miles from Heavener. Farley's colleagues identified it as a bronze coin almost certainly struck in ancient Carthage, a city in northern Africa that was destroyed in 146 B.C. Farley's experts concluded: "There is no question of its antiquity or its authenticity. . . . Indications are that it has remained buried for centuries." This determination precluded the idea that the coin simply belonged to a numismatist who strolled the countryside with his prized possessions and an unfortunate hole in his pocket.

And these weren't the only coins to be found in Oklahoma. Others have popped up, as well, including two minted around 200 B.C., one found by a farm boy in southern Oklahoma, the other scratched up by a hen in the eastern part of the state. The coins, curiously, were identical, both minted in the ancient Italian colony of Thurium. The questions raised by the discoveries were probably best summed up by one of the researchers involved, when he asked, "Is it really possible that a collector of ancient Thurium coins has gone about scattering his material all over eastern Oklahoma to be dug up by farm boys and chickens?" Or, as the question suggests, were these coins, and those like them, lost by those who actually carried them as working currency?

Maybe the only question that remains now is: What will be discovered next?

The Anubis Caves

Evidence seems to be mounting that shows the gun-jumping, land-grabbing Okies of yore may well have been Laters rather than Sooners. Case in point: stone carvings have been found in remote regions of the state that depict ancient symbols and languages, which together suggest there may have been visitors to the plains as early as 2,500 years ago.

The most telling of these petroglyphs lie in an out-of-the-way stretch of private land, the exact location of which remains a guarded secret. Comprising five shallow rock shelters in a short, sandstone cliff side, the site holds some of the most interesting collections of archaic symbology ever studied.

Although others have known about the site for some time, evidenced by graffiti dating to the 1800s, it wasn't truly "discovered" until the 1970s when a number of archaeologists were invited by the landowner to have a look. It was then that the true significance of the site was realized, as Gloria Farley, known for her work on Oklahoma's Heavener Runestone, immediately recognized the cave's most prominent figure as an Egyptian deity. Originally thought to be a mere drawing of a coyote—a position still held by skeptics—the long, conspicuous ears and the flail protruding from its back appear to match ancient images of the jackal god known as Anubis, for whom the immediate cave, and the site collectively, have now been named.

Among the marks covering the back wall of Anubis Cave is a star map comprising the constellations Perseus, Auriga, Taurus, Orion, and Cetus, which are all in their relative astronomical positions.

Scholars became excited at the prospect that the Anubis Caves were used as a solar observatory. Perhaps most interesting among the petroglyphs is an alleged image of Mithras, a sun god once popular among soldiers in the Roman Empire. Mithras appears to be holding a sword and wearing a cape and rayed crown, all items with which Mithras has been depicted in early reliefs and statues. The figure stands atop a three-dimensional cube, believed to represent the earth, and flanks an image of the setting sun.

The northernmost cave, nicknamed Compass Cave, features an asterisk-like symbol carved into the floor, the lines of which precisely indicate the four cardinal directions (north, south, east and west), the plane of the ecliptic (the path the sun follows through the earth's sky), the latitude of the cave's location, and the direction of the sun on the horizon during the summer solstice.

Moreover, the petroglyphs within Anubis Cave line up perfectly with shadows cast by the feature's opening during the spring equinox. Four separate images of the sun, three of which surround Mithras himself, are illuminated and obscured in sequence as the moment of equinox approaches. Just as the sun reaches the mesa dominating the view to the west, the head of Mithras, which itself looks like the sun, falls into shadow along with the largest sun image to his right.

The caves' significance was strengthened when interpreters discerned that several sets of vertical lines carved into the walls were a form of writing called ogham, translating into Old Gaelic. Once translated, the inscriptions spelled out statements like, "In the month of June reaches the illumination this far out," "The sun belongs to Bel. This cavern on the days of the equinox is for the chanting of prayers to Bel," and "Instructions for the Druid. In clear weather the projecting piece of rock eclipses the blaze at sunset. This shadow will reach nearly to the jaw of the image of the jackal divinity."

So, who left these marks? Evidence seems to point

toward a Celtic culture that somehow traveled here from Europe and possibly integrated with Native Americans. Egyptian influence may have infiltrated Europe by way of the Romans and their vast empire. Although the Romans never officially adopted the Egyptian Anubis, he was often associated with Sirius of the heavens and may have somehow carried over from Rome's rule over Egypt.

On the other hand, could the Anubis Caves have been a hoax? If so, it's a highly elaborate one that would have taken a well-educated person a lot of effort to accomplish. It seems unlikely.

Of course, there is much more to the Anubis Caves than can be covered here. Scholars continue to discover symbology amid the petroglyphs that further enrich the story of those who left them here. Will their full secret ever be unlocked? It's hard to say. If nothing else, though, the caves may suggest that the history of this continent isn't as clear as we once thought.

David Campbell's Fortress

The details were vague, but the story itself was too interesting to ignore. It had come from David Campbell in Colbert, Oklahoma, who claimed to have spoken with an old-timer possessing knowledge of some ancient stone tablets he'd found in a cave. The tablets, containing a strange script, had been discovered near a collection of bones belonging to what the elderly man referred to as "little people."

Campbell, a writer and amateur archaeologist, couldn't help but investigate. He and his wife, Sue, went to the home of the elderly man, dubiously named "Mr. Self," and inquired about the find. Unfortunately, the elder denied any knowledge of tablets or skeletons. His granddaughter did, however, point the couple to a few local sites where they might have a look for artifacts.

On their own, the Campbells hiked through the trees in search of anything out of the ordinary. They never found any trace of the tablets or the remains mentioned to them, but they did stumble across a collection of rather interesting stones. Though somewhat worse for wear, the unnatural formations were composed of concentric layers of hardened minerals. The dense black stones, some rectangular and others more amorphous, were all fitted tightly together and appeared to look like cells in a honeycomb.

David recalled accounts of ancient miners who had worked in the area, and thought that he and his wife might very well have discovered the charred remains of an old smelting furnace. The striations in the stones, he believed, were due to repeated and intense heating and cooling. His research revealed prehistoric copper and iron furnaces that had been discovered in Ohio, Georgia, Virginia, New Mexico, and Arizona, and he believed that this was of similar construction. David was familiar with the story of a sixteenth-century Spanish expedition that had traveled as far as eastern Oklahoma in search of the mythical Seven Cities of Gold. He theorized that he and his wife might have stumbled across a fortress and gold-smelting furnace that once stood as one of those fabled seven cities.

Since then, other formations similar to the Campbells' discovery have been found, one about two hundred miles to the northeast in Petit Jean State Park in Arkansas. Often referred to as "carpet rock," such formations are regarded as a natural phenomenon resulting from the fracturing and erosion of sandstone and the influence of quartz and oxidizing iron.

David Campbell's discovery gained intrigue, however, after a comparable site was located near the first, this time allegedly featuring symbols carved into the rock. Investigators began to excavate the site, but it was quickly shut down, bulldozed, and buried, reportedly by government officials. According to someone close to the family that owned the land, the family was told to forget what they saw and were warned not to let anyone else dig there.

The story results in a whole new wormy can of questions that, unfortunately, will probably never be answered.

Healing Rock

As the U.S. Army Corps of Engineers neared the final completion stage of building the new, man-made Skiatook Lake in the late 1980s, members of the Native American Church brought to their attention that an ancient and sacred artifact was about to be lost. The object, once known as Teepee Rock, had not only played an important role in local history, but was said to possess unexplained powers of healing.

Now known as the Healing Rock, or the Healing Stone,

it measures about seventeen feet wide and juts approximately nine feet above the earth, looking much like the tip of an arrowhead. Approach it in the right light and it looks like a pyramid, but just as the cartoon man who appears fat but then turns out to be wafer thin, the stone, upon closer inspection, reveals itself to be only about a foot thick. The unusual thing about the stone is its placement, its apex pointing toward the sky almost perfectly perpendicular to the earth—an orientation that geologists have determined to be the result of entirely natural processes.

According to what little history could be unearthed about the rock, its apparent curative properties weren't discovered until the late 1800s. It was at this time that a Caddo Indian named John "Moonhead" Wilson began to visit the Osage and Quapaw Indians of the area in the hope of establishing a new cooperative religion. Moonhead brought with him the ceremonial Ghost Dance, the ritual use of peyote, and according to many stories, a practice that put him into a deathlike trance for up to three days before mysteriously coming back to life. Wilson reportedly went into this trance and deathlike state at the foot of Healing Rock.

In another story, Moonhead, suffering an unspecified injury, lay helpless against the stone for several days while an opossum licked his wounds and brought him food. Other Indians, suffering various illnesses or infection, were left in the sun near the stone to recover. As recently as the 1940s, people have seen Native Americans carrying someone on a stretcher to the Healing Rock.

Thankfully, the Corps of Engineers recognized the stone's importance and relocated it before it disappeared beneath the surface of the lake. Today, it can be found at the end of a short trail behind the Skiatook Lake Project Office on Lake Road.

Fabled People and Places

Oklahoma is not just a state. It's an indefinable landscape with a history both notorious and peculiar, filled with unusual characters brave enough to venture across its plains at a time when most of the land remained shrouded in mystery.

That's not to say much has changed. Oklahoma is still filled with unusual characters and many of its parts continue to linger in mystery. However, there are those that have revealed just enough about themselves as to remain seductively ambiguous: people who've left behind tales so odd as to make them almost mythical, and locations imbued with histories so marvelous that they approach complete disbelief.

And yet something makes us want to believe. Some part of us, however strange, hopes that these tales of mislaid treasure, of lost underground dwellings, of men impervious to death, are just as true as they purport to be.

ITED
BY
T.BOAG
WHUSKA
OKLA

John Stink, Osage Zombie

By the time Osage Indian Ho-tah-moie was laid to rest in the late 1930s, interment to him was old hat. It was, after all, his second burial. The first one, performed about fifty years prior, just didn't take.

For much of his life, Ho-tah-moie, or Rolling Thunder, lived as a hermit. He refused to take up residence in any shelter provided him and instead slept in the woods. He wandered the area surrounding Pawhuska, always seen with an old blanket over his shoulders and a head scarf tied under his chin. On occasion, he might be spotted in town, sleeping on a Pawhuska sidewalk or bitterly spitting at passersby.

He was not a well man, suffering from an ailment known as scrofula—an actual disorder, tuberculosis of the lymph nodes in the back of the neck—which produced an intolerable odor. Not to mention his only companions were a pack of filthy dogs, about a dozen in all, that surrounded him wherever he went. The Indian's unique aroma earned him the nickname John Stink.

He was not a poor man, though. In fact, John Stink held quite a sum of cash, which he and many of his people had received as compensation for oil pumped from Osage land. He had little use for money, however, and had to be assigned a guardian to look after his royalties and to dole out his allowance for necessities. A cigar for himself, steaks for his dogs, and fifty cents a day for meals were reportedly all he needed.

How did John Stink come to live such a solitary lifestyle? Well, that's the best part of the story. Sometime around 1890, a rash of smallpox broke out among his people and Stink himself became infected. Some say it may have been tuberculosis or simple drunkenness that led to his fate, but no matter the cause, the ailing man was soon discovered alone and unconscious.

Unable to revive him, everyone assumed he was dead. So they carried his body away to sacred ground and, in the proper burial custom, arranged him in a sitting position aboveground and entombed him under a pile of rocks.

His people still mourning his death, John Stink came to, stumbled from his rock pile, and wandered back into his village. Stink was unquestionably confused, but not nearly as much as everyone else. Shocked by the sight of him, and influenced by superstition, many believed Stink had become a member of the walking dead. He even earned another nickname: the Osage Zombie. His people, believing that he was an undead, shunned him.

John Stink lived the rest of his life in virtual solitude. He was allocated a plot of land next to the local country club, where he lived out his days with his gang of canine cohorts. Concerned

citizens built a cabin for him, but he reportedly refused to live in it, though he eventually conceded enough to sleep on the porch.

At the age of eighty, Stink broke his leg, contracted pneumonia, and passed away. He was interred in a mausoleum in 1938, for what everyone hoped would be the last time.

The Wrath of Ella Myers

For two full weeks in 1896, the otherwise tranquil town of Guthrie fell under the spell of hysteria thanks to the death of Ella Myers, a forsaken prostitute. A short series of articles that ran in the *Guthrie Daily Ledger* are the only known records of the event, but if the reports are accurate, residents appear to have been overcome with fear of the woman's restive spirit, apparently outraged at the manner in which her body was buried.

The *Ledger* first reported that the "Cyprian"—a fancy word for *hooker*—was discovered dead on April 5 in a shack along the Santa Fe railroad. The article mentions some concern over the haste with which the body was buried and alludes to a rumor that Myers was actually buried alive, a claim that one Dr. Cotteral, who helped examine the body, denied. Cotteral said he "applied the galvanic battery," presumably to make sure Myers was dead, and concluded along with Dr. Barker, the coroner, that any further investigation would be an unnecessary expense. After all, "the deceased was a cocaine fiend," the paper reported, so it wasn't much of a stretch to presume she had simply died from an overdose.

Within a week, however, residents were reporting that "horrible groans" and "ghastly incantations" emanated from Myers's vacant shack every night after her burial. "Much excitement prevails among the neighbors residing in the vicinity of the haunted house," the *Ledger* insisted, and those living nearby had begun to leave their homes.

George Hardie, "a well-known sport," went to the shack one night to investigate the claims for himself. When he arrived, he discovered the front door locked. When he tried the back door, however, the front door swung open freely, prompting Hardie to go inside. After entering, he was struck several times in the head by an unknown force, a reporter noted, at which point a bright ray of light appeared, revealing a "blood-red hand" clutching a vial.

Others had noted similar manifestations the same week, including three instances of a voice calling out, "Don't give me any morphine! I am sick!" As a result, many were convinced Ella Myers had indeed been buried alive as rumor insisted. Some believed she had even been interred facedown. Moreover, having died without money, the woman would have been buried in the pauper's graveyard, a plot of land that was reportedly nothing more than a soggy parcel along the Cottonwood Creek. "The county undertaker, after slapping a stiff into a box, hurries it to that wet marsh and deposits it about four feet under the ground," complained one resident, indignant at the county's disregard for the indigent dead. No doubt this would have only added to Myers's postmortem angst.

Fortunately for Myers, her half brother, after reading about his sibling's fate in the newspaper, arrived in town just a few days later. He insisted that Ella's body be disinterred so she could be given a more respectful burial. Contrary to expectations, however, Ella Myers's body was discovered face up, with no evidence that she had died trying to claw her way out.

Of course, rumors die hard. Some claimed that, in an attempt to quell the relentless hauntings, unnamed parties had already dug up the corpse, arranged the body in a more respectful repose, and reburied her before officials got there.

The Black Jail

In the late 1800s, years before Oklahoma would achieve statehood, the area was known for its criminal element. There was certainly no shortage of fugitives, thieves, and murderers in the Oklahoma Territory.

As such, the centrally located town of Guthrie was chosen in 1892 as the site of the first territorial prison, an essential development in helping round up and discipline the unruly bandits. Built with eighteen-inch-thick walls of brick and limestone, it was regarded at the time to be inescapable. Its two stories of cells housed up to ninety prisoners at a time. The basement was reserved for particularly disruptive inmates, who were thrown down below to suffer the increasingly popular punishment of solitary confinement.

Even for a prison during that era, Guthrie's facility was considered especially dreadful. The interior was dark and claustrophobic. Comfort was naturally of little concern at

the time. Ventilation was terribly inadequate, according to reports, making the harsh summers of Oklahoma unbearable. Incarceration at the prison was so intolerable that the inmates nicknamed it the "Black Jail."

As testament to the prison's reputation, locals proudly retell the story of convicted felon James Phillips, who stands as the jail's most famous inmate. (This is quite a statement, considering the jail held such well-known criminals as Bill Doolin and the Dalton Gang.) Phillips, who was reportedly imprisoned for murder, was scheduled to be hanged in June 1907. But apparently, as Phillips watched out the window as his personal gallows were constructed across the street, he fell back on his bed and gave up the ghost then and there. The coroner's report allegedly states that Phillips "died of fright."

The Black Jail still stands in Guthrie at the corner of Noble Avenue and Second Street and is said to be haunted by the ghost of Phillips and other former inmates.

Blundering Bandits

There's no denying that the Old West has inspired tales of outlaws whose exploits have inflated them to mythical proportions. Men like Bill Doolin, the Dalton brothers, and Charley Pierce secured their names in history with the daring crimes they committed in and around the Oklahoma Territory. Turns out, however, that there were plenty of other lawbreakers most of us have never heard of . . . and for good reason.

How McCurdy Blew It

Elmer McCurdy, who would in the years following his death be immortalized as a sideshow mummy, was perhaps one of the least capable outlaws in the history of the Old West. His modus operandi was the detonation of safes by high explosive, but despite repeated attempts to master the medium, he never really got the hang of it.

McCurdy's first endeavor into high-stakes crime was the 1911 holdup of a passenger train on the St. Louis Iron Mountain line. Just north of Lenapah, McCurdy and accomplices Albert Connor, Walter Jarrett, and Lee Jarrett forced the train to a stop and stormed the express car to find the safe.

While the others held the train's passengers and crew at gunpoint, McCurdy set a dynamite charge on the safe. Moments later, a deafening blast echoed across the countryside. The men lifted their heads from the ground where they had taken cover, walked to the smoking express car, and discovered the safe undented. Frustrated but determined, McCurdy tried again.

A second explosion rocked the train and again the men inspected the safe. Again, nothing. Another charge was set. What should have taken minutes was now taking well over an hour. It wasn't until the fourth explosion that the safe doors finally swung open and revealed a mound of silver coins, worth about $70,000 today. Problem was, it was all fused together, melted to the inside of the safe by the heat of multiple blasts. The gang came away with only a few scattered coins and a pocket watch stolen from one of the mail clerks.

Later that year, McCurdy formed a new team with two other men and attempted to blast a bank safe in Chautauqua, Kansas, just north of the Oklahoma border, this time with the very unstable explosive nitroglycerin. They pick-axed their way into the bank, set the charge, lit the fuse, destroyed the bank's interior, and totally failed to open the safe. McCurdy set a second charge, but got spooked and ran off before getting a chance to detonate it.

Elmer McCurdy engaged in other criminal undertakings, but sadly the above-mentioned detonations remained his most successful.

Sparks Fly in Sparks

Three years before McCurdy had a go at safecracking, another group of outlaws attempted a stunt very similar to the one in Chautauqua, but with even more bungled results.

In the dead of night, three would-be robbers huddled inside a bank in the town of Sparks, attempting to empty the establishment's safe of its contents. Using supplies they reportedly stole from the local hardware store, they set barbed wire in front of the bank's door to slow down any law enforcement they might encounter, then placed a cup of nitroglycerin on top of the safe, which they planned to detonate by shooting it.

Unfortunately, the candle they placed next to the cup didn't illuminate their target as they'd hoped, and the gang kept missing the target. The prolonged gunfire woke the sheriff, who raced to the bank to stop the thieves.

Even though the barbed wire kept the sheriff outside, a gunfight ensued and at some point a stray bullet struck the nitro, blowing up the safe and the money inside. The robbers, their ears undoubtedly ringing, made a break for it, getting away with only a few handfuls of cash. The trio was apparently, to their benefit, never identified.

The Jennings Gang

Oklahoma's most unsuccessful band of outlaws, however, may have been the Jennings Gang, formed by "Little Dick" West, Patrick and Morris O'Malley, Frank Jennings, and Frank's brother Al, a former lawyer who once served as Canadian County's prosecuting attorney.

The gang's criminal ventures began in Edmond in 1897, when the five men attempted to hold up a Santa Fe passenger train. Edmond turned out not to be the best place to start, because both the Jennings brothers and the O'Malleys were well known there. When the conductor, who had been familiar with the boys for years, opened the door to the express car, he exclaimed, "What do you think you're doing, Al Jennings?" The men reacted by screaming and running into the woods.

Undeterred, the gang tried again, this time in a different county. Outside Muskogee, they attempted to stop another train by piling railroad ties across the rails. It was a proven tactic, but one that worked only when the locomotive was on a section of track that was steep or curved, forcing it to move slowly. The Jennings Gang had instead chosen a long, level stretch. The engineer, who could see the ties and the bandits for miles, hit the steam and plowed right through, leaving the thieves empty-handed and staring at a pile of splinters.

Their next train robbery was more fruitful, but just barely. When a Rock Island passenger train stopped for water north of Chickasha, the Jennings Gang successfully boarded it, but when faced with the onboard safes, nobody really knew what to do. Al had brought two sticks of dynamite but didn't know the first thing about blowing safes. So he laid the two sticks atop the larger safe, lifted the smaller safe on top of that to make a dynamite sandwich and lit the fuses. The ensuing blast blew through the side of the car and simply flipped the smaller safe back onto the floor. With no more explosives left, the gang had to settle for $300 pilfered from the passengers, a pocket watch, a jug of whiskey, and—no kidding—a bunch of bananas.

After that, they tried robbing something a little easier. The gang, minus Dick West, who apparently figured he'd had enough, held up the post office in Foyil. They robbed the customers and the money drawer of some $300, which they jammed in a postal sack, and galloped away. When they stopped to divide up their loot, however, the foursome discovered that they had grabbed the wrong sack. All they'd come away with was a bag full of canceled stamps.

Sixteen days later, the law caught up with the gang, who surrendered without a fight. They'd lost their horses and were broke, hungry, and freezing. The Jennings Gang's reign of terror—or rather, their reign of annoying inconvenience—lasted a pathetic 108 days.

Ghost Mound

Jutting up from the acres and acres of pastureland between Hydro and Colony towers a spectacular plateau that would be hard to miss even with a blindfold on. It rises more than 1,500 feet into the Oklahoma sky, sticking up all by its lonesome for more than a quarter mile out of what is now cow pasture.

Its solitude is what some say give the feature its name—Ghost Mound—a singular monument, desolate and forlorn. Others, however, insist the title's origin is more interesting. In a tale reminiscent of Romeo and Juliet, the summit played a pivotal role in the final scene of a young Indian girl's life. The girl, daughter of a local chief, had given her heart to one of the warriors in her tribe. The two were deeply in love. Her father, however, had promised her to the chief of a neighboring tribe and denied his daughter any say in the matter. Distraught and feeling she had no other way out, the girl climbed to the top of the mound and threw herself from its peak.

When the wind blows, they say, you can hear the young girl's cries. And if you climb to the top yourself, you can find her last footstep preserved in the rock.

Surprisingly, this isn't the only legend tied to the summit. Reportedly, a fortune in gold is buried somewhere near the mound, yet to be located. A group of forty-niners, members of a very small percentage of miners to actually benefit from the California Gold Rush of 1849, were on their way home from the West Coast with a substantial prize when they encountered a group of Indians. With only minutes to react, the men dumped their heavy load and made a run for it. Several of them stayed behind just long enough to stash the gold out of sight, somewhere on or near Ghost Mound. Only a few of the men survived, but having been among those who bolted first, none of them knew where the cache was hidden and were never able to find it. The gold, worth somewhere around $250,000, is presumably still there.

Unfortunately, the mound is now located on private property, so none of you should get any wild ideas about heading out there with a metal detector and a shovel. However, you can view Ghost Mound from E1110 Road, about two miles west of SR 58 and about nine miles south of Interstate 40.

The girl . . . threw herself from its peak.

Lost Treasures

Between 1860 and 1900 the state of Oklahoma (or "Indian Territory" as it was then known) saw more than its fair share of greed. In addition to a fairly major gold rush, Oklahoma was the site of illegal cattle drives, bank robberies, and other nefarious activities. When one place hosts so many dishonorable men—even temporarily—it can only mean one thing. Buried loot.

So much gold and money was loved and lost in late nineteenth-century Oklahoma that an accurate calculation of the losses is impossible to estimate. The conquistadors of the American Southwest might be more acclaimed than the lode busters of the Sooner State, but that doesn't make Oklahoma gold any less shiny. In fact, because of the dearth of publicity for hidden Oklahoma gold, you might just have a better chance of finding some.

Just like George Hardsook did in 1913. Hardsook was digging a trench for a new oil pipeline in northeastern Oklahoma when his shovel hit metal. Upon inspection, Hardsook discovered that the piece of metal was a gold coin. He kept digging. After unearthing more than a hundred pounds of gold coins, he laid down his shovel and returned to town. In one day, a poor laborer became a very rich man. He never found out where the coins were from, or why they had been buried.

Stories of lucky people who stumbled upon buried treasure are interesting, but they're not nearly as exciting as stories of treasure yet to be found. These are the stories that give hope to treasure hunters, thrill seekers, and incurable dreamers. With some quality research, a little patience, and a good pair of hiking boots, anyone could become Oklahoma's nouveau riche. Prospective millionaires might want to start in Devil's Promenade.

In 1867 a German man settled in the northwest corner of Oklahoma, just off the Spring River. He was, by most accounts, a paranoid miser, and spent his days fearing for the safety of his life's savings. He told his best friend, a local Indian, that he was plagued by dreams of ambush and theft. After years of torment, he decided the best course of action was to bury his fortune.

The German and his gold journeyed to the great sandstone bluff locally known as Devil's Promenade. He returned empty-handed and at peace, claiming that stashing his money finally afforded him a good night's sleep. On his deathbed, the German told his Indian friend where he had hidden the gold. He described a small cave on the side of the bluff, and said that a tin box full of gold sat on a shelf inside the cave. The German's dying wish was that the Indian tribe use the gold for themselves. The tribe never located the cave to which the German referred.

Treasure hunters who seek the German's gold at Devil's Promenade should make time to stay around after dark for a glimpse of the Spooklight. If you park four miles south of the tristate junction in Ottawa County and look west, you might be treated to the appearance of a tight ball of light. A scientific explanation of the Spooklight has never been conclusively given, but some of the locals say it's the lantern of the German, forever protecting his treasure.

An even larger treasure remains unfound in Cimarron County's Black Mesa. In 1804, a team of French traders traveled through the Oklahoma Panhandle on their way to New Orleans with six carts full of furs. Underneath the furs were hundreds of gold ingots. After a fellow traveler informed them that New Orleans, and all of the land they could currently see, was sold to the Americans, the Frenchmen knew they had a problem. They knew the Americans would confiscate the gold, and so they decided to bury it until they could arrange its safe passage home to France. They never returned to collect their treasure.

The missing gold was legendary for decades after that,

but it was not the object of any serious quest until a series of markers was discovered in the 1870s. The Frenchmen had constructed a Roman numeral eleven—XI—out of rocks. Exactly six miles to the east and six miles to the north were two other Roman numeral rock formations. For the better part of a century, treasure hunters couldn't decipher what the markers were triangulating in the barren panhandle. But that's because they never found the fourth marker.

In the mid-twentieth century rancher Cy Strong found the fourth marker, resembling a Greek omega and made from the same rocks the Frenchmen used on the other markers, on his land. The four markers formed a thirty-six-square-mile area of nothingness, except for Sugar Loaf Peak in the dead center. Strong was certain the Frenchmen chose Sugar Loaf Peak for their hiding spot, but he was never able to find the cache.

In the annals of lost treasure lore, southwestern Oklahoma's Wichita Mountains appears again and again. In fact, Oklahoma's most mysterious lost treasure is rumored to rest near Elk Mountain behind a giant iron door. The legend began in the 1850s, when a Mexican inherited a map of the Wichita Mountains showing several stores of Spanish gold. After years of searching, he allowed a friend to make a copy of his map and try for himself. The friend formed an expedition, and followed the map to an enormous iron door on the side of a mountain.

On the other side of the door was a cave containing gold bars stacked like firewood and baskets filled with bullion. Just then, a lookout warned of approaching Indians. The Mexican expedition managed to escape, but when they returned they found that the Indians had resealed the entrance and secured it with a large padlock. They marked the spot, planning to return with a greater number of men, but they were never able to find the door again.

In 1910, the iron door was once again found by a boy named Prince. It didn't arouse his suspicion at the time, but in the years that passed Prince found that he couldn't get the image out of his head. He tried to find the door again, but failed. Ten years later, a group of boys found a large padlocked door. One of the boys kept trying to locate the door for the next fifty years, but he never did. A farmer found the door during the Great Depression and ran to town to find people to help him pry it open. He returned to the same spot, but the door wasn't there. Over and over, the door returns, and then vanishes again.

No report of Oklahoma treasure is complete without a mention of Jesse James's lost treasure. In Mexico, the James Gang attacked a Mexican party and stole eighteen burros carrying gold. They fled north, only to walk straight into a Wichita Mountains blizzard. After deciding that the gold was slowing them down, they buried the loot. Jesse James marked the spot by nailing one of the burros' shoes to a tree. The James Gang vowed to return together, and signed a pact etched onto a kettle.

Years later, Jesse James was killed in Missouri. Jesse's brother Frank and another gang member, Cole Younger, separately returned to Oklahoma to recover the gold. Frank was able to locate the burro's shoe, some etched rocks, and other clues left by his deceased brother, but he never found the treasure.

In 1932, a man named Joe Hunter acquired maps that were rumored to lead to the James fortune. The maps led to clues, which led to more maps and more clues. Hunter found the kettle inscribed with the outlaws' contract in 1948, but he died in the 1950s. Other treasure hunters are confident that they have narrowed down the location to the ruins of a James encampment on Mount Pinchot. No one knows for sure how much gold is in the James cache, but most estimate the treasure to be in the millions.

—Craig Robertson

Chinese Underground

It's safe to say most Oklahoma City residents are familiar with the Underground, the series of tunnels running beneath downtown streets that offer subterranean dining, shopping, and haircuts. Originally known as the Conncourse—named after banker Jack Conn—it connects more than thirty downtown buildings via a subterranean network that was dug out in the 1970s. Yet few may know that, as far back as the 1920s, an entirely separate underground system wound its way below the city, which was known only to a certain segment of the populous.

Its existence was discovered around 1921, when the *Oklahoman* reported on an inspection of Oklahoma City's Chinatown by six members of the health department and a police detective, during which the officials were led by a resident below ground and through "a dozen connected caverns." Slipping into a basement below California Avenue, the men were greeted by several Chinese residents who appeared to have been expecting them, leading the inspectors to surmise that word of their presence had spread through the Chinese suburbs. They had no idea anyone had actually been living below ground, but how would they? The underground population may have been larger than they would have ever imagined.

The following year, federal agents discovered another subterranean area, an opium den beneath a Chinese restaurant at 12 S. Robinson Avenue. The *Oklahoman* reported on the raid: "Down a flight of stairs went the

officers . . . and through an oaken door which is (entered) by means of a hanging rope." Inside, they discovered twenty-five men, some unconscious, lolling in a stifling mist. Rumors followed of even more subterranean chambers that included a temple and a cemetery.

A large number of Chinese immigrants had come to Oklahoma in the late 1800s in an attempt to escape intolerance on the West Coast. Thousands who had worked for the railroads were laid off when the lines were completed and the Chinese were subsequently seen as a detriment to the white working class, forcing them to migrate inland to escape racial persecution. Unfortunately, the federal government declared in 1878 that Chinese people could not become U.S. citizens, compelling many to stay well below the radar, possibly even establishing their homes in secretive basements.

Some say the underground city existed only in rumors, which grew more elaborate as the years passed. By some accounts, the tunnels extended from NW Seventeenth Street and Classen Boulevard all the way to the North Canadian River, some thirty blocks to the south. Secret entrances dotted the city like mysterious portals to a forbidden world. Residents with somewhat questionable parenting skills convinced their children that, should they misbehave, the Chinese would kidnap them and take them to their labyrinthine lair, never to be seen again.

TIP BY CLERK LEADS TO RAID

Rum and "Dope" Worth $10,000 Seized in City; Chinaman Held.

NOW the bunks are empty and the 'thandoo lies cold. Draperies are drawn back and the fragrant oder of the poppy preparation is stealing from the darkened room where four chinese kept the lamp aglow and took the thirty second sniffs that spell dreams of the orient—later oblivion.

Frank Wong and Wong On Chong, the latter consignee of three boxes of narcotics and twelve jugs of fine rum are $10,000 poorer after seizure of a prize and the raid of federal officers which took them into a shadowy basement under 13 South Robinson avenue. Wong was arrested.

The tunnels had taken on incredible proportions that some historians originally insisted were really only a couple of disconnected basements. In 1969, however, the folklore received a shot of hot mustard when wrecking crews began demolishing some downtown buildings. In an alley near Robinson and Sheridan avenues, workers discovered a short flight of "expertly handcrafted stone stairs" leading to an old wooden door fastened with an intricate lock and leather straps. Inside lay a long-abandoned maze of rooms, partitioned by walls of brick and wood. It seemed the Chinese Underground, which had been nearly forgotten, was rediscovered.

The ceilings inside the chambers were low, the floors were damp and there was no apparent source of daylight. Abandoned artifacts, including an old stove and papers with Chinese writing, pointed to the mystery space as being a rooming house, laundry, opium den, and gambling space. A second entrance was discovered, and officials hypothesized that the tunnels extended below the rest of the block, but access to them was never found.

Unfortunately, appeals to preserve the discovery as a historic site were rejected and the whole thing was covered by the Cox Convention Center. The find did, however, prove that the secret Chinese Underground did exist, at least to some extent. It also raised speculation that other secret chambers may yet lie below the streets of downtown Oklahoma City, their back doors just waiting to be spotted down some forgotten alleyway.

The Great Manure Feud of 1888

Here's a "Hatfields and McCoys" story that's full of BS and yet remains, unlike most Sooner yarns, entirely true.

Sometime in the late 1880s, a family by the name of Eldridge settled into the Oklahoma Panhandle, then known as No Man's Land, and established a cattle ranch near present-day Hardesty. A short time later, a second family, this time by the name of Johnson, rolled in and set up their home right next door.

Seeing as there was plenty of room for everyone at the time, relations between the Eldridges and the Johnsons started out pretty friendly. The Johnsons allowed the Eldridges' cattle to graze on their land, and in return the Eldridges let the Johnsons cross their property to gain access to the river. Life on the prairie was all sunshine and buttermilk.

With the arrival of the cold season, however, things quickly changed. Relations between the two families went south right along with the temperature. In fact, things got so bad, the argument escalated into gunfire. Why? They were fighting over meadow muffins. Cow flop. Manure.

Back then, you see, cow dung was a valuable asset. Not for fertilizer, but for fuel. Dried cow chips burn well, produce a lot of heat, and are reportedly not as smelly as one would think. In a place where there just wasn't that much firewood to be had, the patties were precious property.

Problem was, both the Eldridges and the Johnsons were collecting the chips for their own. And since the Eldridges owned the cattle, they argued that they owned anything that came out of them. The Johnsons, on the other hand, figured that if it fell on their property, it belonged to them. In response, the Eldridge family cut off the Johnsons' access to the river. Soon thereafter, several of the Eldridges' cattle were found dead. Words flew, then bullets. One of the Eldridge boys, twenty-two-year-old Silas, was shot in the back of the neck with a .50-caliber buffalo gun. Sometime later, twenty-year-old Charley Johnson was shot and killed, almost certainly, according to an ancestor, at the hand of an Eldridge.

The big poo to-do finally ended when a vigilante committee, which had taken it upon itself to reestablish order in No Man's Land, forced both families to leave the territory.

Beer City

The number of Oklahoma towns that have sprung up and disappeared over the course of the state's history is almost endless, but few are as legendary as Beer City.

The reason for the settlement's name isn't hard to guess. It was, quite literally, a town built for drinking. When the panhandle had yet to become part of the Oklahoma Territory and was still known as No Man's Land, Beer City popped up in the lawless strip of terrain to satisfy the vices of men working in and around Liberal, Kansas, where alcohol was prohibited.

The town reportedly was never platted and never had a single church, school, or post office. There were only saloons, dance halls, gambling houses, and brothels, all serving up whiskey and beer, as well as moonshine manufactured in a nearby cave. Women of ill repute moved from nearby towns just to work there. Some even commuted. It was, as some called it, the "Sodom and Gomorrah of the Plains."

As one might expect, it was not an entirely safe place to live, work, or visit. In a town where there was plenty of booze and virtually no law, crime and violence thrived. Hustlers and pickpockets were an ongoing problem, especially for the exceedingly inebriated. Many businesses built drunk pens in the backs of their establishments to hold their intoxicated for safekeeping until they could sleep it off and start the cycle over again. Still, formal law enforcement was never very welcome. According to one story, the people of Beer City, having tired of the interference by a sheriff from a nearby town, lured the officer to one of their bars on false pretenses, cornered him, and shot him to death. Practically the whole town participated; that way, no one could prove who actually killed him.

Beer City lasted for only two years. When No Man's Land was assigned to the Oklahoma Territory in 1890, the town simply dissipated. Nothing of it remains today.

Bathsheba

To some, an entire town populated exclusively by women may sound like a fantasy realized, but when its residents are quick to raise a loaded barrel in the direction of anyone with a Y chromosome, that daydream pops like a cartoon thought bubble.

Such was the town of Bathsheba, a tent city that supposedly existed somewhere between Perry and Enid shortly after the Cherokee Strip Land Run in 1893. According to a report coming out of Kansas at the time—neither the author nor the publication of which has yet been pinned down—the village was inhabited entirely by females who were so opposed to the presence of the opposite gender that not even billy goats, bulls, or tomcats were tolerated inside the community. A farmer who lived nearby said that some of his chickens once roamed into the settlement and the single unfortunate rooster among them was promptly slaughtered "with druidistic rites."

Bathsheba, sometimes spelled Bethsheba, though presumably named for the biblical figure, appeared fairly organized for a small tent city. They had appointed a mayor, a town council, and a chief of police, despite the fact that the population at its height reached only thirty-three women, twelve of whom deserted after the first week. (Another was booted out after it was discovered she owned a razor.)

The reporter responsible for chronicling the town's existence, himself a man, was forced to make all his observations of Bathsheba and its residents using binoculars just as an anthropologist might study wild game. He once got too close and the police chief fired a shotgun at him. Lucky for him, she missed.

The all-female settlement, however, was short lived. When the reporter later returned to gather more details for his article, the residents had already pulled up stakes and moved on. No trace of the town, save for the single uncredited Kansas article, has been uncovered.

The Secret Life of John Wilkes Booth

The date was April 14, 1865. The War Between the States was nearly at an end, with Robert E. Lee having formally surrendered to Ulysses S. Grant just five days earlier. President Abraham Lincoln, who was in good spirits, celebrated the excellent news by accepting an invitation to a play.

Of course, anyone who's made it through fifth-grade social studies knows what happened next. John Wilkes Booth, actor and Confederate sympathizer, made his way into Lincoln's theater box and shot the president in the back of the head with a single-shot Deringer pistol.

Booth had counted on a quick getaway, but had trouble when he leaped from the box and clumsily caught his riding spur on a U.S. Treasury Guards flag, tumbling to the stage and breaking his leg. Nevertheless, after shouting that infamous cry, "Sic semper tyrannis!"—the Virginia state motto meaning "Thus always to tyrants"—Booth ran outside, mounted the horse that was waiting for him, and rendezvoused with fellow conspirator David Herold in Maryland.

After staying the night with acquaintance Dr. Samuel Mudd, who reset Booth's broken leg, Booth and Herold fled for Virginia, where they were discovered several days later hiding out in a barn. Surrounded by Union soldiers in the early morning hours, Herold surrendered, but Booth stood his ground. As the soldiers began setting fire to the barn, a sergeant named Boston Corbett spotted Booth through a gap in a wall and fired at him, striking him in the back of the neck. Booth succumbed to his wound a few hours later and was eventually buried in a family plot in Baltimore, Maryland. (Cue the suspenseful music.) Or was he?

Thirty-eight years later, a man by the name of David E. George would raise doubt concerning the fate of Lincoln's assassin. In January 1903, in a long narrow room on an upstairs floor of the Grand Avenue Hotel in Enid, Oklahoma, George made a startling confession. He was dying, and although a doctor had been called to his bedside,

there was nothing the physician could do; George had ingested a fatal dose of strychnine. As the dying man drew his last breath, he confessed that David George was just an alias. His real name was John Wilkes Booth, and he had killed Abraham Lincoln.

None of the locals really seemed to know that much about George. He was a self-professed house painter and devoted barfly, that much they could say—though he was fond of quoting Shakespeare, which he did at length when he was on the drink, which raised speculation that he may have once been very familiar with the stage. Was it possible that he was who he claimed to be?

The evidence began to pile up. Upon examination of George's body, doctors noticed scars that matched those

Booth would have had. He had also suffered a broken leg sometime in the past, just above the ankle, as Booth had when he leaped to the stage at Ford's Theatre. Plus, he shared Booth's height and features, and was of the proper age. Moreover, a minister by the name of E. D. Harper revealed that, during a previous suicide attempt, George had confessed once before to being Booth.

Still, nothing came of the matter. And since no one came forward to claim the body, the local mortician mummified George, dressed him up and set him on display in the front window of his funeral parlor/furniture store. Despite George's supposedly astonishing revelation, he remained little more than a minor curiosity.

The mystery grew, however, when Finis L. Bates, a lawyer from Memphis, heard about George's claim, traveled to Enid to see the corpse for himself and identified it as the man he once knew as John St. Helen. St. Helen, he said, had been a friend of his back when he worked in Granbury, Texas, in the 1870s. Furthermore, at a time when St. Helen was gravely ill and believed he was lying on his deathbed, he confessed to Bates that he was the man who killed Lincoln and proceeded to describe the whole affair in detail. St. Helen recovered, however, and left town, supposedly for Oklahoma. Bates, who spent years investigating the claim, tried to bring the incident to the attention of the U.S. War Department, but he was dismissed.

Since then, more than a handful of theorists have concluded that it's plausible, if not entirely likely, that John Wilkes Booth actually escaped following the assassination of America's sixteenth president. Many believe Booth was involved in a conspiracy with the U.S. government to have Lincoln killed and was allowed, even helped, by the military to make his getaway. The man who was killed that night in the Virginia barn was either a patsy or someone simply shot by mistake. Oddly enough, there have been some clues, although yet unsubstantiated, that Boston Corbett, the man credited as Booth's killer, also lived out his final days in Enid, which raises some interesting questions about a possible association between him and David George. In recent years, a group of researchers, joined by several members of the surviving Booth family, petitioned to disinter the man buried in John Wilkes Booth's unmarked plot in Maryland to prove whether or not he's really the man he's supposed to be. Unfortunately, their request was denied. So, the mystery, at least to many, is still unsolved.

As for David George's mummy, Finis Bates acquired it from the funeral parlor in Enid and toured the country with it, putting it on display and renting it out to carnivals. It even made an appearance at the 1904 St. Louis World's Fair. Following Bates's death, the mummy changed hands several times and was eventually lost.

The hotel in which David George made his confession, however, still stands in Enid at 205 S. Grand Avenue. Today it's the site of Garfield Furniture.

SURRATT. BOOTH. HAROLD.
War Department, Washington, April 20, 1865,
$100,000 REWARD!
THE MURDERER
Of our late beloved President, Abraham Lincoln,
IS STILL AT LARGE.
$50,000 REWARD
$25,000 REWARD
$25,000 REWARD
EDWIN M. STANTON, Secretary of War.

Unexplained Phenomena

We live in an age of science and reason, it's true. Advances in research and technology have brought us ever closer to understanding our own bodies, our environment, and even our universe. It's an exciting era.

Still, there's excitement in the unknown, as well. Being confronted with events that confound our sense of logic is stimulating to both our imaginations and our emotions. And luckily, there are mysteries still to be had, even in our own backyards. Strange aural phenomena, unexplained lights, dancing orbs, even something as common as the tornado can tack sizeable question marks onto the ends of things that we previously knew to be factual. Even with so much knowledge at our disposal, there's still plenty of opportunity to tip one's mental equilibrium if you know where to go.

The Tri-State Spook Light

Judging from the stories dating back to nineteenth-century Oklahoma, you'd think that one in every five relationships ended with one person killing the other, that the most common cause of death among settlers was decapitation, and that pioneers went looking for things only in the dead of night. Then again, tales of mild-mannered townsfolk who ran feed stores and died uneventfully of old age in their beds don't usually get passed down through the generations.

Without these fantastic narratives, we might not have anything to talk about as we slouch in our car seats on darkened back roads waiting for mysterious dancing lights to make an appearance—a popular activity with people living in northeast Oklahoma. This is, after all, the location of the Spooksville Triangle, a region famous for unusual nighttime phenomena. Stretching between Miami, Oklahoma; Columbus, Kansas; and Joplin, Missouri, the region is rife with unexplained lights that taunt visitors and elude rational explanation.

The most famous of these luminous entities is the Tri-State Spook Light, which actually lies just outside the designated triangle along East 50 Road, just this side of the Oklahoma–Missouri state line. Locals say that if you park your car about a half mile west of the border and face the Show-Me State, you'll see a show you'll never forget.

According to witnesses, the light emerges from the trees along the shoulder and floats out above the roadway. It always appears as an orb, but varies in both size and color, usually measuring from somewhere about the size of a volleyball to as much as five feet in diameter. Sometimes the light will change in both size and color right before your eyes, apparently depending on its mood. On occasion, multiple orbs will even appear together, dancing and leap-frogging like puppies in a pet-shop window.

The phenomenon is typically shy, though, and will dart off if you honk your car horn or turn on your headlights. Yet some allege to have encountered the light up close when it approached their vehicles as though suddenly curious about its audience. A few have said the light even entered their cars, at which point the astonished passengers felt an intense warmth radiating from the orb. In one case, the light hitched a ride on a school bus taking kids home from a carnival, jumping out when it apparently reached its destination.

The earliest verifiable report of the light dates back to 1936, but many claim that locals have known about it as far back as the mid-1800s. Native Americans may have been aware of it even further back than that. As such, numerous legends have attached themselves to the phenomenon. In one case, a young girl was said to have been lost at night while looking for stray cows. Her mother, who searched for her by the light of a lantern, was so upset by the loss that she continues her search in the afterlife. In another story, the lantern is said to belong to a prospector who was decapitated in a mining accident. Another recounts the tale of a soldier whose head was blown off by a cannon ball during the Civil War. Then there's the Seneca Indian who got into an argument with his ax-wielding wife and—you guessed it—lost his head. A more romantic version of the story tells of two Indian lovers who were unable to marry and leaped to their deaths. They continue to seek each other nightly.

Naturally, many people have attempted to explain the lights scientifically. In the 1940s, the U.S. Army Corps of Engineers came to have a look, as did a scientist from Kansas City, Missouri's Midwest Research Institute. In 1969, a professor from Southwest Missouri State

University performed his own study. In the years since, numerous scientists, ufologists, and documentarians have conducted investigations with varying levels of scrutiny and technical expertise. No one has come up with a conclusive answer for the light.

That's not to say that myriad theories haven't been proposed, of course. Swamp gas is a popular one, as is static electricity. Some are convinced that mineral deposits are at the root. Ball lightning, plasma, and natural phosphorescence round out the more far-reaching explanations. More often than not, though, skeptics insist that it's just the result of distant car headlights refracted by the atmosphere, although that doesn't explain the reports that originated before the advent of headlighted vehicles.

Regardless, it seems the light doesn't stick to one spot. In addition to East 50 Road, otherwise known as Devil's Promenade, reports indicate that you're likely to catch it playing to the north over on East 40 Road, as well. You might also catch it at Devil's Promenade Bridge to the west, where East 57 crosses Spring River, especially when the Quapaw tribe holds their annual powwow nearby. However, East 50 remains the most popular viewing area and the one most everyone will point you to when asked.

When inquiring about directions, though, don't be surprised if the locals correct you on the name. "Tri-State Spook Light" is more the phenomenon's politically correct moniker, as multiple towns in three different states claim the spectacle as their own. In Missouri, you might hear it called the Hornet Spook Light, the Neosho Spook Light, the Seneca Spook Light, or the Joplin Spook Light. Kansans say it's appeared on their side of the state line, also. In Oklahoma, the towns of Quapaw, Miami, and Peoria have all staked naming rights, so you might as well call it what you want.

Spook Light Spotting Is a Family Affair

My mother was raised in northeast Oklahoma during the Depression. Most summers in the early 1960s she and I and my older brother would venture up there from Texas. Even when I was little, I remember all of us driving out of Fairland, Oklahoma, to this deserted country road where we would sit for hours waiting for the Spook Light to appear. There were the usual explanations: swamp gas, car lights refracted somewhere, and so on. My mother told us her father used to see it when he was a kid, before cars were invented. His generation believed the Spook Light had something to do with lost and wandering Cherokee spirits. Others claimed it was the ghost of a Civil War soldier with a lantern, out looking for his decapitated head.

My favorite story involved a couple of policemen who witnessed the light come close enough to pounce on the hood of their patrol car, then the trunk, before disappearing.

Most of the time I remember falling asleep in the car, waiting and waiting, then waking up on the way home, my mother telling me if they had seen the light or not. Finally, one night when I was about six, I got to see it for myself; it was exactly as everyone had described it to me over the years. It started out way down the road and it took a while to get your eyes focused on it. What was cool was hearing other car doors opening and realizing about five or six other families had come out there late on a summer evening for the same thing.

I was frightened at first, but that faded as the phantom light came closer and more focused in intensity. I could see why some people described it as the front light on an approaching train. Except as a train light grows in intensity and illumination, it also increases its circumference, which helps you to keep it in perspective as to its proximity. The Spook Light, however, grew only in illuminated intensity; it never grew in size. It consistently appeared to be the size of a bowling ball.

This first time I saw it was cool because I really thought this thing would dance or bounce around like I had always heard. I wasn't disappointed, because the closer it got, the more you could see that it wasn't taking an entirely straight course; it veered and dipped ever so slightly.

As my family and I watched it approach, I heard the excitement of the other families around us, particularly the random *boo*, and the high shrill squeak from some poor little kid, followed by laughter. But I didn't take my eyes off the Spook Light. What happened next was the part that made that night even more memorable.

The light just veered off to its left in a wide arc, cutting across a field, but fast, like a big round rocket hitting a booster stage, and BOOM. Everyone sort of oohed and aahed together when that happened. It was the only time I observed the light seeming to change in its size and intensity as it faded off. I did see it other times later, but it was never as cool as the first time. —*Nick Beef*

The Birth of the "Flying Saucer"

Reports of UFOs extend far back into history, certainly, but in the mid-twentieth century, they remained few and far between. As the summer of 1947 came into full swing, however, things quickly changed. It's difficult to say exactly why that specific year would result in such an explosion of reports, but it's generally accepted by those who study UFO phenomena that 1947 marked the inauguration of the unidentified flying object into mainstream culture.

Among the earliest sightings of that year is that by pilot Byron Savage, who spotted an object traveling over Oklahoma City in May. The object appeared at dusk, but there was still enough light present that Savage could make out what he described as being "frosty white," perhaps even "silvery," "perfectly round and flat," and larger than any aircraft existing at the time. Savage, who was standing in his yard, said it moved about three times as fast as a jet and disappeared to the north after about twenty seconds. Savage's sighting even predates that of Kenneth Arnold near Mount Rainier, Washington, the first sighting widely reported in the popular media and the one responsible for giving us the term *flying saucer*.

The following month, at least two more reports surfaced out of Oklahoma. One was by a traveling salesman who spotted six objects shaped like washtubs flying in formation above Yukon, west of Oklahoma City. The other came from a man in Walters, southeast of Lawton, in which two saucers repeatedly passed each other, back and forth, at around 10 P.M.

In July, several reports came from various parts of the state, including Harrah, Enid, and Anadarko, in which a handful of witnesses saw a fast-moving object that changed colors. In Norman, the dean of the University of Oklahoma School of Engineering, W. H. Carson, spotted an unusual object flying across the sky in the clear of the afternoon. Joined by his wife and three neighbors, the group then saw two more similar objects follow the same path. Carson said it was difficult to determine their exact shape, but that they flew very high, very fast, and without producing any sound. A woman in Oklahoma City named Patsy Morgan saw a bright light above the city that same day, which appeared to come from some sort of shiny, reflective craft. Paul Skvork, another OKC resident, described seeing something similar that evening, which he equated to a "ball of fire."

Such sightings continued to pop up from across the United States, a surge of UFO phenomena that eventually culminated in the world-famous July 3 report of an alien crash-landing outside Roswell, New Mexico. Such a flood of activity wouldn't be seen again for nearly twenty years.

The object appeared at dusk, but [it was] . . . larger than any aircraft existing at the time.

Flight 655 (Not)

Although the sudden commotion of 1947 would be unmatched for years to come, that doesn't mean activity ceased entirely. In the early morning of July 17, 1957, for example, a U.S. Air Force bomber crew was running exercises over the south-central United States when the six men aboard the aircraft found themselves engaged in an involuntary game of cat and mouse with what remains an unidentified entity. The object first appeared on one of the airplane's three radar screens, which showed that an unspecified craft moved up from behind the jet, crossed in front, then disappeared toward the rear. Since the signal mimicked the frequency characteristics of ground-based search radar common at the time, the operator dismissed the incident as a technical anomaly despite its unusual movement.

Moments later, however, the pilot and copilot spotted a bright bluish-white light coming almost directly toward them. Even though they couldn't see the standard red and green navigation lights indicative of all aircraft, they assumed it was just another plane and prepared to take evasive maneuvers. The light, however, almost instantaneously changed course, zipped across their flight path at a speed unmatched by any aircraft of the day, and blinked out.

The crew was able to continue tracking the object after it reappeared on their radar, having turned up in the position at which it previously went dark. At that point, it appeared to be matching the bomber's course and speed as though it were observing them. Upon contacting technicians on the ground, the air force crew discovered that, at that point, ground stations were picking up the mysterious body, as well.

When the object changed course once more, the bomber pilot attempted pursuit, but could never get very close before it disappeared again. For an hour and a half, while covering more than seven hundred miles, the crew tracked the object both visually and electronically. At times, it even appeared as multiple entities. Finally, somewhere near Oklahoma City, the object vanished entirely, never to return.

Oddly, in a report filed by Project Blue Book, a now-defunct U.S. Air Force study of unidentified flying objects, the thing that flew circles around the bomber and repeatedly vanished and reappeared was dismissed simply as American Airlines Flight 655, a commercial plane that had flown some six hundred miles away.

Rock Spectacle

Imagine sitting on your porch, enjoying a cool summer breeze, when out of nowhere a flurry of rocks begins pelting the side of your house. Such is the story of the McWethy family of Centrahoma, a rural town about halfway between Ada and Atoka in southeastern Oklahoma. It's a mystery that began on the evening of June 15, 1990, when Bill and Maxine McWethy were enjoying the summer evening along with their daughter Twyla and granddaughter Desiree. Even after Bill called out to the suspected miscreant to knock it off, the rocks just kept coming. And they continued unabated for the next twenty-four hours, clattering against the siding and breaking windows.

The attack persisted off and on for the next few weeks. One night, the McWethys assembled nearly fifty people around their house, and no one could identify where the projectiles were coming from. Initial speculation pointed to Oklahoma's own Bigfoot, a creature notorious for pitching rocks at unsuspecting humans, but such a beast would be hard-pressed to tromp around unseen.

Oddly, the McWethys aren't the only ones in recent history to have experienced such an event. In 1983, even before the McWethy incident, an Arizona family named Berkbigler suffered an identical attack after moving into their new home in Tucson. Rocks flew from the surrounding desert, striking their home repeatedly, but even with help from friends, reporters, the sheriff's department, and a helicopter pilot, the tormented family was unable to spot the source of the flung rocks. More than one hundred years before that, a similar occurrence took place outside Leavenworth, Indiana, at the home of the Benham family where, according to an 1870 newspaper article, "stones weighing from two to four pounds are being constantly hurled at the house . . . at all times of day and night." Sentries were placed outside the house to catch the troublemaker who was responsible, but not a single rock would be thrown until everyone stepped inside. As soon as a rap was heard against the house, everyone rushed outside, but still no one could catch the culprit. At one point the unknown aggressor took to knocking on the front door, but even when someone waited inside with his hand on the doorknob, ready to pounce at the first sound, not a soul was seen.

Everyone rushed outside, but still no one could catch the culprit.

Eventually, the McWethys' mystery deepened as rocks were replaced with other items, including screws, nails, coins, and eventually bottles and eggs. What was even more unsettling was that, when watched carefully, the objects appeared to be materializing midflight. At one point, objects began appearing inside the house, as well, such as handfuls of pebbles that seemed to be dropped from the ceiling onto the kitchen table. Stones inexplicably showed up under Twyla's bed sheets, which themselves began flying off the bed at night. Ultimately, it appeared the McWethy family had drawn the mischief of a poltergeist.

After paranormal investigators were called in, one researcher caught what sounded like a faint voice on audiotape that said, "This is Michael," and a psychic claimed that she could sense a disturbed spirit by that very name. Although there has been no real substantiation of such a ghost's existence, the McWethys have since then referred to the source of the mysterious events as coming from Michael. Besides, it's as good an explanation as any proposed so far.

The Surge of 1965

Perhaps it was the Cold War. Maybe it was the Space Race. It could have been America's rising counterculture, or possibly the Beatles' recent "invasion." Whatever the cause, it appears that intelligent aliens took a great interest in the United States beginning in the summer of 1965, resulting in one of the largest, if not the largest, swell of UFO sightings in history. And it began right here in Oklahoma.

On July 11, at about 4 A.M., two teenagers who probably shouldn't have been awake at that hour spotted two UFOs flying over the capital city. Possibly the same objects, though their number had increased to three, were seen again in the same area by other witnesses the very next night. Nine days later, separate witnesses reported unusual lights in the sky, this time for three full nights in a row. What at first seemed to be mere coincidence started to look like a full-fledged event.

Then things really started to take off. Based on reports starting in late July, Oklahomans were hard-pressed to look up and not see something strange hovering overhead. Objects were spotted both visually and on Air Force radar near Wynnewood. Witnesses in Oklahoma City saw a strange round object with wings drifting close to the ground in the 600 block of NW Sixty-third Street. A man fishing on Lake Hefner said he saw a saucer-shaped craft emerge from the water and fly away. Objects looking much like children's tops began to show up in virtually every major city.

When an officer at Tinker Air Force Base saw something unusual in the sky, he called upon another officer to verify what he had seen. Together, and with the aid of a telescope, the officers confirmed that it could not have been an ordinary celestial body. After all, the craft, which was saucer-shaped and rimmed with pulsing lights, was seen traveling speedily at a forty-five-degree angle and visibly passed in front of observable planets.

Meanwhile, that same night, witnesses all over Oklahoma, as well as many others across the Midwest, marveled at brightly lit objects of various shapes and colors dancing in the night sky. As many as eight at once appeared over Ardmore. They glowed, circled, flickered intensely, and moved in unpredictable patterns, some skipping about and disappearing in a flash, others hovering in place for as much as an hour. Such reports continued throughout the summer and, according to some, didn't really taper off until well into 1967.

Unfortunately, this unprecedented wave of sightings was, on the whole, dismissed by the Air Force, which was responsible at the time for investigating such reports, even though members of their own staff reported having seen UFOs themselves. Oklahomans, however, knew what they saw.

The Smith Photo

Out of the rash of UFO sightings that cropped up in the summer of 1965 came what many consider one of the best photographs of an unidentified object ever taken. Captured by fourteen-year-old Alan Smith, the craft was spotted hovering high above Tulsa on the evening of August 2, or perhaps past midnight on August 3.

The image (shown here) is the second known photo to be taken of an unknown aerial object above Oklahoma and is believed to be the first-ever nighttime photograph of a UFO using color film. It depicts a multicolored object displaying segmented areas of red, green, and white light in an otherwise darkened sky. According to young Smith and the four other witnesses who saw the object, it appeared to them as a blob of light that shifted in color, although the photo seemed to reveal more detail. According to various reports, the object traveled from east to west, at one point apparently moving toward the witnesses, and emitted a faint, high-pitched whine.

Skeptics have somewhat convincingly compared the shape of the object to a type of Christmas decoration popular at the time, which was basically a light with a rotating wheel of colored filters. They insist that it was an underexposed shot taken around the holidays. Numerous photographic experts, however, have determined the image to be authentic, and the photo, which has been published in numerous books and newspapers, as well as in *Life* magazine, remains one of the most intriguing UFO images ever captured.

They glowed, circled, flickered intensely, and moved in unpredictable patterns, some skipping about and disappearing in a flash, others hovering in place for as much as an hour.

Tornadoes: Freaks of the Storm

Lying smack dab in the heart of Tornado Alley, Oklahoma is unfortunately all too familiar with the deadly destruction of swirling vortexes. Oklahoma sees, on average, fifty-four tornadoes every year, and at least since 1950 the state has never gone a full calendar year without suffering at least seventeen.

In 1999, as all Oklahomans are sure to remember, an unprecedented 145 tornadoes swept across the state. Of those, 90 occurred in the month of May alone, 60 of which struck in a single day, May 3. This included the costliest tornado ever recorded in U.S. history, which covered thirty-eight miles, took the lives of thirty-six people, and damaged or destroyed eight thousand homes, causing an estimated $1 billion in damage. It set the world record for the fastest wind speed ever recorded on earth: 318 miles per hour.

And although intense study of cyclonic events has been ongoing since the 1950s, we are only just beginning to understand how these destructive spectacles work. Even with major advances in radar and satellite technology, tornadoes remain a virtual mystery. They strike wherever, whenever, usually with very little warning. Prediction is a matter of educated, though inexact, guesswork and the best projections are still made by storm chasers out in the field, closely watching the clouds.

Oddities discovered in the aftermath of a tornado are the stuff of legend. Cattle turn up marooned on roofs and lodged in treetops. Tree trunks are found impaled by stalks of wheat. Entire swimming pools are sucked dry, and metal buckets are blown inside out. Chickens, it seems, take the brunt of tornadoes' mischief, always being stripped bare of their feathers or thrust inexplicably into milk bottles, their heads poking out the top. Such improbable incidents are surely a key reason newspapers once referred to twisters as "freaks of the storm."

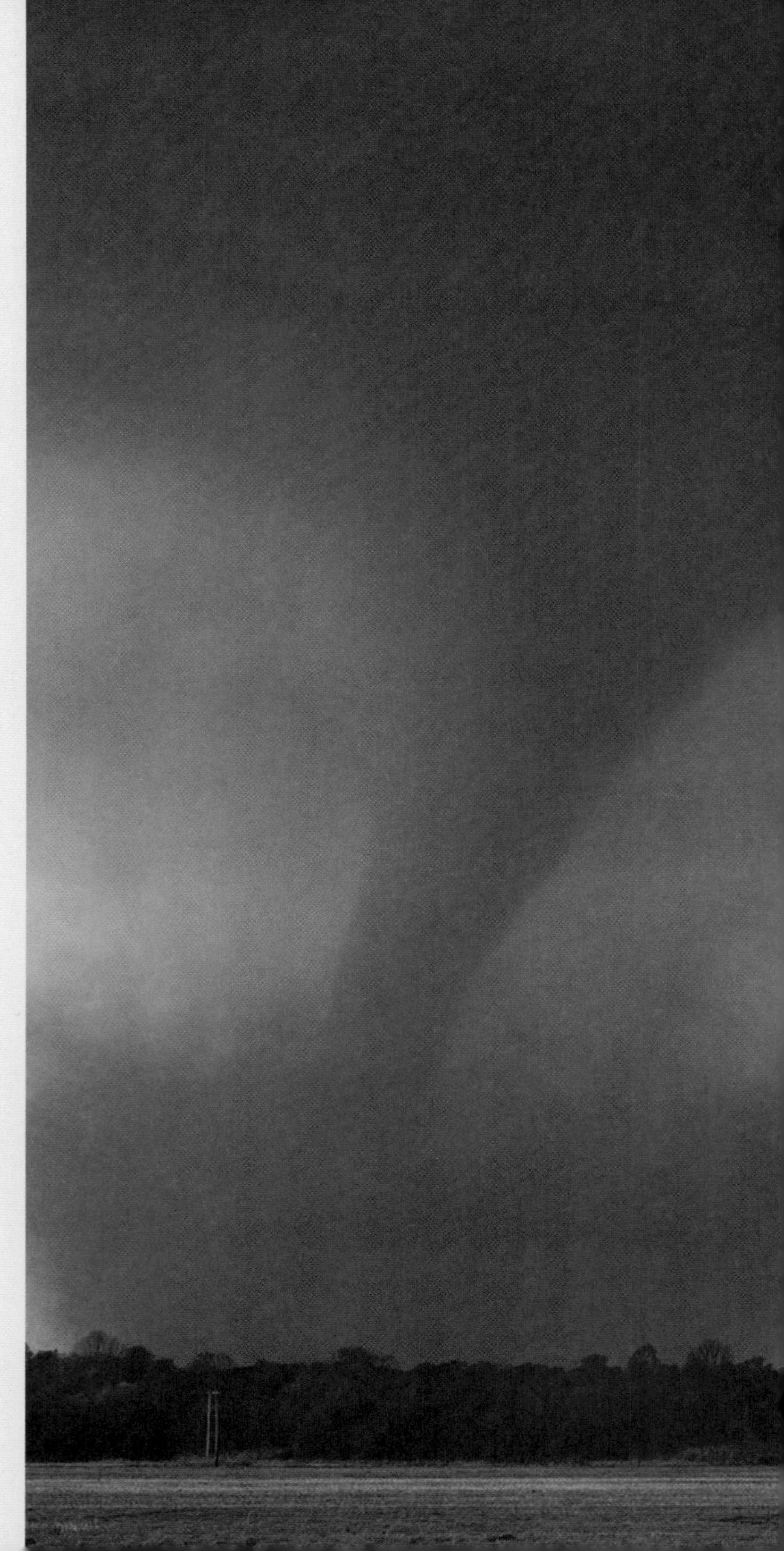

Many incidents are mere hearsay, but some benefit from photographic proof. A picture taken in 1883—among the first of its kind—depicts a six-inch-wide timber run fully through a tree. Others show a table fork turned into a deadly projectile, twisted and stuck prong-first into a pole, or the blade of a shovel thrust six inches deep into a tree trunk. A photo taken after a tornado that hit Moore, Oklahoma, in 1999 shows a large truck twisted completely around a utility pole as though it were a twist tie.

Tornadoes boggle the mind. They can lift entire homes from their foundations and flatten whole towns in a matter of seconds. A twister recorded in 1919 lifted several seventy-ton train cars off their tracks as they traveled along at sixty miles an hour; one, a passenger car carrying 117 people, was heaved eighty feet and dropped in a ditch. In another incident, a tornado picked up a locomotive, spun it 180 degrees and set it back down on an adjacent track. A tornado that struck Minnesota in 1919 split open an enormous tree, then tossed in an automobile and slammed the tree back together again, crushing the car like a huge vise.

In some cases, it's the astonishing lack of damage that garners the most attention. Tornadoes may churn up miles of terrain uninterrupted, or leap impulsively from earth to sky and back again, sparing a single home amid blocks of leveled houses. They cut through dense forest in a turmoil of debris, carving out entire corridors featuring naked trees on one side, and lush undamaged landscape on the other, as if nothing ever happened.

Tornadoes can crush a two-story house, yet leave a milk bottle standing upright on the front porch. They can rip away an entire wall of a downtown store, as one did in Kansas in 1915, but leave the shelves of canned goods that were standing against the wall untouched. That same Kansas tornado also blew a necktie rack for forty miles with ten ties still attached.

Other tornadoes have carried whole crates of eggs five hundred yards without cracking a single one, absconded with a jar of pickles that was dropped twenty-five miles away completely undamaged, and made off with a bank's cash drawer that was discovered sixty miles away with nothing missing. One of the more amazing oddities, which was captured on film after a twister struck Ada, Oklahoma, in 1973, is of an unbroken phonograph record lodged halfway into the side of a downed telephone pole.

An observer caught in a 1912 storm saw a utility pole plucked from the ground and bounced down the street like a pogo stick. Another story recalls a tornado that blew open a barn door, pushed a wagon out, turned it around, blew it back in and shut the door behind it. In 1919, a steamer trunk was discovered in an unroofed attic and traced back to a completely different attic several blocks away. And in 1958, a woman was yanked from her home and thrown sixty feet, where she was deposited next to a record of the song "Stormy Weather."

Yet some of the most astonishing stories following a tornado are those of extraordinary survival. The so-called Tri-State Tornado that struck Illinois, Missouri, and Indiana

in 1925—which still holds the record for the world's longest track of destruction and remains the deadliest tornado in U.S. recorded history—performed an unusual act of mercy when it destroyed a school in West Frankfort, Illinois, yet repositioned its sixteen students only 150 yards away and left them unharmed. In 1936, more than forty employees at the Cooper Pants factory in Gainesville, Georgia, ran for the stairs as a funnel struck their building. One woman, Mrs. Boyd Shaw, caught her dress on a sewing machine and became inextricably entangled. As the ceiling collapsed, Mrs. Shaw was torn free, picked up, and carried a block away with only minor injuries. She was the only one to survive. In 1955, nine-year-old Sharon Weron and the horse she was riding were snatched up by a twister as they were trying to flee. Sharon was carried one thousand feet before landing softly on her stomach, "just like a plane." Her only injuries came from the hail that followed.

In Woodward, Oklahoma, a schoolboy got the shock of a lifetime in 1947 while taking a bath just as a tornado hit his house. The twister lifted away his entire home, except for the floor and the bathtub, which was held in place by the plumbing, leaving the boy sitting naked in the rain.

In 2006, nineteen-year-old Matt Suter was plucked from his trailer, sucked out through a hole torn in the roof, and tossed almost a quarter of a mile, wearing nothing but his boxer shorts. It's estimated that, when he landed, he hit the ground at thirty miles per hour. Because he was knocked unconscious by a flying lamp just before he was picked up, however, his body remained limp, allowing him to absorb the impact evenly and walk away without so much as a single broken bone. Investigators later measured the distance between the trailer and Matt Suter's landing spot at 1,307 feet, conferring him with the unofficial record of longest distance carried by a tornado and living to tell the story.

One of the most heartwarming stories, though, comes out of Bridge Creek, Oklahoma, after a series of twisters ripped through eighty miles of the state in 1999. As a police officer was assessing the damage amid a flattened neighborhood, he spotted something next to a tree. At first he thought it was a doll, but as he pulled the figure from the debris, it started crying. Ten-month-old Aleah Crago and her family had been huddled in their hall closet when a tornado annihilated their home, ripping Aleah from her mother's arms and throwing her a hundred feet away, into the mud. Aleah's mother, who also survived, had assumed her daughter was dead, but the infant was returned to her arms just hours later as she was being treated at a hospital. The officer who found Aleah called the girl a true miracle baby.

Of course, the veracity of such amazing stories as these is often difficult to corroborate, save for the few cases that benefit from photographic evidence or verifiable, firsthand accounts. It just goes to show that there's no predicting what people, or tornadoes, are capable of.

Shaman's Portal

Out in the Oklahoma Panhandle lies Beaver Dunes State Park, a recreational playground centered on hundreds of acres of gleaming silica sand dunes, where visitors can camp, hike, swim, and dune-buggy their way across the vast sandy hills. There's a reasonable entry fee, so the only real downside is the slight possibility of being captured through a mysterious human-snatching gateway.

It's called Shaman's Portal, said to have swallowed more than a handful of unsuspecting travelers and vacationers over the last few centuries. The exact spot where the disappearances have taken place has not been determined, but it's fair to say that, wherever it is, anyone who's stumbled across it simply hasn't reported back.

If the accounts are to be believed, the first recorded occurrences date back to the sixteenth century when conquistador Francisco Vázquez de Coronado traipsed across the continent from Mexico, passing through Arizona, New Mexico, Texas, Oklahoma, and Kansas, looking for the famed Seven Cities of Gold. A friar on the expedition allegedly wrote in his journal about the loss of three men when camping near the dunes in Oklahoma:

> *It was the work of El Diablo. That night by the sandy hills we had been warned by the natives to avoid, we lost three able bodied men of valour: Juan Viscaino, Marco Romano, and Juan Munoz. They had been hunting game for the men when the three ill-fated men were taken from us in a lightning bolt of green.*

The "lightning bolt of green" coincides with the bright-green flash of light more recent observers say accompanies a victim's abduction, an indication that the same phenomenon has endured for at least half a millennium.

In 1894, settler Nancy Wright is said to have vanished amid the dunes attempting to rendezvous with her lover. In 1977, Bill Gruendyke, a camper from Colorado, disappeared as well, leaving behind both his vehicle and campsite. The night before he vanished, locals reported seeing those telltale flashes of green radiance. One morning in 1997, a group of young campers from Kansas woke to discover one of their companions missing. Again, a fellow camper reported seeing an emerald light the night of the disappearance.

The source behind the phenomenon, often referred to as Oklahoma's Bermuda Triangle, is yet undetermined, but there are several theories. Some believe it may be some kind of interdimensional portal focused on an infrequently trampled spot amid the dunes. At the other end of the theoretical spectrum is the idea that the disappearances are the result of boring old sinkholes. As for the flashes of green light, they may simply be discharges of static electricity; visitors to similar sand dunes regularly experience small shocks due to the friction of wind and sand grains.

The most popular theory, however, involves the existence of a UFO buried somewhere among the sand hills. A number of years ago, a group of relatives attending a family reunion claimed to have seen a crowd of military-looking personnel digging out—or possibly covering up—something alien, late at night within the park. The family was spotted by the uniformed men, who detained them for several hours and warned them not to talk about what they saw. Following up on the story, a researcher named Dr. Mark Thatcher investigated the area in the 1990s and hired a geologist to test soil samples. The two men found unusual levels of ionization and electromagnetic radiation, which the scientists equated to similar findings at both the legendary UFO crash site in Roswell, New Mexico, and the Bermuda Triangle. However, they too were approached by officials who produced government credentials—remember, it's a state-run park—and warned them to cease and desist, an admonition they evidently took to heart. Dr. Thatcher has since fallen off the radar.

In an attempt to get to the bottom of the story once and for all, Tammy Wilson, founder of the paranormal research team Eerie Oklahoma, sent out some feelers in 2006 hoping to gather more information. In return, she was contacted via e-mail by an individual using the alias Davis Humes, who warned her not to visit Beaver Sands and to forget anything she knew. Humes listed a number of researchers, including Dr. Thatcher, who had disappeared as a result of their investigations, and advised Wilson that it would be in her best interest to move on, as well.

After several exchanges between Humes and Wilson, Humes claimed that it was all a hoax that he himself instigated in 1997 as a psychology experiment about the nature of urban legends and conspiracy theories. He said he abandoned the experiment long ago, but thanks to the Internet, the mystery of "Shaman's Portal" took on a new life of its own. Having received this admission by Humes, Tammy Wilson considered the matter closed.

The only question that remains, of course, is whether the confession was genuine or simply a last-ditch effort to head off further scrutiny by discrediting the legend as a simple practical joke.

Little Bang Theories

On the afternoon of February 28, 1990, residents of Nowata were rocked by an unusual blast originating somewhere south of town. No one had any idea what could have caused the explosion, and since nobody saw anything actually blow up, there was little investigation.

However, when local landowner Bill Mitchell tried to find out why the water level was unusually high in Double Creek, which runs through his property, he discovered a large blast site along the creek bank. As Mitchell told the *Tulsa World*, it looked like "a giant mole went all under the ground. There is no telling how big a hole is under there. You can hear water falling. . . . In one place the water was shooting up a couple of feet . . . like a fountain."

Mitchell said it would have taken an immense amount of pressure to cause such damage. Having worked in the oil fields most of his life, he speculated that it may have been the result of a gas pocket, but he admitted that it would have had to be a tremendous one to move things the way it did.

This wasn't Oklahoma's first inexplicable explosion. Back in 1948, residents all across the northwestern portion of the state had witnessed an explosion "of atomic proportions" high in the sky. The crews of two B-29 planes reported seeing a ball of fire just prior to the explosion, which they said occurred well above their altitude of ten thousand feet. The detonation, which was described as a "fiercely brilliant white flash," generated a wide cloud of smoke. Many thought it was some kind of massive airline disaster, and astronomers surmised that it might have been an exploding meteor, similar to that which allegedly caused the Tunguska Event, a devastating blast in remote Siberia, Russia, in June 1908.

Nearly fifty years later, in 1995, central Oklahoma would be stymied by yet another blast, this time in Kingfisher, only two weeks after domestic terrorism brought down the Alfred P. Murrah Federal Building in Oklahoma City. This explosion was prefaced by a bomb scare. No bomb was found, but then, just forty-five minutes later, a thunderous report could be heard up to thirty miles away. Problem was, nobody could tell where it came from and there didn't seem to be any damage.

A man was later arrested for making the false bomb threat, but still no one could figure out the origin of the actual explosion. Both the Air Force and the Federal Aviation Administration said no planes in the area had been traveling at supersonic speeds, which ruled out a sonic boom. The county sheriff's department had no luck in solving the mystery, either. The blast still remains an enigma.

Yet another loud boom was recorded on February 2, 1999, at around 7:30 P.M. in Elk City. Similar to previous blasts, it shook window panes and prompted numerous phone calls to authorities. Oddly, another noise had caused a bit of a stir just the week before when citizens reported a sound like that of a rocket taking off. Of course, there was no apparent cause for either incident. Even ufologist and president of a UFO-research group Jim Hickman, who lives in nearby Elk City, could offer no probable source.

Why so many acoustic events in the Sooner State? Like most unusual phenomena, it's probably impossible to say. Then again, maybe these sorts of things go on all the time around the world. Maybe Oklahoma is the only place still quiet enough for residents to hear them.

Center of the Universe: Tulsa

The Bermuda Triangle. Stonehenge. Crop circles. The world is so wondrous and complicated that there are countless mysteries science has yet to solve. There are places on this earth that seemingly defy all we know about its natural machinations, and restore awe and splendor to a jaded populace. This blessed plot, this earth, this realm, this . . . Tulsa.

One of the country's most intriguing mystery spots sits comfortably in downtown Tulsa atop a pedestrian bridge, connecting First and Archer streets via Boston Avenue. The anomaly, which Tulsans modestly call "The Center of the Universe," is located directly within a thirty-inch concrete circle on the ground, surrounded by thirteen concentric rows of worn bricks. Why thirteen? Only the helpful aliens know, but this genuine abnormality cannot be easily dismissed.

Actually, the circle that marks the Center of the Universe was not an original feature of the bridge. Tulsa built the bridge in the 1930s to carry cars over the railroad tracks, but closed the span to automobiles in 1983 after a fire damaged a warehouse below. After that, it was refurbished as a pedestrian walkway. The architect of the project claims to have intended his circle design as a metaphor for the linking of the north and south sides of town, but that seems too pat. The circle, in fact, marks the location of an auditory oddity found nowhere else.

To experience the Center of the Universe phenomenon at its fullest, go with a friend. Sit in the middle of the circle and face any direction. Have your friend stand on the rim of the outermost circle of bricks. If you speak in a normal tone of voice, you will not sound any different to your friend just a few feet away, but to you, your voice will sound amplified and tinny. The more you try to make sense of the sound quality, the more bizarre it'll sound to you. Then, when your friend speaks to you, he will hear your echo but not his own. How could that even be possible? The Center of the Universe consistently tickles visiting schoolchildren and vortex seekers until, of course, it begins to unnerve them.

Just to add to the spot's inscrutability and panache, the Center of the Universe is flanked by a sixty-foot abstract sculpture of a totem pole called *Artificial Cloud*, or sometimes *Unity*. American Indian artist Robert Haozous claims to have erected the structure to commemorate Tulsa's 1991 Mayfest, and not to act as a landing beacon for intergalactic ships, or to summon Nessie.

Tulsa's municipal leaders dismiss the Center of the Universe as a "fluke," or at most, a simple "whisper chamber." One doubter speculates that an expansion joint that bisects the circle underneath the bridge vibrates with the sound of a nearby voice, causing a slightly delayed, metallic echo.

Wait, we hear the echo now. It's saying, "Hogwash."

—Craig Robertson

Bizarre Beasts

Oklahoma, with its acres upon acres of prairie, grassland, and forest, harbors a diverse menagerie of fauna. Antelope, bison, alligators, and big-eared bats make up but a small fraction of the virtual statewide zoo that's made the nation's twentieth largest state a popular destination with both hunters and wildlife spotters.

There are, however, some creatures said to roam within Oklahoma's state lines that have yet to make the official list at the Department of Wildlife Conservation. Elusive and mysterious, these enigmatic beings have also made Oklahoma a terminus for cryptozoologists in search of curious beasties.

So, the next time you're scouring the back roads of the Sooner State for interesting sights, be sure to keep your camera handy. You just might come across one of the region's peculiar, unclassified wildcats, shapeshifting "manimals," or even Bigfoot himself.

The Okiepus

Taking advantage of a pleasant autumn day, four young friends head out for a brisk swim amid the waters of a remote and quiet lake. With no one else around, the two couples take advantage of the solitude and swim out to the wooden platform that floats offshore, which they claim all to themselves. Unfortunately, their isolation proves to be their doom as the foursome encounters an unidentifiable creature that quickly pulls one of the swimmers beneath the surface and to her death. Unable to call for help, the remaining three are left stranded on the platform until the creature methodically snags them all from between the cracks and, one by one, yanks them under.

It's a story that only master of horror Stephen King could make believable. Yet, these events, which King described in his short story "The Raft," may occur closer to the plane of reality than one would care to imagine.

Similar incidents have allegedly occurred in the waters of Oklahoma—more specifically Lake Thunderbird, Lake Oolagah, and Lake Tenkiller. The predator in this case, however, is not a dark, oily slick as King described, but an as-of-yet-unidentified freshwater octopus.

These creatures, which have been described by only a handful of surviving witnesses, are usually said to be leathery, reddish brown in color, and as large as a horse. Some reports depict them as measuring up to twenty feet long and more closely resembling a shark with tentacles, although no one has really gotten a reliably clear view of the animal.

It's impossible to tell just how many drownings may have been caused by the sinister cephalopod. Between 1988 and 2003 (the most recent statistics readily available), Oklahoma experienced an average of sixty-six submersion injuries per year, most of which were fatal, and it's not always possible to clearly determine the cause. In some instances, however, nearby swimmers claim to have seen the victims struggling amid the splash of what appear to be tentacles.

Internet accounts of ancient Native American octopus tales in Oklahoma's lakes unfortunately must be dismissed, as each of the three lakes purportedly inhabited by the beasts is man-made and date no earlier than 1953. However, that doesn't negate the possibility of such creatures having lived among the rivers that feed them, which may explain how they got there in the first place.

Of course, it's worth noting that no species of freshwater octopus has yet been classified, which means that either Oklahoma is home to one unique beastie, or the invertebrate in question has been misidentified. Some have suggested that the Oklahoma Octopus might in fact be a eurypterid, a class of arthropods believed to be extinct, though perhaps lurking below the water's surface like the coelacanth, a fish thought to be extinct for the last 65 million years until one species was discovered happily swimming off the coast of South Africa in 1938. (A second species was identified in 1998 in the waters around Indonesia.) Others, however, think the Okiepus is more than likely a breed of freshwater jellyfish such as *Craspedacusta sowerbyi*, which has been discovered in lakes and reservoirs all over the world, including the United States.

Bigfoot

He's big, he's hairy, he's smelly, he has a bad attitude, and he's not your aunt Carla. Yes, as hard as it might be to imagine, that figurehead of enigmatic beasties, Bigfoot, lurks amid the forests of Oklahoma.

In the Himalayas, he's known as the yeti. In the Pacific Northwest, his name is Sasquatch. In Arizona, they call him the Mogollon Monster, and down in Texas, people refer to him as the Big Thicket Wild Man. Here in Oklahoma, he has a list of different monikers: Boggy Bottom Monster, Kiamachi Bigfoot, Nowata Monster, Millsap Monster, and sometimes the Abominable Chicken Man, a nickname earned for his predilection toward consuming farmers' poultry.

Descriptions of the creature vary slightly from sighting to sighting, but generally he's said to be about eight feet tall, covered in long, dark fur and looking something like a cross between a man and an ape. His feet leave distinct footprints, some measuring up to twenty-seven inches long. Most notable, at least to those who encounter him, is the stench he emits—a distinctly trenchant smell, which has earned him yet another nickname: Skunk Ape. The odor is so pervasive, in fact, that Bigfoot hunters often use it as an indicator that they're on the right track, as they can smell him long before they ever see him.

One of the beast's more intriguing characteristics, though, is the unusual vocalizations he's said to make. According to researchers, Bigfoot's calls, unlike those of most animals, comprise a variety of distinct sounds. Most common seems to be the whooping cry, similar to that of some primate species. Campers have recounted hearing nearby calls consisting of a long "whooooo" followed by three short, high-pitched "whoops," which are frequently answered with similar calls from much farther away, as if two creatures are trying to locate each other. Bigfoot also reportedly communicates with whistles, screams, and deep grunts. More frightening is his "roar," a deep, deafening bellow that's been described as something like the call of a bear and crow combined, and at least as loud as a truck horn. This particular sound is usually heard from a short distance, leading some to believe this is meant as a territorial warning. Even more interesting, however, is Bigfoot's speechlike articulations, which come out as garbled or "bubbly" but sound like some primitive language, which may indicate a higher intelligence than one might initially suspect.

Most encounters with the beast, thankfully, remain fairly benign. In numerous reports, the creature has been spotted with his face pressed to a cabin window, his reddish brown eyes calmly investigating its inhabitants like a hirsute Peeping Tom. Some have run across him while hiking through the woods, occasionally coming within yards or even footsteps of the beast, but with nary a response. Hunters have reported spying him standing among the trees, harmlessly watching them as though he's been studying them for some time. However, like most of the people who witness him up close, Bigfoot is quick to startle and will typically run off into the brush when spotted.

Still, a number of encounters have reportedly turned violent. In an incident that took place in 1951, an eleven-year-old boy named Billy Ludlow saw a tall, hairy creature near the Little River, which chased him and his friends all the way to the his grandmother's cabin, where it tried in vain to break down the front door. In a similar event in 1999, Tim Humphreys of Honobia caught a Bigfoot staring into his house, followed by screaming and beating on the outside walls. Humphreys later spotted a whole group of the creatures in the woods, one of which charged him before he shot it, forcing the aggressive monster to flee. In another episode that took place in Talihina in 1970, a high-school boy, who was cruising the back roads with some friends, wandered into the woods to take care of some personal business when he was frightened, and reportedly assaulted, by a large creature that was thereafter known as the Green Hill Monster. When the sheriff later investigated the area where the encounter took place, he discovered a number of deer whose necks had evidently been snapped in two. The sheriff subsequently prohibited anyone from going into the woods at night.

Most of the time, though, Bigfoot proves to be little more than an elusive nuisance. His favorite pastime, apparently, is to throw rocks at humans. Numerous encounters with the creature begin with a volley of pebbles hitting the sides of houses and barns. Hikers have been confused by the sounds of large stones plunking into bodies of water they happen to be walking near and countless campers have had rocks thrown into their campsite from the darkened woods as the hapless recreationists sit about the campfire. Oddly, the big knuckleballer never actually hits anyone with his projectiles, indicating that he has either really bad aim or a streak of mischief as broad as his shoulders.

Oklahoma has become such a hot spot for Sasquatch activity, it seems, that it even has its own annual fair. Held in early autumn, the Honobia Bigfoot Festival brings together serious hunters and casual enthusiasts alike from across the country to enjoy man-ape–themed food and fun. It also features a conference hosted by numerous experts in the field offering up-to-date information and advice on tracking the beast. In the past, the festival has even sponsored a Bigfoot-hunting excursion into the Kiamachi Mountains, although as yet none of the participants have sniffed him out. Then again, as conference director Farlan Huff has put it, "You don't find Bigfoot. He finds you."

Bigfoot Calling

I decided if ever there was a place where Bigfoot might live, it could be this ranch located in the Arbuckle Mountains of Oklahoma. There is plenty of wild game, woods, and clear running streams. Imagine how you might react if you made a "Bigfoot call" in the woods at night, and one came!

That's what happened to me while I spent the night at an isolated hunting cabin during July of 2004. Since I was by myself and no one could laugh at me for doing so, I made a Bigfoot call as best I could from watching a Bigfoot documentary on television. After I made the call something hit a tree with what sounded like another tree. The sound was so powerful! I ran back inside the cabin where I already had all of the lights off.

Soon I heard heavy footsteps coming to the cabin and then I could hear deep voices mumbling. I didn't get much sleep that night and the rest of my visit to the ranch was spent at the main house. My return visit the following month was very exciting. This time I brought a motion sensor camera and my beginner's luck paid off: I got a photo of an adult red-haired female Bigfoot with a juvenile. I realize everyone will take my story with a grain of salt, but for me this photo is proof positive that Bigfoot is real. *—Farlan Huff*

Flying Rabbit

Several years ago I was looking through an old scrapbook and I noticed several articles from a Tulsa, Oklahoma, paper saying that several people had spotted a flying rabbit over the city. One article had a picture of a rabbit being held by a young boy. So far I haven't found anyone living that remembers it, including the Tulsa Historical Society. Maybe you could check into it for me. *—James Gore*

The Deer Lady

Most world cultures have a femme fatale of folklore, a mysterious woman who lures unsuspecting men to their deaths. The ancient Greeks have the sirens, Latin Americans have La Llorona, and Oklahoma's Native American tribes have the Deer Woman. Director John Landis transformed the story into a modern, hard-boiled mystery for Showtime's "Masters of Horror" series, but he failed to capture the spirit of the original Native American legend.

Each tribe makes minor alterations to the myth, but the basic structure of the story is the same throughout Oklahoma. To celebrate a successful hunt, the tribe has a powwow. The men and women dance around a roaring fire, and the drums echo through the dark valley. A young warrior takes a break from dancing to get a drink of water when he notices a flicker in the distance. He walks away from the warmth of the tribe's camp, and as his eyes adjust to the darkness he realizes that the flicker is the shape of a dancing woman.

The woman's clothing is ornate and colorful, her jewelry of shining gold. As the warrior watches her, he becomes entranced by her beauty and grace. She glides along the surface of the ground effortlessly. At times she seems to float closer to the warrior, but when he approaches the woman she seems to drift away. The more the warrior watches her, the more he can't look away.

The warrior begins to run toward the woman, desperate to see her face. When he finally catches up with her, he is much too far from the tribe for anyone to hear or see him. When she finally stops, he approaches her carefully, gazing into her large inky eyes, like the eyes of a doe. She smiles and retreats, easily dashing through the thorny brush. The warrior races to catch her, but she is too fast. Far from home, the warrior pauses to rest before journeying back to the safety of the tribe.

The woman appears abruptly in front of him. Her face is wet with tears, and her expression is one of remorse. The warrior starts to reach out to her, but stops when he sees two hooves beneath her skirt. The warrior backs up as he watches the woman transform, her face morphing into that of a doe. He trips over a rock and falls to the ground, and the deer is immediately on top of him. The warrior tries to fight against the animal, but she is too strong. She tramples him as he calls out for help that will never come. Broken and dying, he lifts his head for the last time as he watches her run off into the valley, shifting from deer to woman and back again. Her beauty provides the warrior a last comfort as he dies alone on the cold ground. —*Craig Robertson*

The Thing from Tahlequah

Reading newspaper archives from the early 1900s seems like it might be the driest of all hobbies, but we should all be grateful for those unsung library moles who endure the tedium and frustration of loading a microfiche machine, for it is they who uncover the most marvelous of articles.

A prime example is an item once buried deep in an issue of the *Oklahoman* published in November 1920. Boldly featuring the word *monster* in its title, the article recalled an incident said to have occurred near the eastern Oklahoma town of Tahlequah in 1842. The "thing," described as reptilian, reportedly lived in a cave of unknown depth, which opened onto a bluff overlooking the Illinois River. For reasons unexplained or inexplicable, the creature left its home and started making its way across the prairie north of town, an action that unnerved the locals enough to call in well-respected elder and noted warrior Archibald Campbell.

Through the snow and ice, a messenger raced to retrieve Campbell, who took up his knife and his gun, and gathered a group of brave trackers to hunt down the beast. When the posse reached the prairie north of town, they discovered a broad track that had been cut clearly through the snow. The track, the men said, appeared "as if some animal the size of a bear had been dragged along." It remains unclear if the description was meant to convey the size of the creature itself or if perhaps the beast had been so powerful as to actually take down such large game, though either conclusion would have been reason enough to hunt it down.

Unfortunately, the creature had a considerable head start on the men. When the party reached the Grand River several miles west they got a glimpse of the monster.

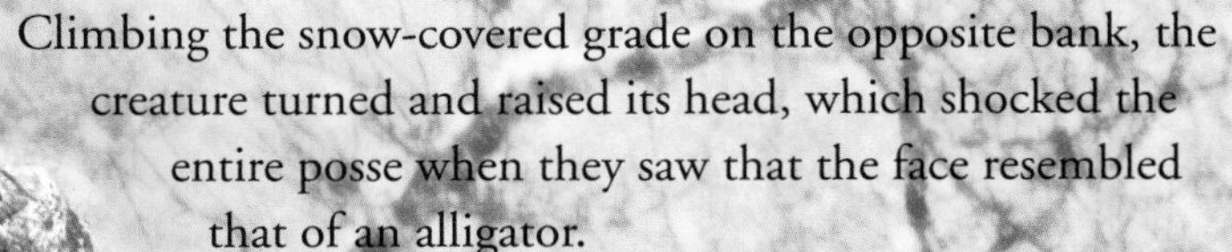

Climbing the snow-covered grade on the opposite bank, the creature turned and raised its head, which shocked the entire posse when they saw that the face resembled that of an alligator.

Regrettably, the late hour forced the party to camp for the night before continuing its pursuit. Moreover, by the next morning many had decided to drop out and return home. Campbell, however, backed by a few indomitable hunters, forged on.

Given the path left in the snow, not to mention the horrible stench it was said to produce, the posse found no difficulty in tracking the creature. By late afternoon, they spotted him once again. Before they could get close enough to take aim, however, the men were stopped by a group of Osage Indians.

The Osage, who were familiar with the creature, had caught sight of it as well and intercepted the hunting party to warn them not to continue. Insisting that the creature's thick scales were impenetrable by their bullets, they said continuing the chase would have been futile. Besides, they said, it was not a creature to be trifled with.

The article conveyed few details of the ensuing conversation, but "so urgent were the appeals" that the Osage convinced Campbell and his bloodthirsty group to turn back.

Local history has since recorded no other sightings of the creature, though it has been suggested that the beast may have turned south and sought refuge in Mexico. It's also possible that the creature may have traveled as far as South America, which may have, in fact, been its original home. Interestingly, ancient artifacts uncovered from the Chiriquian natives who once lived in Panama are rife with images of a deity whose body was that of a human and whose head was that of an alligator.

Crypto Cats

Gauging from the number of sightings, Oklahoma appears to be virtually crawling with large unidentified felines. Though there is little to no hard evidence to support their existence, it seems everyone and his neighbor has spotted one of these big cats roaming the countryside.

Now, we're not talking about the usual bobcats or mountain lions here. And that looks to be the point exactly. Few people are precisely sure of what they did see, but they know what they didn't see. The mysterious beasts, according to reports, are larger and huskier than native species and are totally black.

Oklahomans in virtually every part of the state have run across the big black cats. Drivers have swerved to miss the animals, stopping briefly to get a view of the abnormally large and darkly colored felines before the creatures dart off into the brush. Some ranch owners have witnessed the cats skulking about their acreage. One resident says he was able to watch a mystery cat for several minutes as it stalked a group of deer on his property. Yet, despite numerous reports such as these, experts deny that any such beast exists.

Now, before we get much further, let's clear up a few things. Mountain lions, cougars, pumas, panthers: these are all the same thing. In fact, the same cat has more than forty names in the English language alone. For our purposes, however, we're going to stick to *panther*. These panthers, which are unusual in Oklahoma, but not unheard of, are slender and measure about eight feet, including their lengthy tail. They're generally yellowish or reddish brown in color. Bobcats, which are quite common in the area, are well known for their spots, which cover an otherwise tan to grayish brown coat. They measure about three feet long and feature a distinctively wide face, pointed ears and a stubby tail.

With this in mind, the mystery cats witnessed by so many residents are unlikely to be simple cases of mistaken identity. Occasionally, one of these cats is described as having spots, but is much too big to be a bobcat, not to mention its thick, "ropelike" tail. Many believe the creature at first to be a dog, its size being comparable to a Great Dane, but its features are distinctively feline.

As already mentioned, however, the cat is often said to be uniformly black. And this is where the sightings become so unusual. Although there are a number of recognized panther subspecies, none has ever been recorded as having an all-black coloring. The term "black panther" is actually a misnomer, which refers to melanistic jaguars or leopards, not panthers. An actual black panther has never been scientifically documented.

So, could the mystery cat in fact be a jaguar or a leopard? Well, first off, leopards don't even live on this continent, and jaguars, while native to the Americas, certainly don't reside in Oklahoma. In fact, the only jaguars known to live in the United States are a small population in Arizona. Besides, black jaguars, even on the whole, are exceedingly rare. So, to find a jaguar, especially a black one, skulking around the suburbs of Tulsa would be nigh impossible, which is certainly why the Oklahoma Department of Wildlife Conservation denies any existence of such a cat.

Still, there are too many reports across the state of the large black cat to simply ignore the possibility. So, what could it be? Some have suggested that it may be a northerly migrating jaguarundi, an odd-looking, medium-sized cat that normally lives south of Texas, looks something like an otter, and sports a coat that can be blackish to brownish gray in color. Others think it might be some kind of bizarre hybrid such as the jaglion, the pumapard, or the popular liger. Some propose that it might even be something that escaped from Hugo in southeast Oklahoma, which has long been known to serve as the winter home for generations of circus folk.

Then again, there are some close encounters with the beast that are a bit harder to explain. In some circles, the ebony animal is known as the Ozark Howler, a fear-provoking feline that prowls Arkansas, Texas, and Missouri, as well as Oklahoma. Those who've gotten a better look say its dark fur may, in fact, have a reddish hue, as do its eyes. Moreover, it proudly displays small horns, or features that appear like horns, as well as something resembling a beard. Its yowl, which gives the creature its name, is a bone-chilling sound that's much closer to a woman's terrified scream than any kind of roar or growl.

Unfortunately, there have yet been any reliable photographs of the Ozark Howler or its counterparts, as most encounters are fleeting and occur at night. And, honestly, those are probably moments in which one is least likely to hold anything steady, much less a camera.

The Ishkitini

Tales of men who can metamorphose from human to animal form have permeated Native American legends for centuries. These skinwalkers, as they are often called, are traditionally practitioners of arcane customs who wear the pelts of various fauna and engage in acts of terror on unsuspecting victims, though many believe there are those who literally transform into the animals themselves.

Often described as some kind of half-human beast that has assumed the physiology of a wolf, coyote, bear, or any number of other creatures, the skinwalker is said to travel at extreme speeds, terrifying human prey in the dark of night. In recent decades, stories have been about shape-shifters overtaking vehicles traveling along back roads, evidently simply for the sinister pleasure of striking terror in the hearts of drivers and passengers, though no one has yet slowed down to see what the creature's intent might really be.

Of the more feared incarnations of the skinwalker, however, is the Ishkitini. Commonly referred to as the "Stigini" due to an apparent misinterpretation in pronunciation, the Ishkitini is a manifestation of the horned owl and is considered a much maligned harbinger of death. Unfortunately, the legend of the Ishkitini is a difficult one to pin down, reportedly due to the reluctance of most Native American elders to discuss the creature. From what can be gathered, though, it's evidently the foulest of fowl.

The call of the Ishkitini was a sure sign that death was imminent among those who heard it. The death would be quick, and unavoidable. According to some accounts, the screech, which sounds much like that of the common owl, is only to be feared when there is no answering call, an indication that the creature is seeking to take a life. Frequently, however, the call is described as more of an otherworldly shriek, much like that of a banshee, starting out as a sort of growl that crescendoes into a birdlike howl.

The Ishkitini appears to be a legend of Choctaw origin, though evidence suggests the Creek Indians are familiar with the creature, as well. From the vague details gleaned from younger tribe members, who are more apt to discuss the creature openly, a person takes on the form in one of two ways. In the first, a warrior must kill someone, cut out his heart, and bury it next to a tree, a ritual that would allow him to take on the form of his choice. The second, which seems related more specifically to the Ishkitini, requires the shape-shifter to vomit up his internal organs. To kill the creature, one must either shoot it with a specially prepared medicine arrow or destroy the organs while they're outside the body.

Rumor has it the area around Bird Creek Church in Sasakwa is a good place to hear the call of the Ishkitini, or perhaps even encounter the creature if you're the type of misguided person who would want to do such a thing. It might be advisable in such a situation, however, to take a can of lighter fluid and a match along with you just in case you stumble over a pile of guts.

The Thunderbird

For every dominion, there is a mysterious creature the world has yet to quantify. Below the sea swims the Loch Ness Monster, on land stalks the chupacabra, and high up in the mountains lumbers the majestic yeti. And if we consider each of these to be the ruler of its domain, then the sovereign of the sky must certainly be the mighty Thunderbird, an enormous flying beast resembling something from the age of the dinosaurs.

A surprisingly large creature, the Thunderbird's wingspan is said to measure up to 160 feet wide and its body more than 90 feet long. The beast has been described as featherless and somewhat dragonlike, possessing a serpentine body, two powerful, clawed feet, and the face of an alligator. According to Native American mythology, such gigantic creatures could shoot lightning from their eyes, and the flapping of their massive wings produced a roar like thunder, hence its name. Still, though it would be hard to miss, the Thunderbird remains highly elusive.

The creature made its first appearance in Western lore in 1890, when a story out of the historic town of Tombstone, Arizona, reported the slaying of one such beast. In an article published in the town paper, the aptly named *Epitaph*, two cowboys were said to have encountered the creature, chased it on horseback, then gunned it down with a volley of rifle fire. Today, the fate of its carcass is unknown, but several men purportedly saw the corpse up close and even posed alongside it for a now misplaced photograph.

However, this would not be the only reported sighting of the terrible Thunderbird. Such encounters have continued to surface even up through modern times and have cropped up across the West and well into Oklahoma. According to author and Fortean investigator Cullan Hudson, settlers in the southeastern portion of the state were briefly terrorized by a giant bird, which the pioneers were so mystified by that they regarded it as a supernatural apparition. In another incident, a similar beast kidnapped three children from a small community near Clarita, causing residents to confine their offspring indoors, while braver neighbors tried to hunt the creature down. Unfortunately, most who tried to kill the bird only got themselves sliced to death by its razor talons. Eventually, a local rifleman finally brought an end to the Thunderbird's reign of terror.

It's believed the townspeople buried the monster in a nearby river bottom, where its bones are presumed to still exist.

THE REDNECK CAPITOL
PLAY IN THEIR OWN ENVIRONMEN
ROUTE US 66
INSANITY AT ITS Finest
TEXACO
LUCILLE'S
HISTORIC HIGHWAY

Local Heroes and Villains

Okies, Boomers, Sooners—I don't care what you call them, they're weird. And in a book like this, that's a compliment.

It seems that Oklahomans like to consider themselves pretty average folk, friendly and conventional. In my experience, they also have an irresistible impulse to run to the top of the nearest grassy mound and shout, "Hey! Over here! Look past my frayed baseball cap and sleeveless flannel shirt. I've got something to say!"

Usually, that something is a welcome deviation from the norm. Sometimes the Okie drive to stand out leads them to contribute some pretty amazing things to our national culture; other times it leads them to commit horrendous misdeeds to scar an otherwise magnificent history.

Still, either way, these individuals' exceptionality has secured their stories a well-earned retelling.

Harley and Annabelle

"Lord Almighty, God! Get in here, ya good-lookin' pervert! Welcome to America!"

From your first step through the screen doors at the Sandhills Curiosity Shop, you realize the curiosities aren't the hundreds of old signs and antiques covering the walls. It's the two living characters.

"We want to welcome you to Erick, Oklahoma, the redneck capital of the world!" cry Harley and Annabelle, in voices explosive enough they might scare off the meeker visitors. Dressed in red-and-white-striped overalls—what they call their "redneck tuxedos"—they let you know from the get-go that you're in for a unique experience.

It's hard to describe just what Harley and Annabelle are all about. There's guitar-playing, singing, and storytelling, to be sure, but it's not your usual family-style hootenanny. It's more an interactive event, full of inappropriate humor and general madness. The "Music Makers" call it "insanity at its finest."

They heat up quickly, as does the old building in which they play, jam-packed with upwards of sixty tourists at a time, all laughing, singing, and cheering in the sweaty, un-air-conditioned former meat market that serves as redneck central. Yet nobody complains. Anyway, Harley's accommodating: "If it gets too hot for ya, feel free to take off yer clothes!"

The show is an all-out cyclone of classic tunes, free beer, sandwiches, and sexual innuendo, punctuated by bear hugs and an R-rated version of Bobby Troup's song "Route 66" that starts off: "Get your bumps, kicks, grinds, tricks"—and a couple of other –ick words we can't share in a family book—"on Route 66." At the end of every show, the floor is littered with coins, paper plates, and empty cans, the detritus of genuine roadside fun and hospitality.

Surprisingly, this most popular of Route 66 attractions was never something Harley or Annabelle had imagined being a part of. It was pure serendipity. Harley, a seasoned musician, had moved back to his hometown of Erick in the mid-1980s to "clear his head," and he set himself up in the old brick-fronted building on Sheb Wooley Avenue. Annabelle, on a visit from California, stopped in shortly thereafter to have her guitar tuned and, having succumbed to Harley's unique charm, never left.

From there, the two tried their hand at running an antiques shop, a music shop, and a health-food store, none of

which worked out. They had about three people a year walk through their doors, which, according to them, included themselves and nobody from Erick.

Finally, after they ate all their own stock, there wasn't much else to do but entertain themselves. As they were strumming away on their guitars, a man walked into their shop and asked if a few people could come in and stretch their legs a bit. The duo were happy to oblige, and spent the next hour or so playing for an impromptu audience, who began clapping along and tossing cash their way.

"The building was cram-packed full of people," Harley recalls. "They picked up these tambourines, started playing 'em, jumpin', hollerin', kickin', screamin', havin' the damnedest time you ever seen." By the time the group left, Harley and Annabelle had made more money than they had from their previous businesses combined. As it turned out, the group was a busload of visitors from England on a tour of Route 66. The tour guide asked if he could bring by another crowd in a couple of days.

That was 1999. Today, the duo estimates they see some three hundred tour groups a year from all over the world. They've been featured on international television and have been invited to the governor's mansion. They've even been visited by the heads of Pixar, who incorporated some of Harley's personality into the character of Mater from the 2006 movie *Cars*.

Oddly, Harley and Annabelle don't consider themselves extraordinary in any way. "We ain't good at nothin'. We can't do nothin'," they like to say. "We're just what we are." Lucky for them, and us, that happens to be a slice of good old American weird.

God's Insurance Policy: Jesus as Underwriter

I'm beginning to think "Chutzpa" is a lost book of the Bible. The things people try to get away with in the name of religion seem to get more and more bizarre as the years go by.

Take, for example, a story that surfaced in 1994 out of Oklahoma City. A woman was stopped for a traffic violation, and when she was asked to present her proof of insurance, as law dictates she must carry, the driver handed over a document labeled "God's Insurance Policy." The paper looked legitimate in every way, except for the fact that the issuing agency didn't legally exist.

When questioned, the woman revealed that she had presented the insurance form twice before, once during a separate traffic stop, and another time when renewing her vehicle registration, both without incident. She said her boyfriend had obtained the coverage for her at the amazing cost of $285 a year, which was too good a deal to pass up, though apparently not too good to believe. Further investigation turned up several other drivers who were carrying the policy and at least three tag agencies that had accepted the documents for license renewal.

The documents appeared, at cursory glance, to be genuine. They were printed on perforated carbon paper and recorded the date of expiration, policy name, and the make and ID of the insured vehicle. According to the police officer who first suspected the document to be forged, it "was perfect in every detail to an authentic insurance verification form." The only technical problem was that every form subsequently discovered shared the same policy number: PS91MT6.33, an obvious scriptural reference to Psalm 91 and Matthew 6:33.

The mastermind behind the insurance scam was sixty-year-old James E. McCuiston, known to his clients as "Brother Jim." He had sold the policies to at least fifty people, with the assistance of, according to him, "God the Father, through his son, Jesus Christ, the Holy Spirit, and a computer."

Brother Jim insisted that he had not established his insurance company for the purpose of making money, and that the policies provided "God's protection, not man's protection." As made clear by the fine print on the back of the forms he had issued, security from vehicle accidents came from the faith of the policy holder:

> *God's insurance policy, issued by the Father, Son, and the Holy Ghost, and backed by the power of God, is not founded on a philosophy of fear as typical insurance, but on a foundation of faith in God's word.*

Not fearing, only believing, brings protection and is reality, even as fear allows accidents and is reality: so according to your faith be your reality.

All accidents, then, would be caused by the insured's lack of faith—and could result in a claim's rejection.

When a warrant was issued for McCuiston's arrest, the accused said he would follow "man's law."

"The Lord had made it clear that I am accountable to man physically and accountable to God spiritually," he said. There was no word on whether God appeared in court to testify on his behalf.

Morrison's Circus

You'd think when an entire town gets duped into handing over a large sum of money to a complete stranger and getting nothing in return, they'd do their best to forget it ever happened. In Wetumka, though, they considered it cause for celebration.

On a hot August day in 1950, a well-dressed stranger by the name of F. Bam Morrison sauntered into town and introduced himself to the locals as the advance man for Bohn's United Circus Shows. He was there to let everyone know the show was headed through their burg and to make sure arrangements were made.

Wetumka, which had a population of about 2,500 at the time, was naturally thrilled that the big top had chosen their town as the next stop. On Morrison's advice, a local grocer eagerly ordered one hundred pounds of hot dogs and dozens of cases of soda. The Meadors Hotel reserved twenty rooms for the performers. Farmers delivered a truckload of hay to the chosen circus grounds to feed the elephants.

Meanwhile, Morrison himself sold $250 worth of advertising that was to be printed up in the circus program. He enlisted the local Boy Scout troop to sponsor the event and reportedly sold plenty of advance tickets to the show. While he was in town, he was granted a free hotel room and complimentary meals at the Wide-A-Wake Cafe. A couple of doctors provided medical service in exchange for free passes.

As soon as Morrison felt everything was in order, he departed town, assuring folks that Bohn's Circus would be headed down Main Street in just a few days.

When the day came, residents young and old lined the sidewalks in anticipation of the coming parade. Wetumka buzzed with excitement. Everyone waited . . . and waited . . . and waited. Pretty soon, fanfare turned to confusion, which then turned to agitation. Realization began to set in. They'd been had.

F. Bam Morrison, whose initial probably stood for "Flimflam," had taken the entire town for a ride and got away scot-free. Rather than grumble about it, though, Wetumka figured they'd make the best of it. After all, they already had the food and drinks, and everyone was gathered together ready for a celebration. So, they had one, right then and there. They christened it "Sucker Day" and have been celebrating it almost every year since.

One year, officials even tracked Morrison down and invited him to be the grand marshal. He reportedly sent his regrets—from jail.

Andrew Hartley Payne

Long before there were sports drinks, designer running shoes, and breakfast cereal endorsements, there was C. C. Pyle, a pioneer in sports promotion. The P. T. Barnum of athletic marketing, Pyle was both revolutionary and shamelessly ostentatious in his promotion of athletes and their accomplishments. He was also known to be a little dodgy, earning himself the nickname "Cash and Carry" Pyle.

But this story isn't really about him. It's about the Oklahoman he made famous and the grandiose way in which he did it. C. C. Pyle's opus, a coast-to-coast marathon that would last nearly three months and pass through thirteen states, would be known as the Transcontinental Foot Race of 1928. A roving promotion engine, the event was devised as a huge moneymaking scheme the likes of which had never before been organized.

Pyle formulated his grand competition to make a profit at every conceivable angle. From Los Angeles to Chicago, he would follow the newly completed Route 66, soliciting money from the Highway 66 Association ostensibly to finance road improvements. He instigated bidding wars between towns vying to have the race pass through their neck of the woods, bypassing the losers. He even hired a traveling carnival to set up wherever the race stopped for the night and took a cut of the proceeds. Runners themselves were charged $125 to compete, then asked to pay 50¢ a night for bedding and 50¢ per meal while attending the mandatory training camp set up three weeks before the start of the race. The event was a virtual cash machine.

When the gun was fired on March 4, 1928, 199 competitors crossed the starting line. Among them were Pyle's golden boy, Arthur Newton (the most famous distance runner of the time), an American who held the record for skipping (eleven thousand times), a Hindu philosopher, a one-armed man, a ukulele player, hikers, letter carriers, barefoot runners, and an actor who looked like Moses. Some quickly became media favorites and earned nicknames like "The Sheik" and "Wildfire" Thompson.

Then there was Andrew Payne, a quiet nineteen-year-old Cherokee from Foyil, who had to borrow the money from his parents to be there.

From city to city, runners were followed by an army of track officials, personal trainers, doctors, nurses, dieticians, and miscellaneous support crew. Pyle constructed a $25,000 double-decker bus, christened *The America*, to lead the procession, a mobile mansion that became a story in itself, pimped out with an observation deck, living quarters, writing tables, hot and cold water, showers, and air-conditioning. It was followed by a dedicated darkroom car that produced a stream of publicity photos, as well as a mobile radio station that broadcast a play-by-play of the day's events.

The average distance covered in a day's run was forty-one miles, longer than a single Olympic marathon. Competitors' daily times were tracked and added up as they progressed. When they reached camp for the night, where Pyle's carnival had been set up, the leaders were paraded onstage to the cheers of the midway crowd. Some told stories, others sang or told jokes. Many, like Andy Payne, simply grabbed a hot meal and hit their tents.

All did not go as planned, however. By the third day, about 30 percent of the runners had already dropped out. As the race passed through the Southwest, the region's population proved too scarce to support the operation financially. Often, townsfolk simply watched the race from the shoulders of the highway instead of paying to enter the fairgrounds that night. Moreover, Pyle skipped towns that didn't pony up enough in sponsorship, sometimes leaving his own runners without proper accommodations. In a blow of bad publicity, Pyle's star, the famous Arthur Newton, threw in the towel before he crossed into Arizona.

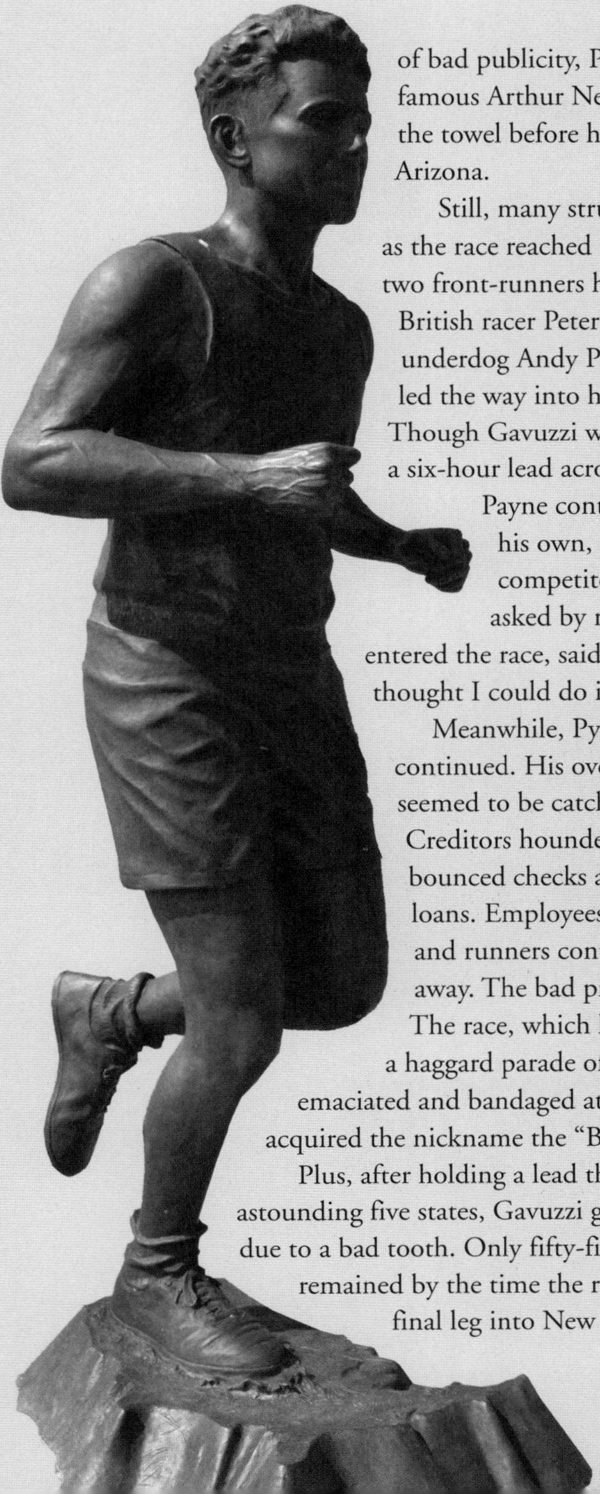

Still, many struggled on, and as the race reached Oklahoma, two front-runners had emerged: British racer Peter Gavuzzi and underdog Andy Payne, who led the way into his home state. Though Gavuzzi would soon gain a six-hour lead across the Midwest, Payne continued to hold his own, a humble competitor who, when asked by reporters why he entered the race, said simply, "I just thought I could do it."

Meanwhile, Pyle's troubles continued. His overachievement seemed to be catching up to him. Creditors hounded him about bounced checks and defaulted loans. Employees were quitting and runners continued to fall away. The bad press mounted. The race, which had become a haggard parade of increasingly emaciated and bandaged athletes, had acquired the nickname the "Bunion Derby." Plus, after holding a lead through an astounding five states, Gavuzzi gave up in Ohio due to a bad tooth. Only fifty-five runners remained by the time the race reached its final leg into New York. On top of it all, there was no ticker tape in the streets of Manhattan, no throngs fighting for autographs, no brass band to greet them. Only a few hundred onlookers gathered inside Madison Square Garden, where the leaders slowly stumbled in and Pyle forced them, as a finale, to run an additional twenty miles on an indoor track.

In the end, Andy Payne emerged as the clear winner by 15 hours, 35 minutes, and 39 seconds. He had endured a full eighty-four-day run, completing an unheard-of 3,422.3 miles. Yet his victory was bittersweet. Too many had already lost interest in the race. His name echoed through a nearly empty auditorium and the *Saturday Evening Post* later announced, "The winner, if anybody cares, was Andrew Payne." Almost a week passed before he even got his prize money, which Pyle held without explanation. When Payne finally received his check for $25,000, in front of what the *New York Times* titled "the smallest crowd in history of the Garden," a fight nearly ensued when it was momentarily snatched back.

His payment quickly recovered, Payne returned to Oklahoma, paid off the mortgage to his family's farm, bought his parents a new house, and purchased a car for himself.

Sending a Message to "The Man" in Oklahoma

In Perry, Oklahoma, there is a rancher by the name of David Nemechek, who apparently has a beef with the local government. Sometimes referred to as the "X-Files" ranch, sometimes the Conspiracy House, David Nemechek's home has been turned into an ever-growing statement against the government of Noble County, its law enforcement officers, and the city of Perry itself.

Just from reading the signs, the story seems to go like this: David Nemechek moved to Noble County with his family. After a period of time, something happened, either to get him on the bad side of the law, or to get the law on the bad side of him. That is when strange things started happening: cattle started getting mutilated and murdered, harassing phone calls were placed, strange drumbeats were heard in the middle of the night, threats on his family's lives occurred, and many other things happened. It would seem that David did not appreciate this, so he fought back the only way he knew how: by posting signs in his front yard.

Some are small, with short lines, saying simple things such as "We are whistleblowers" and "Stop your lies." Some are long, telling the complete story of what seems to be going on. Some are on wood, hand painted and painstakingly crafted. Some are on steel, with stick-on letters forming the message. The signs form what looks like a giant ransom note, pieced together from various sources, all lined up along his property.

The first time I came across this place was on my way out to one of the Indian hospitals in the state to work on their computers. It was just random luck that I happened to take the road I did and came by Mr. Nemechek's home. It felt creepy, but I was so curious that I slowed down as much as I could to read them all. Taking the time to read them is a dangerous sport, however, as the road is highly traveled, as well as marked by the county sheriff with signs warning against stopping on the side of the road.

Everything I have read about this place tells me that Mr. Nemechek is a nice man, who encourages people to read his signs and such. I, however, was quite creeped out by the place. Of course, like I said before, it didn't help that I was being followed by a police officer at the time of my visit. I do, however, plan on going back for more pictures.

—*Colby Weaver*

Dr. Maurice Doreal and the Brotherhood of the White Temple

If ever Oklahoma had a black sheep in its family, it would have to be Claude Doggins. Founder of one of the most laughably bizarre cults in history, he's undoubtedly among the top Sooner sons we'd rather forget.

Born near Sulfur Springs around 1898, Doggins became interested in science fiction at an early age. He engrossed himself in fantasy literature, reading and rereading stories of lost civilizations and ancient, mythical creatures. It was an obsession that would continue throughout his life, resulting in a collection of titles that, by some counts, numbered around thirty thousand.

For reasons unclear, Doggins renamed himself Dr. Maurice Doreal, then was contacted by two "Masters" following one of his lectures. According to Doreal, these Masters, members of a race of tall, blond, and blue-eyed aliens, took him miles beneath California's Mt. Shasta to an underground dwelling called Telos. There, he witnessed an advanced civilization where survivors of Atlantis lived in homes of white marble and a foreign metal called "orichalcum." They ate from gardens of strange fruits and illuminated their subterranean world with a ball of light composed of rays from the sun and moon.

These Atlanteans, he reported, were once at war with the Lemurians, a race of shape-shifting, humanoid lizard people. The two sides nearly destroyed each other, eventually fleeing underground for survival. Reportedly, there are a number of groups like these, all living beneath Earth's crust in places like the Gobi Desert, the Yucatán, and Canada.

According to Doreal, the most important of these sites is Shamballa, a temple located beneath the capital of Tibet. Naturally, Doreal himself visited said location and witnessed a vast library composed of spools of golden wire that hold the history of everything mankind has ever done, and ever will do.

(In case you're curious, the spools have a motor that causes the golden wire to flow past a crystal, in which images of history appear. By turning a spool sideways, the viewer can trigger a holographic version of the image. This technology, we hope, will someday replace Blu-ray.)

Doreal also claimed to be privy to the Emerald Tablets of Thoth, an abridged history of mankind compiled thirty-six thousand years ago by an Egyptian priest-king and recorded on slabs of indestructible material formed through "alchemical transmutation." According to Doreal, the tablets were written with ancient characters "which respond to the attuned thought waves of the reader and which release much more wisdom and information than the characters do when merely deciphered." But, of course, any true student who possessed "the light" within would have no problem releasing the wisdom from Doreal's $30 hardbound English translation, too.

Based on said tablets, Doreal went on to form the Brotherhood of the White Temple in 1930 in a place he called Shamballa Ashrama, a retreat tucked away in the Colorado Rockies where he presided over the brotherhood in golden robes. He convinced his thousand or so followers, who referred to him as "The Voice," that they would survive a great atomic war that would commence in May 1953.

The 1950s came and went, of course, and not so much as a bottle rocket threatened the brotherhood. Doreal himself died in 1963. Still, the Brotherhood of the White Temple lives on and invites anyone interested in learning more about the "Divine Path of Light," or Dr. Doreal's wacky underground adventures, to join their retreat, enroll in their college or, if money is tight, become a mail-order "disciple of the Avatar" for only $3 a month.

Carlton Cole Magee, Inventor of Space Time

It's thanks to Carl Magee that the convenience of street-side parking is no longer convenient. That lollipop-shaped apparatus that demands silvery nourishment before displaying its permissive green flag—the parking meter—was his idea. Patent number 2,118,318.

The world's first was installed near the southeast corner of Park and Robinson avenues in downtown Oklahoma City. It was one of about 150 that were mounted curbside, thereafter demanding a nickel for one hour of car time between newly painted delineations.

At the time, Magee was better known as an accomplished lawyer, editor of the *Oklahoma News*, and an integral player in a 1920s White House bribery investigation known as the Teapot Dome Scandal. Yet, the position that would solidify his place in history came when he was a member of the Oklahoma City Chamber of Commerce and was appointed to a traffic committee established to solve congestion in the capital city.

Automobiles were becoming more and more common in the early 1930s, and businesses were suffering as a result. An influx of drivers were filling downtown spaces and leaving their cars all day long, making it difficult for shoppers to find a place to park. Some business owners were deliberately taking up convenient spots in front of their competitors' shops. Lack of parking space was forcing patrons to take their money elsewhere.

To establish order and make sure spots were regularly cleared, Magee developed the Park-O-Meter. It was reliable and had the benefit of paying for itself. By intent, it was more a deterrent to space hogs than it was the money-grubber that most believe it to be.

Still, the public's response was mixed. When the first meters went into service on July 16, 1935, Magee tried to soothe motorists with an announcement in his newspaper explaining the device and insisting it ". . . treats all alike. It knows no favorites. The public will like it." And some actually did. Others were less receptive.

"Gypometers" they were called, "newfangled nuisances," "a combination of an alarm clock and a slot machine . . . for further socking the motorist." Years later, one newspaper columnist would refer to the invention as a perfect example of "man's inhumanity to man."

Some patrons protested. Two couples reportedly paid their nickel, set up a folding table and sat down to play bridge. Others were just confused. One little boy supposedly fed a meter expecting to get gum.

Overall, though, the gadgets were a success. Magee, along with partner Gerald Hale, established a manufacturing company, and in one seven-year period sold some seventy-one thousand units. Today, an estimated five million meters serve cities across the United States. Of course, today they take more than a nickel. Although parking meters are now made with circuit boards instead of clockwork timers, they still pretty much look like Magee's original lollipops.

Jimmie Ray Slaughter

Let's talk about warning signs. In the aftermath of grisly multiple murders, people often try to examine the events leading up to the tragedy. Was anything out of the ordinary? Was anyone acting strangely? Were there any signs that could have tipped people off that something was out of the ordinary? In the case of killer Jimmy Ray Slaughter, the answer is a resounding, "Yes!"

Slaughter worked at Oklahoma City's Veteran's Administration Hospital with Melody Sue Wuertz. In July 1991, neighbors discovered the bodies of Wuertz and her infant daughter in their home. Each had been shot twice in the head with a .22, and Melody's body had been partially mutilated. Police found curious symbols carved into the flesh of her stomach, including an upside-down cross. After a rigorous six-month investigation, police arrested Slaughter for the ritual murders.

What made the police think Slaughter was their man? Warning signs, my friend.

Slaughter was a bit of a workplace lothario, and Wuertz was one of several coworkers who had short flings with the then married Slaughter. In fact, Slaughter was the father of Wuertz's daughter. A few months before the murders, Wuertz began legal action against Slaughter in an attempt to collect child support. (Public and documented feuds with her ex shortly before her demise? Warning sign.)

Though Slaughter pleaded not guilty to the murders, coworkers claimed that he was angry at Wuertz for trying to ruin his marriage, and that he was openly interested in Satanism. When police searched his home, they found a ring with occult symbols, Satanic magazines, more than a hundred candles, a large assortment of knives, and .22-caliber bullets.

What followed was the longest trial in the history of Oklahoma County. At one point, Slaughter's wife was arrested as an accomplice, but the prosecution was unable to submit any concrete proof that she had any knowledge of his crimes. Though Slaughter continually restated that he did not kill the Wuertzes (he was also charged with numerous counts of perjury), witnesses kept coming forward with rather damning testimony.

Cecilia Johnson, a nurse who worked with Slaughter, was the grand jury's key witness, and the biggest ignorer of warning signs in history. She testified that Slaughter said he "wished they [the Wuertzes] were both dead." (Ding! Warning!) She retold his anecdotes of past animal mutilations, and how Slaughter claimed to have killed three Mexicans during a south-of-the-border drinking binge years earlier. (Ding! Ding!) Once, while Johnson and Slaughter were shopping together, Slaughter commented that an oriental bowl he saw "would make a good blood bowl." (Ding! Ding! Ding!) Johnson later became despondent over her testimony, and committed suicide.

Almost two years after the murders (during which Slaughter confessed to an inmate that "a demon" told him to kill the Wuertzes), the jury found Slaughter guilty of double homicide. Slaughter died by lethal injection on March 16, 2005. He maintained his innocence to the end.

—*Craig Robertson*

Kevin Ray Underwood

When Kevin Underwood answered a facetious question about cannibalism in an online profile, he probably didn't imagine prosecutors would one day use the joke as evidence to send him to his death.

Underwood, a twenty-six-year-old grocery-store shelf stocker living in Purcell, was arrested in April 2006 for the murder of his ten-year-old neighbor Jamie Bolin. Bolin had been missing for two days when detectives followed the trail to Underwood's apartment, where they found the girl in his bedroom closet. Underwood was quick to confess. "Go ahead and arrest me," he told the police. "She is in there. I chopped her up."

The girl had been stripped naked and her lifeless body was stuffed inside a plastic tub. A towel had been shoved inside to soak up blood and the container sealed with duct tape. The ten-year-old's neck showed deep cuts where Underwood had attempted to sever her head from her body.

According to reports, Underwood had targeted other residents of the Purcell Park Apartments (shown here) where he lived, but the young girl ultimately made for an easier victim. Bolin lived with her father in the unit upstairs from Underwood, so she passed by his door regularly, making it easy to lure the girl inside to play with a pet rat, then beat her over the head with a cutting board and smother her to death.

Officers found meat tenderizer and barbecue skewers that Underwood apparently purchased in anticipation of the crime. He had also bought a hacksaw. The Purcell police chief later told reporters, ". . . this appears to have been part of a plan to kidnap a person, rape them, torture them, kill them, cut off their head, drain the body of blood, rape the corpse, eat the corpse, then dispose of the organs and bones."

When a story like this surfaces, the perpetrator, at least for most of us, is a complete mystery, totally removed from any frame of personal reality. All we know about him is what the newspapers tell us, along with the usual quotes from family and neighbors predictably describing him as quiet or boring. In this age of the ubiquitous Internet weblog however, insight into the mind of a random stranger is as easy as typing in a search field.

Using the pseudonym "subspecies23," Kevin Underwood had been maintaining an Internet presence since September 2002. To the few who read it, it doubtlessly seemed much like any other twenty-something's blog, an intermittent diatribe about how work sucks, how the girl he likes doesn't like him back, and how you have to drive to Texas to get decent porn. Up until April 2006, his were little more than frivolous rants. After his arrest for murder, however, certain glaring passages assumed frightening importance.

"I find myself becoming more and more detached from the world," he wrote in one passage. "I walk around like a zombie, with a blank expression on my face." He described his loss of personality and a continuing withdrawal inside himself. "I wish I could be like I used to be," he concluded. "I wish I could be human."

He wrote often about his depression and apathy. Many entries focused on unrequited love or a self-diagnosis regarding his social phobia. On occasion, Underwood would go so far as to hint toward murder or suicide. At one point, he flippantly commented on a group of people making noise outside his apartment, whom he planned to tell off. "And then I'll kill them, with that shopping cart that someone has left out in the parking lot." In most cases, this would sound like a sarcastic vent by a frustrated kid, but in retrospect, it becomes alarmingly sinister.

"My fantasies are just getting weirder and weirder," he confessed in another entry. "Dangerously weird. If people knew the kinds of things I think about anymore, I'd probably be locked away. No probably about it, I know I would be."

Then, of course, there was his personal profile. That's where he had added the survey question that reporters would repeat again and again following his arrest: If you were a cannibal, what would you wear to dinner? "The skin of last night's main course," he answered.

In the months to come, investigators revealed that Underwood continued his online activities immediately following his gruesome crime. Even as Bolin's body lay in his bathtub draining of blood, he chatted dispassionately with a friend about petting squirrels. In a chat session the next day, he talked about the missing girl and how she ". . . seems like a very nice, trusting kid, and that's probably what got her in trouble, if she's not a runaway." Feigning innocence, he wrote, "I'm afraid the cops would come into my apartment, and see all my knives and swords and the horror movies . . . and suspect me." He admitted to being sick to his stomach and added, "I know I didn't do anything, but I felt like I did." This as Jamie Bolin lay stuffed in his closet.

In the murder trial that followed in 2008, it took only twenty-five minutes for the jury to find Underwood guilty of first-degree murder. A week later, they sentenced him to death. He remains on death row.

As for the blog that has given us an unprecedented insight into the killer's state of mind, it remains available. Under the title "Strange Things Are Afoot at the Circle K," it can be found at http://futureworldruler.blogspot.com. Spend a little time flipping through it and see if it doesn't make you think twice about the sorts of things you confess in your own blog.

Lucille Hamons, Mother of the Mother Road

About an hour west of Oklahoma City, outside the town of Hydro, stands a small, two-story building, quiet and vacant. It rests just off the shoulder of historic Route 66, the highway celebrated in story and song, crowned by author John Steinbeck as the "Mother Road." The business has been closed for nearly a decade now, but travelers still go out of their way to stop by.

The station's namesake, Lucille Hamons, opened up shop in 1941, renaming the previous business, Provine Station, to Hamons Court. With her husband away on business most of the time, she ran the fuel station, the shop, and the five adjacent motel rooms herself, making a home in the modest second-story unit just above the gas pumps.

Lucille did that for fifty-nine years.

In the beginning, Route 66 was bustling. Lucille's little pit stop provided motorists with fresh gas, a clean room, or a cold drink. With Route 66 covering two-thirds of the country, and postwar America booming with automotive travel, it was a good place to be.

Sometimes, travelers who came through were down on their luck, still suffering from the Great Depression. Lucille would offer them a free room, maybe some sandwiches. When they were out of gas, she'd fill them up. If they were desperate for cash, she'd offer to buy something from them. She made so many trades for broken-down cars, she said, that people started to think she was opening a salvage yard. "I never refused anybody," she told one reporter. "I guess that's why I never got held up." Lucille became well known for her roadside Samaritanism.

Over the years, Route 66 grew obsolete. When Interstate 40 came through in the 1960s, the on-ramp was built just ahead of the station, diverting motorists away from the gas station. Lucille closed the motel rooms and began stocking much less merchandise. Eventually, she stopped pumping gas, too, and instead started selling beer. She was never entirely comfortable with it, but she refused to close shop.

In the 1990s, after thirty years of ups and downs, business started to pick back up. Route 66 had recently been decommissioned, and interest in the historic byway began to grow. People who had encountered Lucille in decades past started retracing their steps and came by to tell her how she had helped them so long ago. Her name and her story appeared in newspapers and in Route 66 books and TV programs. Lucille stopped selling convenience items and started selling souvenirs. Out of demand, she had pictures made to autograph for visitors.

She wrote a book about her life, which quickly became a hit. In 1997, her business, which she renamed "Lucille's" after the original sign blew down in the 1970s, was added to the National Register of Historic Places. Two years later, Lucille herself was inducted into the Route 66 Hall of Fame. Then, in 2000, a call from Washington, D.C., brought news of her greatest honor: The Smithsonian Institution wanted to acquire her original neon sign to include in their museum. Lucille was officially part of Route 66 history, an icon of the highway.

Sadly, Lucille died just a month later, at the age of eighty-five, in her bed above the shop. Her funeral procession followed the road she overlooked for nearly six decades, stopping briefly at her service station for a final farewell. Nearly one hundred cars, filled with family, friends, and fans, followed behind.

Lucille's headstone, a gleaming white monolith engraved with a Route 66 highway shield, remembers her as "The Mother of the Mother Road." It was a title she had given herself, but nobody argued.

Lucille herself was inducted into the Route 66 Hall of Fame.

Nannie Doss

She was known as "The Giggling Granny," a lovely woman who was never seen without a twinkle in her eye and a smile on her face. Her laugh, a trademark of sorts, was infectious and charming. She was just the sort of jovial woman you would expect to see in a frill-lined apron, whistling while setting a pie on a windowsill to cool. Except she'd be whistling Chopin's "Funeral March" and the pie would be laced with arsenic.

Nancy Doss, who went by the nickname Nannie for most of her years, was a killer—a bespectacled, unremorseful murderess. When she was arrested by Tulsa police for the death of her fifth husband, her confession was punctuated with the most pathetic, though genuinely honest, explanation: "He wouldn't let me watch my favorite programs on the television."

As investigators found out, Nannie was responsible for as many as eleven murders throughout her life, including previous spouses and her own family members. And she didn't appear to regret any of them.

It's believed her first victims were her own daughters. At the age of sixteen, she married Charley Braggs, and within six years the couple had four girls. But the marriage was not what Nannie had hoped for. Charley's mother, with whom the couple lived, was overbearing, and Charley always yielded to his mother's wishes. Second, Charley turned out to be a drunk and a philanderer. He would often disappear for days on end, reportedly on a drinking binge with some other woman. Nannie herself began turning to liquor and the comfort of other men.

And so the children were quickly becoming a chain holding Nannie to a marriage she deeply regretted. In 1927, their two middle daughters died simultaneously of suspected food poisoning. Nannie was never charged with their murders, but it's widely believed that she was responsible.

Charley quickly bolted for the hills, after which Nannie took her two surviving daughters and found a home elsewhere. She also began sifting through personal ads, looking for someone new in whom she could place her affection. She was known for being a romantic, always looking for love and taking pleasure in romance magazines and the attention of the opposite sex.

Therefore, it didn't take long for her to snag a new husband. In 1929, she married Frank Harrelson. But, again, her *amour*—a word she was fond of using—turned out not to be the knight she longed for. Frank was an alcoholic. He was constantly in and out of jail, and subjected his wife to both verbal and physical abuse. Nannie endured the marriage for years.

Nannie turned her attention to her grandchildren. Melvina, Nannie's older daughter, already had a son and, in 1945, gave birth to a baby girl. Sadly, the child died an hour after delivery, in Nannie's arms. Doctors reportedly could not explain the death, but Melvina, in a state of anesthetized stupor, thought she may have seen her mother pierce the child's head with a hatpin. Melvina was unsure whether the vision was real or a drug-induced hallucination, but when she later told others about what she may have seen, her husband and sister recalled seeing Nannie toying earlier with just such a pin.

Melvina's son Robert was the next to go. He died six months later while his mother was out of town and the toddler was left in Nannie's care. Doctors concluded his cause of death to be asphyxia, but the details were sketchy. As for heartbroken Nannie, she cashed a life insurance policy she had quietly taken out on the boy.

How she had gotten away with all this is anyone's guess. Perhaps it was the smile and the girlish giggle that conveyed her innocence.

On September 16, 1945, after sixteen years with her

abusive husband, Nannie discovered Frank's liquor jar buried in a flower bed. She pulled it up, topped it off with rat poison, and waited. He was dead that evening.

After that, murder seemed to come easily to Nannie Doss. She married again in 1947, this time to Arlie Lanning, after knowing him only two days. Like the others, he was a drunkard and a womanizer. And like the others, he died with Nannie by his side. This time, it was coffee and prunes that did him in, in 1950. Poison, it seems, was becoming Nannie's preferred modus operandi.

Two months later, the widow's house burned down. Had it not, it would have gone to Arlie's sister per his will, but the tragedy left Nannie with a fat insurance check instead. Nannie then moved in with Arlie's mother, but she soon died mysteriously in her sleep. So Nannie moved in with her own sister, who also died in her sleep.

In 1952, at age forty-seven, Nannie claimed her fourth husband through one of the matchmaking services she had repeatedly turned to for romance. This time, it was Richard Morton, a retired businessman who would turn out to be broke and sleeping with another woman.

His comeuppance would be delayed, however, with the arrival of Nannie's mother, Louisa, who came to live with the couple after losing her husband. But it was a short delay; after only a couple of days in her daughter's care, Lou came down with unexplained stomach pains and died.

Three months later, so did Richard.

Then came Sam Doss. Unlike the others, Sam was hardworking, faithful, and loving. Unfortunately, he was also highly frugal and set in his ways, pinching pennies and decrying anything he considered frivolous, like the romance magazines and television programs Nannie so loved. And so, Sam mysteriously acquired severe stomach pains that put him in the hospital for three weeks.

Yet he survived. The same day he was discharged, Nannie served him up a special treat that finally did him in. Surprised by Sam's death after leaving the hospital, doctors performed an autopsy and discovered enough arsenic in his system to kill a team of horses.

In the police interrogation that followed, Nannie confessed, with a giggle, what she had done. Investigators exhumed the bodies of her husbands, as well as her mother, her sister, her grandson, and Arlie Lanning's mother. Her mother and her previous husbands were loaded with arsenic. The others appeared to have been smothered. Nothing was ever proven in the cases of her two daughters or her granddaughter, but the state had enough on her already.

Surprisingly, four psychiatrists pronounced her sane and fit for trial. On May 17, 1955, Nannie pleaded guilty in a Tulsa court of law. She spent the rest of her life in an Oklahoma prison, known by many as Arsenic Annie.

Before she died of leukemia in 1965, Nannie Doss was visited in prison by a newspaper reporter. Ever the jovial woman, she told him, "When they get shorthanded in the kitchen here, I always offer to help out. But they never do let me."

Patrick Henry Sherrill, Going Postal

On August 20, 1986, Patrick Henry Sherrill entered his place of employment at 7 A.M., a half hour late. Letter carriers in Edmond usually arrived at the local U.S. Post Office at 6:30 to sort the mail, but Sherrill had not planned for a day's work. His coworkers probably took little notice of Sherrill as he entered the building wearing his standard-issue USPS uniform and carrying his mailbag, even as he began bolting the rear exits of the building. Less than fifteen minutes later, Sherrill had murdered more than a dozen people before turning the gun on himself.

Sherrill was a quiet man who bounced from job to job, lived with his mother well into adulthood, and earned the nickname "Crazy Pat" from the neighborhood children, possibly due to his bizarre habits of mowing the lawn at midnight and peeping through the neighbors' windows. After the killings, police searched his apartment and found numerous sets of neatly folded military camouflage uniforms and stacks of *Guns and Ammo* and *Soldier of Fortune* magazines.

Sherrill was never a "people person." He quit every job he ever had, usually just before he would have been terminated. He never made friends with coworkers, and he often argued with supervisors. The day before the murders, Sherrill got into a heated argument with Bill Bland, his immediate supervisor, over Sherrill's spraying a dog with Mace while walking his route. (The dog had been chained behind a fence with a locked gate.) Luckily, Bland overslept the following day and was not present when Sherrill came to work.

After securing the back doors, Sherrill pulled a .45-caliber semiautomatic pistol from his mailbag and began firing into the noisy place, where trays and carts were being slammed around, so the morning shift look little notice of the gunshots until the bodies began to fall. Someone shouted, "He's got a gun!" and all started running for cover. Some postal workers fled through the front doors, some hid in closets, and at least one locked himself into the stamps vault, but far too many could not escape or hide.

Sherrill started in the supervisor's office, but after finding it empty, he began to walk methodically through the building. He took careful aim at everyone he saw, killing fourteen and wounding six more. When Sherrill found five postal employees huddled in a cubicle, he killed each of them, pausing to reload partway through. All fourteen victims were shot in the chest, the marksmanship of a shooter who once earned the Marines' "expert" rating. Sherrill ended the slaughter by going into the break room and shooting himself in the head. The entire ordeal took only a few minutes. An hour later, window service would have started and the lobby would have been filled with postal customers.

Today, a memorial statue, featuring a yellow ribbon of remembrance, stands on the southwest corner of Edmond's North Broadway Post Office. A plaque lists the names of the fourteen victims. Sherrill's name does not appear on the memorial, but he is remembered in a more abstract way. Since his demented spree in 1986, approximately thirty more people have been killed in eleven other postal-related shootings across the United States. As a result, Sherrill has been credited with inspiring the now familiar but macabre term *going postal. —Craig Robertson*

Sylvan Nathan Goldman

Walk into any grocery store and what's the first thing we do? Grab a shopping cart. We don't even give it much thought. Unless we get one with a wobbly wheel, we're barely conscious of the contraption.

But there was a time when people were forced to actually *carry* their groceries. Armed with little more than a hand basket, shoppers walked around literally burdened by their selections. God forbid you had to lug a whole gallon of milk or—yikes!—a watermelon through the store.

Enter Sylvan N. Goldman, grocery entrepreneur and Oklahoma genius. One night in 1936, while sitting in his office, he concocted an idea. If only he could relieve the consumers of their encumbrances, he could alter the shopping experience forever! And, of course, increase his profits.

He realized that, in general, the customers who visited his chain of grocery stores typically bought only as much as they could carry. To get them to buy more, he'd have to somehow increase their load capacity.

His idea came from a folding chair. He figured that, if he attached wheels and added a second seat, one could set two baskets on it and cart around twice as much, with little effort. After checkout, the baskets could then be stacked together and the cart folded up and out of the way. With the help of an associate, he worked up a prototype and called his invention the Folding Basket Carriage.

Shoppers weren't impressed. Despite ads that touted "the newest innovation in shopping" that promised no more "having to carry a cumbersome shopping basket on your arm," nobody wanted to use it. Women compared it to an unwieldy baby carriage and men saw it as an affront to their masculinity.

To convince shoppers to use the device, Goldman hired confederates. He planted shills in his stores, both men and women of varying ages, to push the carts around, pretending to shop. Like monkeys, consumers mimicked them. The basket carriage became a hit!

Today, thankful shoppers can worship at the feet of Goldman's statue at the Science Museum Oklahoma in Oklahoma City. He's the one pushing the bronze shopping cart.

Personalized Properties

B*ack when Oklahoma was just a "territory,"* when pioneers were just discovering there was plenty of terrific land to settle, homesteaders labored to build homes that were uniquely theirs. With a hammer, a saw, and their own two hands, they erected dwellings distinctive to themselves and their lifestyle.

A hundred years later residents are carting mass-produced furniture into their prefabricated, homogeneous tract homes. These days, suburbs are stamped out like gingerbread men, and a lot of people seem to like it that way.

There are, fortunately, a few Oklahomans who have shirked convention and insist on dwellings that are unique to their own personalities. Sometimes they're just fun, and sometimes they're way-out oddball. Of course, sometimes they're just plain crazy and a little bit troubling. But at least they're different.

Ed Galloway's Totem Poles

When Ed Galloway retired and moved from Sand Springs to Foyil in 1936, he wasn't content with the conventional house he had built for himself and his wife. Their home was nice enough, sure, but there was something missing. Something for the yard. It needed . . . a lawn ornament.

Crafting something pleasant and attractive would be no problem for Galloway. After all, he had spent much of his life working with wood. After he returned from military service in the Spanish-American War, he took up a career as a wood carver and for twenty-five years taught furniture making at Charles Page's home for orphans and widows in Sand Springs. He was a skilled maker of fiddles, too, though he spent far more time making them than playing them. In fact, of the three hundred intricately decorated fiddles he carved, none was ever strung. Fiddle making was simply a way to demonstrate his skills and to showcase the grains of various types of wood.

Couple his skills with his interest in American Indian culture, and voilà. Galloway decided he'd make a totem pole—in fact, the tallest totem pole in the world at ninety feet high, with elaborate symbols adorning every inch. From the giant turtle supporting its eighteen-foot-wide

base to the nine-foot-tall Indians guarding its spire, it would be covered with some two hundred brightly colored images, and it would catch the eye of every motorist who passed his home.

Yet, curiously, Galloway's medium for the totem pole was concrete, not wood. Why? We don't know for sure, but the result is astounding, especially when you consider the lengths to which the man had to go to create it. Using more than one hundred tons of steel and rock, Galloway hauled twenty-eight tons of concrete one bucket at a time, the final buckets traveling nine stories up before being unloaded.

It was such an endeavor, in fact, that even working on it seven days a week, it took the artisan eleven years to complete. And it was such a sight even from the time he started in 1937 that motorists began pulling off the road straightaway. He started a guestbook in 1940, eight years before the totem pole's completion.

Of course, Galloway didn't stop there. Once he finished the big one, he added eleven or so smaller ones, along with a giant arrowhead and a large decorative tree stump. At the behest of his wife, he also built himself an eleven-sided, ornamental gallery in which he could house the fiddles he carved when it was too dark outside to make totem poles.

Ed Galloway died in 1962. Shortly thereafter, someone broke into his Fiddle House and stole a large number of his fiddles, which have never been recovered. His house and his other creations fell into tragic disrepair. Fortunately, though, after Galloway's relatives donated the property to the Rogers County Historical Society in 1991, dedicated individuals were able to restore everything to its former glory. The Fiddle House has been converted into a museum of Ed Galloway's life and art, and visitors are encouraged to spend an afternoon contemplating the artist's work in what is now called Ed Galloway's Totem Pole Park.

OK County 66

John Hargrove is a fabricator of custom cars, a retired pilot, and, even though he's well into his sixties, an avid long-distance runner. He is also one of Route 66's most dedicated fans.

Just east of Arcadia, at a bend in what is now State Road 66, John lives and works at a virtual museum called OK County 66, an homage to the unique character of the historic highway known by millions as "the Mother Road." "America grew up on Route 66," he says, and he's spent the last few years preserving that part of America's youth by recreating some of the highway's most memorable icons and assembling them all in one spot.

U.S. Route 66, which would become known as "the Main Street of America," was originally established in 1926 and connected the Windy City with the West Coast, passing through eight states. Although it wasn't the very first of the nation's highways, it became the most famous, having been celebrated in books, TV shows, and countless songs. And although it was officially decommissioned in 1985, it's been preserved as a historic roadway in many locations and remains a symbol of American culture.

All along its length, motorists today can find classic attractions that were once an integral part of the Route 66 experience. In California, there's the Wigwam Motel, an inn composed of individual teepee-shaped rooms. In Texas, there's Cadillac Ranch, where a row of old Cadillacs are buried nose-first in a field. In Arizona, there are the towering Twin Arrows and the "Here It Is" Jackrabbit, both icons of roadside trading posts. And here in Oklahoma, thanks to Hargrove, you can see every one of them, and many more, at OK County 66.

John retired several years ago, sold everything he owned, and decided the one thing he wanted to do at that point was to live on Route 66. So he bought a

plot of land outside Arcadia, along the historic highway, and moved there in 2001. Since then, he's built himself a home, a workshop, and a monument to the Mother Road's most recognizable roadside attractions. He's got a two-dimensional version of Catoosa, Oklahoma's own Blue Whale, a sample representation from Elmer Long's Bottle Tree Ranch in California, and a replica of a barn roof painted with a Meramec Caverns advertisement. Most reproductions are authentic, except for Cadillac Ranch, which is represented by a Volkswagen Beetle. Why? "I like small cars," Hargrove says. He refers to his version of the Caddy ranch as "Volkswagen Acreage."

He's continuing to make additions, but he says by the time he hits age seventy-five, he'll be ready to move on to something else. "This is all going to be sold in ten years. I'm going to liquidate everything. Have a hell of an auction." He then plans to spend his remaining years on the road, seeing all the sites he's been replicating.

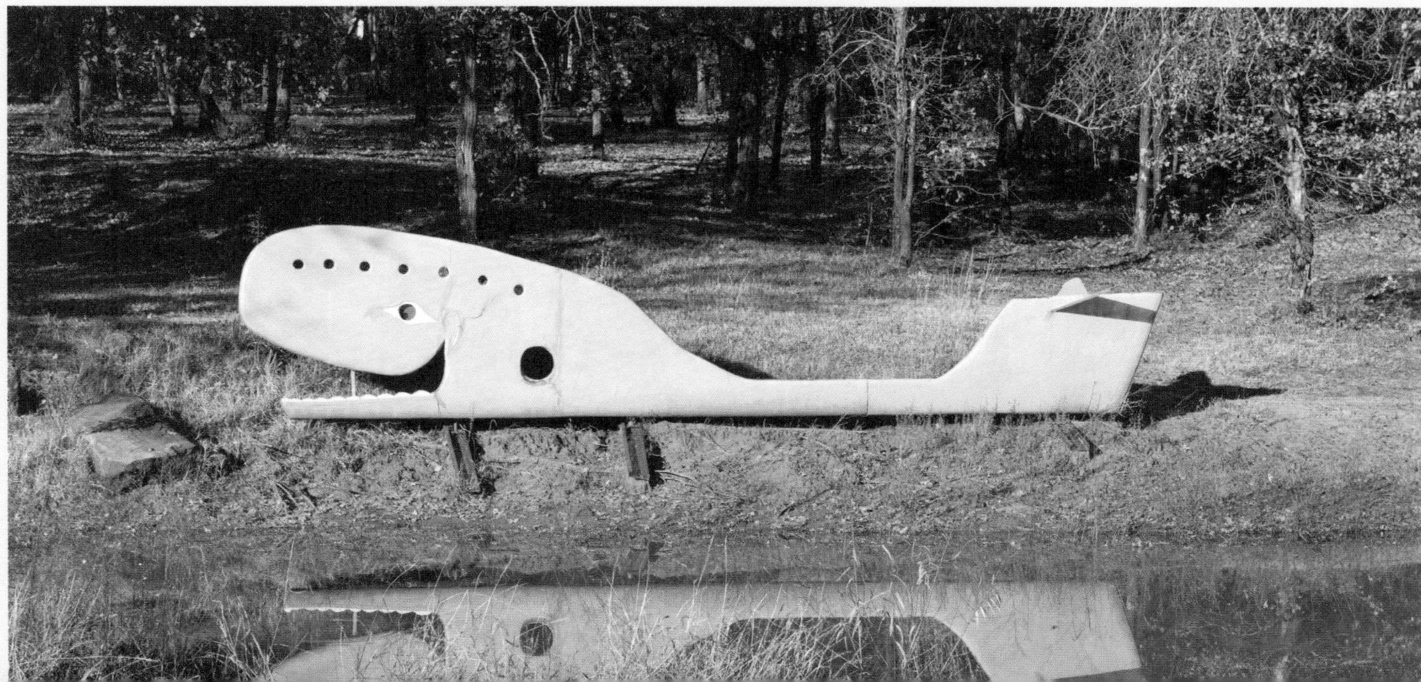

Lowell Burch's Backyard

As a child, Lowell Burch loved visiting Six Flags Over Texas. Those fond vacation memories endured well into his adulthood. When he became a parent himself, not only did he take his own family to Six Flags, but he tried to bring as much of Six Flags as he could back to his family.

The backyard of his Tulsa home is full of re-creations from Six Flags as he remembers them from his childhood, many representing the various cultural themes that once made up the major sections of the park. In one corner is a Mexican-themed pergola. In another stands a wooden fort very much like the former centerpiece of the French section of the amusement park.

Sadly, such motifs, which were meant to embody the actual six flags for which the park was named, have since almost completely disappeared. That's one of the reasons Lowell started his project. He felt that the attraction had lost its true appeal some time ago. He believed it was a much better place when the theme park had actual themes and the thrill of the rides came mostly from one's imagination. He remembered a Six Flags without the towering coasters and corporate sponsorship, back when it featured live animals and park attendants in period costumes.

Back then visitors could ride a genuine stagecoach pulled by real horses, or paddle an actual canoe in the water. The dangerously unstable floating bridge at Skull Island and the leaning Casa Magnetica "gravity house," both attractions that would prove too boring for today's crowd, were among the more popular and memorable spots on the Six Flags Over Texas map. Actors, believe it or not, performed bloody shootouts, hangings, and firing-squad executions. People went to the shows for more than the air-conditioning, and the steam train was more than just a way to get to the other side of the park. That's the Six Flags Lowell wanted to memorialize.

He had hoped one day to add an actual ride or two, and even talked to an out-of-business mall about acquiring their kiddie train. But he was happy with a fish pond and a boat dock reminiscent of La Salle's River Adventure, a 1960s boat ride, or "expedition," through a place filled with angry Indians and animatronic alligators. His favorite re-creation, though, has a fiberglass replica he built of the Speelunker's Cave, a dark, slow-moving, tunnel of love. Speelunker's Cave was inhabited by a race of strange little cone-faced creatures who lived in an underground world of psychedelic black lights and quirky music. There is no water in Lowell's version, but he was working on the lights and the sound system to pump out the iconic music still recognizable to anyone who visited Six Flags before the Speelunkers were ousted in the early 1990s and replaced by Saturday-morning cartoon characters.

Sadly, Lowell Burch was never able to complete his vision. He passed away in 2008. Weather has already started to take its toll on his creations, but his son Scott tries to keep things up as much as he can. "He was probably the most mature person I knew, but he was a kid at heart," he says of his father. "I wish I could have seen what he actually saw and got to experience."

The Cave House

Linda Collier's interest in the unusual house on Charles Page Boulevard started when she was just a kid. "I had grown up passing this as a child," she says. "And I just always thought, 'What is that like inside? What kind of person would own it?'" As it turned out, she would.

Linda bought the landmark Tulsa home in 1997. At the time, it was vacant, falling apart, and filled with mud, vermin, and vagrant droppings. Nevertheless, when the real estate agent opened the door for her for the first time, she realized, "This is supposed to be mine." She saw past the mold and the bugs to a historical treasure that she knew had to be preserved.

For Linda, digging up information on the building has been a labor of love. In fact, much of what is known about the house today is due in large part to her almost fanatical investigations. Linda's tireless research has revealed the house's age, its builders, and a rather interesting history of illegal activity.

Despite the building's somewhat sketchy construction—a fairly haphazard cavernlike facade of chicken wire and concrete—it has survived for a surprising eight decades. Though its exact date of construction has been hard to pin down, documents reveal that it's been in existence since at least 1926. It was built by Tulsa businessmen Joseph Koberling and Joseph Purzer, and served at the time as an open-air restaurant called the Cave Garden.

In about the 1940s, someone added on the more conventional-looking eastern wing, turning it into a residence. Since then, a number of tenants have come and gone, each, it seems, possessing their own little quirks. One woman, known by many as the Key Lady, had a strange compulsion for collecting keys, even to the point that if she saw a person drop one, she might swipe it before its owner could pick it up. Another tenant, Ella Walker, pushed a cart around the neighborhood, collecting scraps of cloth and old bottles and jars. She became known as the Rag Lady, though it's still unclear what she did with all that material. The bottles, on the other hand, turned out to be for the bootlegging operation she and her husband were running out of the house.

The most curious aspect about the Cave House, though, is the secret passageway that's rumored to exist behind the fireplace. Back when it was the Cave Garden restaurant, patrons would enjoy alfresco dining at the picnic tables, but at night, it's said, they would sneak inside to the underground speakeasy for a few drinks. "The story is," Linda recalls, "you would go into the fireplace, down some stairs to the left and then go into a big ballroom." That's where the in-crowd would enjoy booze, gambling, music, and movies. Legend says it was all connected by a network of tunnels that supposedly run throughout the hillside directly behind the house. One of the homes at the top of the hill, Linda says, actually has a tunnel entrance that's been bricked over.

Evidence supports such stories. In the 1970s a previous Cave House owner was performing renovations when he knocked down a column and discovered a cache of silver coins hidden inside. Another resident discovered a secret vault beneath the upstairs floor that held some old bootlegging bottles and a few more coins.

As for the tunnel behind the fireplace, however, definitive proof has yet to surface. With help, Linda tried to knock through the fireplace, but she was deterred by the real risk of structural collapse. She's still certain it's back there, though, and continues to dig up research. She hopes one day to do a proper excavation.

In the meantime, Linda holds tours for curious passersby. She doesn't live at the Cave House, but you can find her there pretty often. Now that it's all fixed up, she likes to spend time with her friends, relaxing, or working on art. It's basically her own little clubhouse. After all, she says, "I never have to grow up over here."

Collings Castle

It's rare that a unique and unusual home ends up as a freely explorable public attraction, but that's exactly what has become of Collings Castle. Located inside Turner Falls Park, just an hour north of the Oklahoma–Texas state line, the multistructure stone fortress graces the side of a wooded hill overlooking Honey Creek.

Sometimes informally referred to as the Rock Castle, the buildings were constructed in the early 1930s by Dr. Ellsworth Collings, professor, and eventually dean, at the University of Oklahoma. It took several years to complete the home, which was built of natural stone collected from the area. Collings used it as a summer home and was well known for the parties he hosted there for friends and colleagues.

The castle consists of several structures, all connected by a series of stairways akin to a life-size version of Chutes and Ladders. It features multiple levels, open-air patios, accessible rooftops, and, of course, a lookout tower. Visitors have described it as both "awesome" and "creepy."

Little has been written about the castle, so it's difficult to say why exactly Collings chose the medieval style, considering he was an admirer of the cowboy life. He even wrote an oft-referenced book on the 101 Ranch, the most celebrated ranch in Oklahoma's history. At one time, the castle served in part as the headquarters and ranch house for his own Bar-C Ranch.

Many who've been to Collings Castle speculate that the professor and his family must have been fairly small people, as the doorways are narrow, the ceilings are low, and the stairs are awkwardly steep, shallow, and cramped. The tower, one of the most popular aspects of the house, is narrow to the point of absurdity. Its windows at the top are just a few inches wide, mimicking archer's slits, but offering only a sliver of what would otherwise be an astounding view.

If you've only got a few moments to check it out, you can see Collings Castle, as well as the beautiful seventy-seven-foot falls, from a lookout point just inside the park. But it's definitely worth your time and the price of admission to explore it all firsthand.

An Open Letter from David Nemechek

If the pen is mightier than the sword, then a paintbrush and several gallons of brightly colored paint must be equivalent to at least a few sticks of dynamite. That's what David Nemechek must have thought, at least. When confronted with what he believed to be a government conspiracy against him and his family, he retaliated by covering his yard in dozens of highly conspicuous protest signs.

The signs, which Nemechek posted on his ranch along Highway 64, about 3.5 miles east of Perry, tell a story both riveting and disturbing. In large, block letters, rendered in all capitals and drafted in ever-switching colors, Nemechek accuses Noble County and its officials of murder, conspiracy, and racism. The narrative, rendered in a disjointed style reminiscent of a ransom note cut from the pages of a magazine, is a little difficult to follow, but the gist is that the government killed several of the family's cattle. The reason, made abundantly clear by Nemechek's billboards, is because a "sick evil yellow bellied lying racist cult religious devil worshippers terrorist clan organization" has a prejudice against the family's Czech heritage.

Since the 1970s, he's posted increasingly verbose diatribes consisting of phrases like "We are whistleblowers," "Your fun and games of hell must stop now," and "Sick evil religious nuts out on a witch hunt using evil witchcraft." Sometimes, the language descends into the incoherent. "How to recognize a warped minded sickies rare disease racist" reads one sign. "Why cow no. 29?" asks another. "Reason my birth May 29, 1929?" The biggest question, it seems, repeated again and again, is simply "Why?"

Sometime in the 1980s, veterinarians from Oklahoma State University tested the livestock that Nemechek claimed had been murdered. They ruled that the cattle had died from bovine leukemia virus, or BLV. To Nemechek this was all just a part of a big cover-up, part of the "smartness games to destroy us." His response, posted on yet another sign: "Your stupid minded racist have a rare disease B.L.V. It stands for bull s*** spread by liars and vicious bastards." Besides, BLV wouldn't explain the alleged attempt on his mother's life, the chemical substance someone allegedly left in his house, and his son allegedly being kicked off the school bus twice, all crimes that warranted even more signs.

Eventually, the courts decided that Nemechek's prolific claims of terrorism, harassment, and "ethnical cleansing" by local law enforcement had gone too far. In 1992, the county sheriff sued Nemechek for libel, which resulted in a judgment against him to the tune of $775,000. Much of his farm equipment was auctioned off to help pay the damages. Nemechek painted over the sheriff's name wherever it appeared on his signs, but posted yet another claiming the judgment was a "bonus bounty" paid to the sheriff by the county's "evil inbred German religious terrorist" in an "unbelievable plot . . . to get rid of destroy-kill this Czech." The signage didn't help his subsequent appeal.

Since then, it looks as if David Nemechek's cause has run out of steam. As of 2009, most of the signs have been removed or have lost bits and pieces to the weather, which has left them making even less sense than before. Unfortunately, the best and possibly the most perplexing of the signs is gone, the one near the front gate that once read, "Thank you for stopping by. Please drive carefully."

Chris Barbee's Yard Art

Just outside Nowata, near the northeast corner of N4150 and E021 roads, Chris Barbee has collected, in every weight and color you can imagine, nearly a thousand bowling balls that he's used to turn his front lawn into one unique and well-hung work of art.

It all started when he retired in 2005 and was looking for something to do. He had fourteen balls that his late wife had once used to decorate a rose garden, but after the roses died, it seemed the balls no longer had a purpose. "I kicked them around and moved them around for two or three years," he said, until finally he came up with the idea of turning them into a fence. "When I started that thing, well, it just caught on fire."

When he was done hand-drilling and hanging the 108 balls that now delineate the yard, he just kept getting more ideas. Since then, he's installed a cross, a giant rosary, wind chimes, an oversized pool table, a big croquet set, and a complete alphabet composed of 265 individual balls. Using an old hay rack, he also constructed a giant, working

Newton's cradle, one of those executive's toys where the balls clack back and forth. His latest project is a small shedlike building with walls covered in bowling balls and roof shingles made from halved bowling pins. Inside will go the more special balls he's collected, where they'll be on display like a sort of mini museum.

Chris says he has no problems with his supply. Once people see what he's up to, they're more than willing to donate however many they've got. Plus, all the bowling alleys in the area now know him by name and volunteer their old balls when they're no longer fit for play. Chris also invites the public to drop off balls in the yard when they come to visit. Once he came home to discover someone had left him fifty-four donations.

What's next? Well, Chris says he isn't short on ideas. Right now, he's planning a peace symbol, an American flag, and a rainbow composed of about three hundred multicolored balls. Plus, someone has already contacted him about some balls they have that look like watermelons, so he hopes he'll soon be adding a melon-ball patch. After that, he isn't sure, but he's enjoying himself too much to quit. "When I finish the tenth frame of my life," he says, "that's when it'll be done."

TULSA

Roadside Oddities

Oklahoma was never blessed with a Grand Canyon or a redwood forest. It doesn't have geysers, volcanoes, or enormous sandstone arches. Neither has it been endowed with a defining architectural centerpiece such as Mount Rushmore or a tourist hotspot such as Times Square.

That isn't to say the Sooner State has nothing to see, of course. Far from it. Its attractions are on a smaller scale, that's all. You can get your picture taken with all manner of interesting things that are scattered across the state. Gaze into one of the world's longest glowing lightbulbs, preen yourself in a mirror that belonged to the twentieth century's number-one bad guy, or walk into the mouth of a floating concrete whale. Perhaps you'd prefer a tour of history's most bizarre pharmaceutical remedies, or a chance at winning first prize at a manure-throwing contest.

Whatever you fancy, Oklahoma has it. And it's guaranteed to be more memorable than a walk through a giant shopping mall and less expensive than posing with a cartoon mouse.

Thar He Blows!

Route 66, the famous highway of legend and lore, is scattered with much-celebrated attractions from end to end, and Oklahoma is home to one of the most distinctive and recognizable: Catoosa's Blue Whale.

Beached along a stretch of the highway running northeast out of Tulsa, the big beautiful whale beams his gaping grin from a pond in a small roadside park. He was once part of a larger attraction that included a concession stand, a petting zoo, a non-petting alligator farm, and a giant boat in the fashion of Noah's Ark. It was all built and managed by entrepreneur Hugh Davis and his wife, Zelta.

The attraction, including the adjacent swimming hole, was already fairly popular, but when Hugh completed the Blue Whale in 1972, the site's popularity skyrocketed. According to Hugh and Zelta's son Blaine, who now lives on the property, "Everybody in the neighborhood, and up and down the road, and everywhere else, started showing up." The whale had a sundeck, diving boards on his tail, slides for fins, and portholes in his head for kids to peek out of.

Unfortunately, by the late 1980s, the Davises could no longer manage the swimming hole and had to shut it down,

along with the Blue Whale. And like the blue whale of the open sea, theirs too began to face endangerment. The wood started to rot, the concrete began to chip, and the paint quickly faded in the sun. Brush swallowed up the park, and the water, left to stagnate, acquired a green skin. Then, of course, there were the vandals who insisted on having their way with things, even going so far as to steal the whale's original baseball cap.

Thankfully, concerned citizens raised money for the Blue Whale's restoration and, by the mid-1990s, returned him to his original condition. That allowed Blaine to officially reopen the site as a Route 66 attraction. The sightseers, after all, had never really stopped coming.

There's still no swimming, though, because the pond retains that green skin.

The Golden Driller

He's loved, he's hated. He's admired and ridiculed. Both "proud symbol" and "embarrassing eyesore" he's been called, and yet there he remains, as he has for more than forty years, unscathed by criticism.

From his full-brim hard hat to his steel-cap boots, he is the embodiment of Tulsa's heritage, a seven-story icon of the petroleum industry. He was dedicated to the men of the oil fields who, according to the plaque at his feet, "created from God's abundance a better life for mankind." Of course, now that the fields have dried up, he stands today more as a memorial.

He came to the self-described "oil capital of the world" in 1953 as a centerpiece for the International Petroleum Exposition, where he was appointed the title of "the Golden Driller." Originally sculpted from gold-painted papier-mâché, he bore a friendly smile and, at least for a roughneck, a surprisingly effeminate hand gesture. Six years later, when the next expo was held, the Golden Driller was re-created, this time climbing a drilling rig. In 1966, the big man made his third and final appearance when he was erected in front of Tulsa's brand-new Expo Center as a permanent installation constructed from steel, fiberglass, and concrete. Weighing more than forty-three thousand pounds, he now sports a size 112 hard hat, size 393DDD boots, and pants with a 576-inch waist.

This latest incarnation's expression is far more stern than in previous creations, resembling a face you might find on an Art Deco–style propaganda poster, and although he's kept the name Golden Driller, his color resembles more of a spicy mustard. Plus, his bare sculpted torso—exposed unabashedly to the so-called buckle of the Bible Belt—has been criticized in the past as being inappropriate for public display. Admittedly, his chest is conspicuously well chiseled, though his more southerly regions remain as ambiguous as a Ken doll's. Still, you could argue that he's just wearing a really tight shirt since, after all, you can't see his belly button, either.

Many are quick to express their negative feelings for the big man, calling him an ugly disgrace to public art. In recent years, some have pushed for his relocation farther into the fairgrounds and out of sight of the street, though without success. Reportedly he's even been targeted by a shotgun, and on one occasion, was stuck in the back with an arrow. Even those who claim to love him have been known to adorn him in giant promotional T-shirts, ugly neckties, Santa's caps, and in one case, a humongous necklace of emasculating "friendship beads."

On the whole, however, the Golden Driller has become accepted as an important and irreplaceable landmark, not only for Tulsa, but for the entire state. In 1979, the state legislature elected him as Oklahoma's official state monument.

TULSA

The World's Largest Peanut?

Despite the engraving touting this monument as the "world's largest peanut," Durant's residents are quick to admit that theirs is, in fact, not. Were it real, they might have something to brag about, but alas, it's just concrete.

The three-foot legume stands in front of Durant's City Hall at the corner of West Evergreen Street and North Third Avenue. According to the plaque, it was dedicated to the peanut growers and processors of Bryan County and it commemorates the region's once having been a leader in goober production.

It also marks the burial site of a time capsule scheduled to be opened in 2023. Together with other items, the capsule reportedly holds a booklet from the Oklahoma Peanut Commission on how to cook peanuts.

As already mentioned, the monument falls far short of being the world's largest. Just months after it was built in 1974, a town in southern Georgia beat it by several feet. Several other towns across the South have built their own giant goobers, as well, and although Georgia's still reigns supreme, each of the others could still mash Durant's into butter.

Perhaps they should consider building the world's largest nutcracker and declare war on their competitors.

Volkswagen Spider

As far as we know, Volkswagen never produced a VW Spider. Rabbits, Foxes, and Beetles, sure, but never a Spider. Leave it to an Oklahoman to fill that gap.

Just up US 77, about a half mile north of Lexington, Volkswagen enthusiast Leroy Wilson installed the fifteen-foot-tall arachnid to watch over his parts business. Constructed from a gutted-out old Beetle and some metal pipe, it threatens passing motorists with its enormous headlamp eyes and blood-soaked fangs.

Wilson's business was once touted as the world's largest dealer in Volkswagen parts, boasting a stock of some 2,500 vehicles. Wilson himself had always been a car enthusiast and raced home-built vehicles in the 1950s and 1960s. He even took part in sixteen cross-country Great Race rallies, each four thousand miles long. Out in the field behind the giant spider, he maintained his own raceway, a dirt track called the Black Widow Speedway.

Leroy Wilson passed away in 2000, and his family sold off the five-acre business shortly thereafter. His spider, however, remains. Out of respect, nobody mentions the arthropod's two missing legs.

Der Führer's Dainties

In the middle of Oklahoma City stands a life-size, outdoor military diorama that would fill any ten-year-old boy with jubilant delight. Jeeps, choppers, howitzers, and airplanes on sticks prevail in a frozen action sequence specially prepared to pull in lovers of militaria to the capital city's own Forty-fifth Infantry Division Museum.

Yet, the real draw to the museum lies inside. Among the astounding twenty-seven thousand square feet of displays covering the history of the Forty-fifth Infantry, as well as other facets of military history, the museum holds what it boasts as the largest collection of Adolf Hitler's personal artifacts on display anywhere.

Salvaged from Hitler's Munich apartment and from his mountain retreat in Berchtesgaden known as the Eagle's Nest, the display includes der Führer's personal bed linens, embroidered with swastikas, as well as his monogrammed napkins and custom tea set. The museum even has the mirror that once hung in the bedroom of the bunker in which he died, the very mirror in which the most vilified man in history once combed his tiny little mustache.

Olson's Two-Headed Calf

It is rarely a waste of time to stop in at a small-town museum. While they may never have life-sized dinosaur models, interactive science displays, or any of the other stuff you'll find at the big-city institutions, it's worth taking a half hour just to enjoy the guaranteed quirkiness you'll find amid the repurposed display cases and handmade placards you're sure to find inside. A startlingly large assemblage of antique clothes irons, the world's most extensive collection of marbles, or perhaps a display on rodeo clowns or a highly detailed model of the Taj Mahal made of toothpicks. You never know what you'll come across.

At the No Man's Land Historical Museum in Goodwell, that special something is the revered yet still bizarre anatomical anomaly known as the two-headed calf. Born in 1932 to local farmer Ed Olson, this taxidermied and glass-enclosed Hereford calf might appear normal in every way, except that it has double the usual number of faces.

The poor thing lived only a few weeks before Olson donated the remains to the museum just as it was getting ready to open its doors for the first time. Eager to add the calf to their collection before the grand opening, curators taxidermied the creature as quickly as they could, but their hasty efforts somehow resulted in the calf catching fire. They apparently rescued their little freak in time, though, and it's been on display ever since.

According to current museum director, Debbie Colson, "There's several museums, especially in this neck of the world, that have two-headed calves . . . but I think ours is prettier."

Tom Mix's Suitcase of Death

Tom Mix was the first real cowboy hero of the big screen. He starred in literally hundreds of films between 1920 and 1935, and has been credited with redefining the Western movie genre with his hard-riding, action-packed performances. Riding to the rescue time and again in his signature ten-gallon hat, Mix paved the way for men like Tex Ritter, Roy Rogers, and John Wayne. Yet, these days, Mix appears to be less famous for his life than he is for his death. Or more accurately, for the way in which he died.

It was October 12, 1940, and Mix was headed to Phoenix, Arizona, on his way west. He had spent the night in Tucson, checking out of his hotel room fairly late in the day. According to reports, he had been up pretty late the previous night drinking in his room with a group of musicians. Leaving the hotel about noon, he tossed his luggage in the back of his Cord convertible. On the way, Mix stopped at a bar for a quick chat with a friend, which turned into rounds of whiskey and a few hands of poker.

Now, there's no definitive evidence to say that Mix was drunk when he finally left the bar, but as he roared up Highway 79 in his yellow roadster, he completely missed the detour signs that warned of construction up ahead. A flash flood had washed out part of the road and a crew was working

on repairing the damage. According to the men on the scene, Mix never even slowed down.

Traveling at eighty miles per hour, Mix's car flew through the barriers, dove into a wash, and flipped. The convertible came to rest on its side. Some say Mix was killed in the impact, but at least one witness reported seeing the cowboy free himself and begin to stand. At that moment, according to the witness, the larger of his metal suitcases fell on him and broke his neck. Legend says the case was full of silver dollars. (Today, a monument to the legendary cowboy stands just about where he got his ticket punched, a seven-foot stone obelisk featuring a profile of Mix's trusty steed, Tony the Wonder Horse, his saddle empty and his head bowed in grief.)

But luckily for Oklahomans with a penchant for celebrity demise, the Tom Mix memorial treasure lies in downtown Dewey at the Tom Mix Museum. There visitors can see the very luggage that beaned the poor movie star in the noggin. Of course, the museum has much more to see, such as a larger-than-life model of Tony the Wonder Horse, and Mix's extensive collection of guns, outfits, trophies, and comically oversized hats. The centerpiece for the truly perverse, however, is the matching pair of custom-made aluminum suitcases, one of which, according to the placard, "crashed forward . . . killing Mix instantly." And if you ask the docent nicely, she'll point out the dent in the shell that may very well have been caused by the impact with Mix's skull.

Some say Mix was killed in the impact . . .

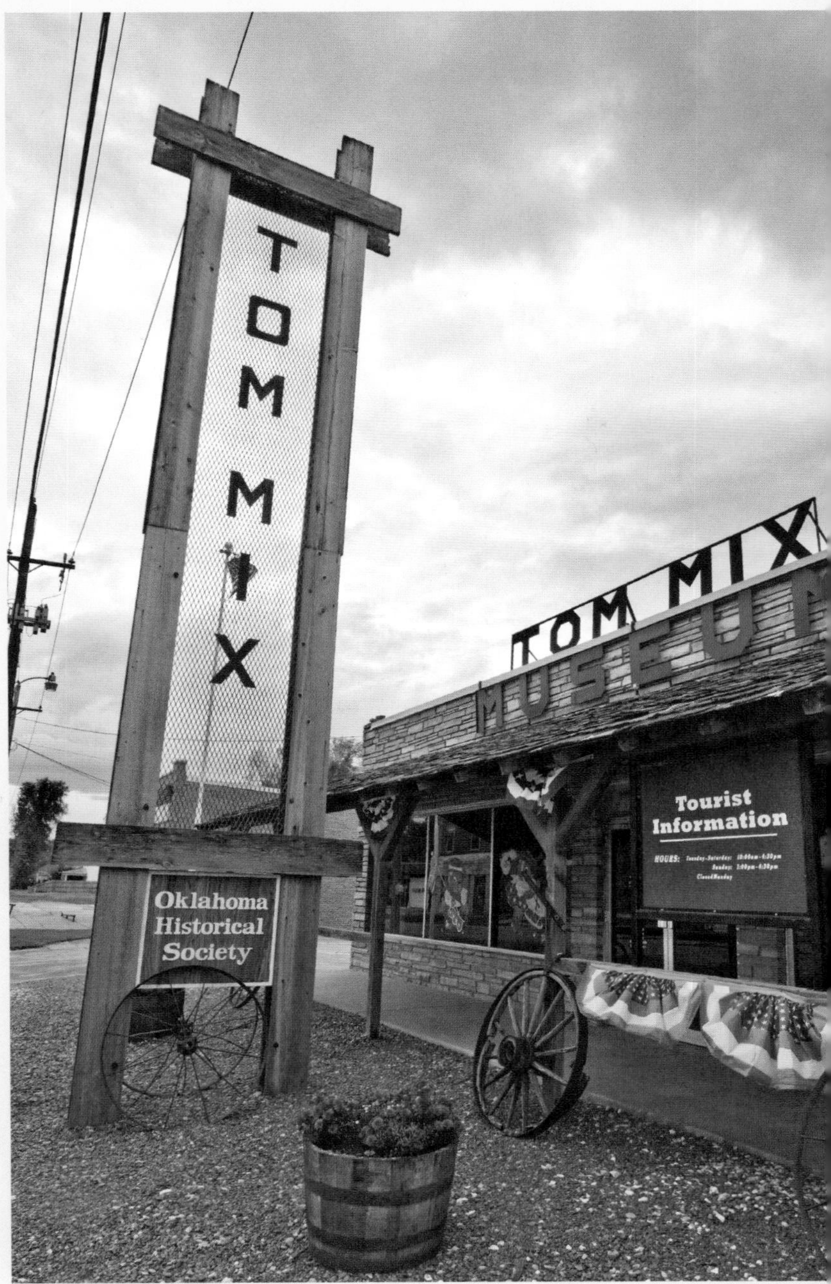

Oklahoma Frontier Drugstore Museum

There's lots of history to be seen in Guthrie, but for good old-fashioned, oddball nostalgia, none of it beats the stuff you can see at the downtown drugstore museum on Oklahoma Avenue.

Walking through the door is like stepping into a genuine, pre-statehood pharmacy. It's been arranged just as you might have seen it in the early 1900s, complete with a vintage, though sadly non-functioning, soda fountain. Apothecary cabinets, chemistry glassware, stacks of antique prescription slips, and vintage ads make up just a small portion of the enormous pharmaceutical antique collection amassed here. Adorning the shelves are leech jars, frighteningly pointy medical instruments, those weirdly ambiguous glass globes filled with colored liquid and several boxes of "rectal dilators" in both plastic and metal.

You could spend hours perusing the thousands of vintage drug packages, an amazing percentage of which still contain their medications. Vials, jars, boxes, and bottles, stacked several rows deep, fill dozens upon dozens of shelves extending all the way to the back of the building.

Bold lettering and brightly colored caricatures hawk pills, powders, and tonics offering dubious remedies for every ailment. Apparently, there wasn't a disorder that couldn't be cured with items like snake root, horehound, quassia chips, soap-tree bark, or imitation hemlock. Heaven help the patient who was prescribed sperm oil or mammary substance.

Before the pharmaceutical industry became the exclusive playground of multibillion-dollar corporations, it seemed that just about anyone could get into the game. Pharmacists stocked all kinds of products with names like Acker's Black Medicine, Mother Gray's Aromatic Leaf, Dr. Kilmer's Swamp Root, and Allan's Fever Drops. Then there were the ones with the more marketable names like Corn-o-Cide, Fink's Magic Oil, Bald-No-More, and Odo-Ro-No. Actually, it's hard to imagine how some could have been prescribed with a straight face. A couple of companies even marketed household medications under the brands "666" and "Sa-tan-ic."

Many come from a time when you could easily acquire substances now considered highly dangerous. Pharmacists regularly recommended cocaine and heroin before they were deemed illegal. You can still find historic samples of them in a glass case at the museum, along with liquid cannabis labeled for the treatment of "nervous depression . . . melancholia . . . wakefulness . . . delusions and forgetfulness." Of course, if the remedies themselves ever became a problem, for $1.50 you could pick up a bottle of "Reliable Cure for the Opium and Morphine Habits."

Sure, it's easy to dismiss products like Worm Syrup, Nerve Tea, or Lovotti's Blood Purifier (for "constipation, liver complaints, impure blood, boils, pimples, tired feeling, headache and all ailments caused by a sluggish liver") as simply quack medicine reserved for a time long-passed—y'know, when consumers didn't know any better. But walk into any of today's drugstores and see if you can't spot fast-selling pills that claim to turn fat into water or sticky pads that pull toxins out through your feet and you might just ask yourself if things are all that different.

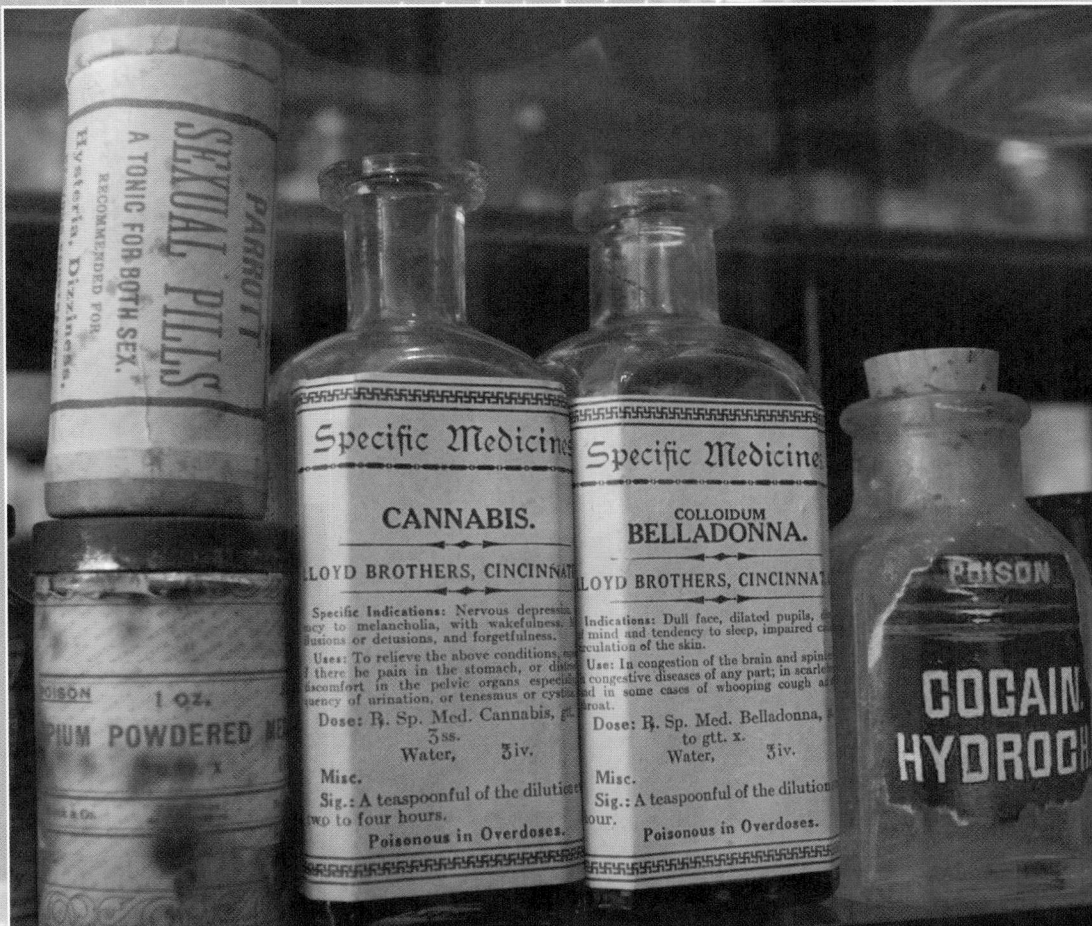

Frogs of Rock

We've all seen figures in clouds, maybe a face or two in the tiles on our bathroom floor. Heck, the news is filled with people who swear they've spotted images of holy figures in tree stumps and oil stains. A grilled cheese sandwich with the vague likeness of the Virgin Mary once sold on eBay for $28,000. People just can't help but see patterns amid chaos. It's in our nature. In fact, there's a term for just this type of experience. It's called *pareidolia*.

And Oklahomans, it seems, suffer from a rather specific form of the phenomenon—what you might call amphibial pareidolia. More simply, they see frogs. Take, for example, at least two boulders that, in one way or another, resemble hoppy little critters.

The smaller, and goonier-looking, of the pair rests along the north shoulder of E1570 Road, southwest of Ada. Though he's widely known as the Lightning Ridge Frog Rock, he probably wouldn't look much like anything at all without the thick coat of dark green paint and the goofy grin. Still, the kids love him all the same and are always excited to spot him from the backseats of their parents' cars as they travel the lonely stretch of road over which he presides. Nobody is quite sure who painted him initially, but reports indicate the little guy has been there since at least the 1950s.

Farther north and west of Tulsa sits an even larger version, this one known simply as Frog Rock. Measuring twenty feet from nose to butt, he sits on an embankment overlooking Keystone Lake. Though the locals are all aware of his existence, his history is difficult to trace, since pretty much all anyone knows about him is that he's been there "for years." Nevertheless, the big guy is obviously well loved, as unsung citizens take it upon themselves to repaint his fading shades of green every few years. The gravelly path on which he sits has even been officially named Frog Road.

Cimmy the Dinosaur

No Man's Land might not be the sort of place you'd imagine as a former Jurassic Park, but if you could travel back a few epochs, that's exactly what you'd see. About 150 million years ago, the Oklahoma Panhandle was a tropical swamp inhabited by numerous species of dinosaurs.

In 1931, fossils left by such beasts were discovered about eight miles east of Kenton. A member of a highway maintenance crew, who was patrolling Highway 64, accidentally snagged part of a bone with the blade of his road grader. As a result, scientists soon discovered that the entire site was a virtual gold mine of paleontological finds and eventually unearthed some eighteen tons of fossils, including an apatosaurus femur nearly six feet long that was deemed the "prize fossil bone of the Southwest."

The man who led the fossils' excavation had hoped many of the bones would become part of the new Black Mesa park recently established in the area, but it did not come to pass. Local historian Norma Gene Young, along with her husband, Bob, funded the construction of a steel-plate version in 1984 in the nearby town of Boise City. At sixty-five feet long and thirty-five feet high, it's intended to represent the true scale of the apatosaur whose femur had previously been discovered.

The big rusty beast, which stands at the north end of town, was named Cimmy by an elementary student in honor of Cimarron County, where the fossils were found.

Hooker, OK

Anybody who's driven through Oklahoma knows there are plenty of place-names to invigorate one's fourth-grade wit. Beggs, Greasy, and Happyland are a few prime examples. On a particularly long and weary drive, even names like Slapout, Bowlegs, and Felt can elicit a few giggles. Yet, there's one town that can join us in our sophomoric amusement, to stand up and take pride in the unignorable double entendre that is its postal designation. It is the Sooner State's very own Hooker, and—forget that this is the Bible Belt—the people here are proud of it!

In these parts cutthroat tourism is a necessary evil, and every town does its absolute best to pull motorists off the highway and convince them to spend their holiday cash. Hooker, Oklahoma, has adopted what has to be one of the state's cleverest and certainly least expensive tourism ventures ever conceived. When you've got a name like it does, there's no need to build the World's Largest Cornhusk or the nation's first pillowcase museum. All you need is a stack of T-shirts and a nine-year-old boy willing to come up with a few catchy slogans.

The Hooker Chamber of Commerce itself is mostly a gift shop, where the shelves are always well stocked with shirts, mugs, and magnets sporting any of a dozen irreverent catchphrases, such as "Support your local hookers" and "Hooker, OK: A location, not a vocation."

In 1967, Hooker organized a baseball team—the Horny Toads—and citizen Jack Goosen built them a field on which to play. A T-shirt memorializes his efforts. It says, "Jack Goosen field: He built it and we came." Catchy, huh?

Admittedly, the rest of Hooker could put a bit more effort into taking part in the joke. After all, there are plenty of opportunities for droll business names. There is a Hooker Health Club and the Hooker EMS (their motto: "Here to serve"), but surprisingly there's no Hooker Hotel, no Hooker Church and no Hooker Storage. I mean, it seems like a wasted opportunity not to at least open a Hooker Wash or a Hooker Drugs.

What say you, Oklahoma? Are there any other towns out there daring enough to cash in on their suggestive names? Mounds? Bushyhead? How about you, Fallis? Are you up for the challenge?

Flung Dung in Beaver

Like Hooker, the town of Beaver is ripe for prurient puns. Yet town officials have opted not to capitalize on such lewd humor.

Since 1970, Beaver has made a name for itself entirely unrelated to its given moniker. Yes, folks, Beaver is the World Cow Chip Throwing Capital. That's right. They're poop pitchers. Flop flingers. Turd tossers. And they're more proud of it than you might think.

Every April, when the fragrance of wildflowers has filled the air, chip chuckers young and old compete in what is inarguably the crappiest discus throw ever organized. Dung-dashing hopefuls battle it out to try and best one another for the farthest distance thrown—and maybe, just maybe, beat the all-time world record set in 2001 by fecal flicker Robby Deevers. His manure cake traveled more than 185 feet.

The historic relevance of the contest, as told by the Beaver County Chamber of Commerce, is a bit tenuous. When pioneers came to the Great Plains, they found there was little wood available for cooking and heating. They soon discovered, though, that dried cow manure made for a decent fuel. Not only did it burn, but it did so with plenty of heat and no odor. And so—and this much is true—cow chips became a valuable commodity. As a result, families scoured the fields for precious patties and, according to Beaver's promotional masterminds, made a game of seeing who could toss their finds into the family wagon from the farthest distance. Thus was born the annual Cow Chip Throw.

Right along the main thoroughfare, visitors can stop for a photo with the local fiberglass mascot, Big Beaver. He is, of course, brandishing a giant meadow muffin.

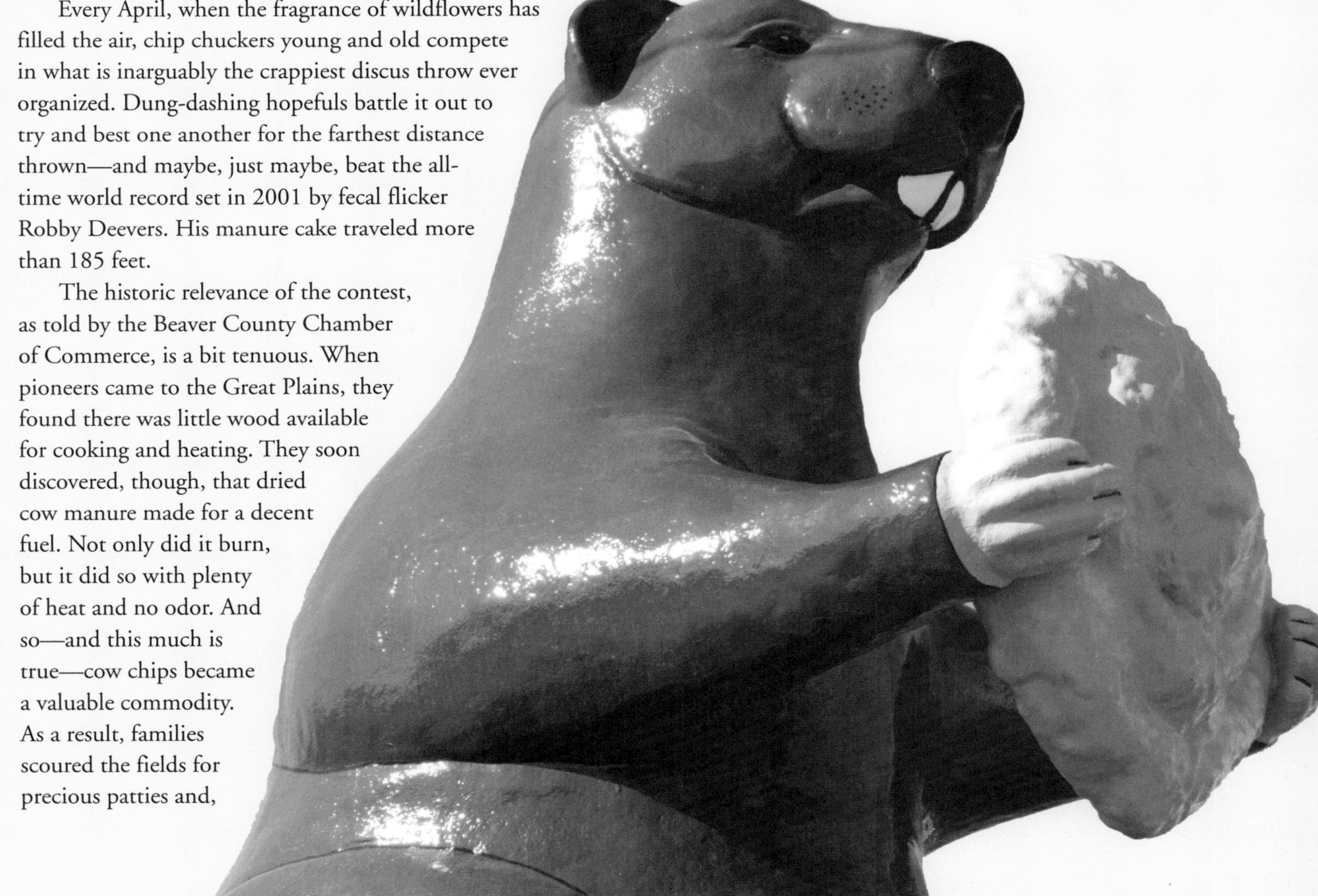

Place of Prayer and Bible Walk

According to the hand-typed notice posted inside the gate and protected by glass and chicken wire, the Open Air Place of Prayer and Bible Walk was erected for rest, reflection, prayer, and spiritual refreshment. Those traveling between Talihina and Whitesboro are probably thankful for the clarification, since most of them likely wonder why, here in the middle of nowhere, someone has chosen to build an unattended holy respite amid pasture and ambling livestock.

The park, which actually makes for a nice, quiet little roadside pit stop even for the less reverent among us, consists of five separate installations, each an embodiment of biblical narrative. Taking center stage is the Bible Walk, a circular pathway outlining the major events of the Bible and circling three life-size crucifixes. Then, to the left, there's the Biblical Museum, Christ's Empty Tomb to the right, the Lord's Prayer monument and the Ten Commandments monument taking up the rear and, delineating the front of the property, a row of teetering brick arches that represent the Seven Churches of the Apocalypse in the book of Revelation.

It's tough to say just which installation takes the prize for most divine, but it's probably fair to say that the museum and Christ's tomb take the lead for most beguiling. The tomb, built of stucco and cinder blocks, is intended to be a reproduction of the burial chamber from which Jesus was found to be missing following his resurrection. Inside, you'll find two aging and balding department-store angels brashly proclaiming through a handwritten note, "Why seek ye the living among the dead? He is not here but is risen!" The famed stone that once sealed the tomb has been rolled back for your viewing convenience, also revealing the rarely mentioned glass security door to which God's messengers presumably held the key.

The Biblical Museum, while perhaps not as spiritually stimulating, is certainly more time consuming. It consists of only three glass-enclosed displays, but stands to be more thought-provoking than even your largest of historical exhibits. The first display, titled "Holy of Holies" is a simple replica of the Ark of the Covenant. Yes, it's similar to the invaluable relic once coveted by Indiana Jones, but this one is topped by two plastic dolls with papier-mâché wings. The second and third displays, "Old Testament" and "New Testament" respectively, are filled with inexplicable detail. (From "inexplicable" one should infer "curious" and "perplexing.")

Some of the elements are not so difficult to decipher, like the whimsical porcelain frogs that represent the second of the plagues imposed on Egypt or the den of tiny lions surrounding what is presumed to be a prostrate Daniel, but others are more puzzling, like the harp-plucking angel that looks suspiciously like a 1970s Mattel superhero, Noah's cardboard-box ark filled with animals who all look like they were hit with a wave of knockout gas, and the band of gorillas who appear to be in a fit of laughter over their mate who's run head-on into a post.

Still, it's worth a visit should you be in the area, if only for the tranquil solitude amid distant cattle moos. You'll find it southeast of Talihina, about a mile and a half down SR 63.

Praying Hands

It was to be Oral Roberts's greatest achievement, the opus of the man who had already become world famous for his missionary efforts and his televised tent revivals. The City of Faith Medical and Research Center, as it would be called, would be the latest and greatest addition to his eponymous Tulsa-based university, comprising three soaring towers dedicated to faith and healing.

The idea came to him directly from God, who, according to Roberts, spoke to him in 1977 and told him to erect three buildings, twenty, thirty, and sixty stories high. Together, they would be the new holy center of medical study and treatment. More than 200 million square feet of floor space would house research facilities, examining rooms, and offices for the three hundred doctors who would come to work there and exactly 777 hospital beds for the million patients who would take advantage of the City of Faith's services every year. Topping it all off would be a gargantuan pair of magnificent bronze hands, lifted in prayer at the facility's entrance.

The total cost for the endeavor was projected to be somewhere between $250 million and $400 million, money Roberts didn't have. Being a man of faith, however, he went ahead with the ground breaking and began construction on his enormous towers anyway. Besides, he explained, Jesus told him everything would work out just fine. The encounter, as he described it to his followers, occurred at the construction site, where Christ appeared to him in a vision, looming above the towers and standing nine hundred feet tall. The gigantic Jesus picked up the sixty-story tower and told Roberts to stoke a fire under his followers, who were sure to contribute the necessary funds.

Roberts's disciples responded, but not nearly to the degree to which he had hoped. When the City of Faith opened in 1981, the interior remained 80 percent unfinished. Only a portion of the clinic and research towers came into use, and even three years later, only 130 of the projected 777 hospital beds were ever utilized. Not even a third divine visitation, which Roberts said occurred in 1984, was enough to save the project. After serving a total of twenty-seven thousand patients and running into the red every single year, the City of Faith closed shop in 1989. It was later renamed the CityPlex Towers, stripped of its religious ornamentation, and rented out as commercial office space.

Today, the only vestige of Roberts's City of Faith is that colossal pair of hands, which, at sixty feet tall and weighing thirty tons, is the largest bronze sculpture in the world. Moved in 1991, the hands stand at the entrance to Oral Roberts University.

Leedey's Leaning Tornado Tower

In the spring of 1947, on the last day of May, a tragedy befell the town of Leedey. In a storm that had already terrorized nearby Gage and Arnett, Leedey lost six of its own as the tempest morphed into a tornado that swept in from the north and leveled much of the town.

Fifty years later, a second tragedy struck, this time in the form of a memorial to those poor souls. Revealed during Leedey's week-long Roll of Thunder commemoration, the odd little monument stands today in Leedey Park, a rusting spiral of steel shaped vaguely like a mannequin leg from a pantyhose display. In an apparent attempt at realism, its creators tossed in a bizarre mélange of objects, the presence of which only add to the twister sculpture's absurdity. Among them you can find a tricycle, the head of a rake, a boot, an old can of neat's-foot oil, and for reasons unexplained, a string of rotting Christmas lights.

Boise City Bombing

Boise City, in the far west end of the Panhandle, was bombed in World War II. And we bombed it ourselves.

Shortly past midnight on July 5, 1943, the crew of a B-17 bomber took off from Dalhart Army Air Base in Texas and set off for Conlen, just to the northeast. Their mission was to make a late-night run on a bombing range about twenty miles away, where their target would be marked by lights. The flight's navigator, who was replacing a man on sick leave, got lost by twice that distance and somehow ended up over Boise City. He then mistook the lights surrounding the Cimarron County Courthouse for their target's bull's-eye.

Down below, a few residents were still up and about. A local newspaperman had just finished a long day at the print shop. A handful of truckers were catching a late dinner at the Liberty Cafe. The last showing of *The Forest Rangers*, starring Fred MacMurray, had recently let out, and a group of soldiers were walking their dates home.

Then, amid the quiet night air, they heard the hum of an engine, a long slow whistle, and a bang. A practice shell filled with ninety-six pounds of sand and four pounds of explosive—just enough to make a nice little boom—struck the ground. Those who were awake ran for cover. Those who weren't jumped from their beds. The city, they thought, was under enemy attack.

For thirty harrowing minutes, the bomber crew circled the square, dropping practice bomb after practice bomb. The doors of the Baptist church were blown open, its windows shattered. One projectile fell directly behind a gasoline

tanker, a rig belonging to one of the men at the café. He dropped his meal, hopped in the truck's cab, and sped out of town, never to be seen again. The shells blew holes in the street three feet deep.

It was Frank Garrett, an employee at the local utility company, who finally brought the ordeal to an end. Jumping from his bed, he pulled his pants on over his pajamas, ran to the Southwestern Public Service building, and pulled the master switch that doused the city's lights. That's when the bomber crew realized something was amiss and cut their mission short.

In all, five bombs blew holes in Boise City's pavement, though luckily no one was hurt and the only real property damage was to an old garage. The bombs all landed within ninety-three feet of the courthouse, save for a sixth that fell away as the bomber left the scene.

The crew's navigator was subsequently ousted and the rest of the men were given a choice: undergo court-martial or head to the front lines. They chose battle, and eventually earned the lead position in an eight-hundred-plane assault in the first daylight bombing run on Berlin. They even became one of the most decorated crews of the war.

In 1993, fifty years after the attack, the good-natured men and women of Boise City honored the event with a memorial. At the junction of Highway 385, Highway 287, and Highway 412, just yards away from the courthouse, they planted a replica bombshell in a miniature concrete crater, tilting it, of course, back toward Dalhart. Officials tracked down the surviving members of the B-17 and invited them to the celebration, but they all declined.

Atomic Annie

The date: May 25, 1953. The place: Frenchman's Flat, Nevada Test Site, about sixty-five miles northwest of Las Vegas. The event: Desert go "boom!"

In a series of nuclear tests called Operation Upshot-Knothole, eleven devices of varying yields and delivery methods were detonated to gauge their effectiveness and viability. The second-to-last, codenamed Grable, resulted in an explosion equivalent to fifteen kilotons of TNT. It wasn't the largest blast, nor the most destructive, but it was unique in that the warhead was fired from a howitzer. That's right: a great, big atomic cannon.

With nuclear weapons becoming the prime choice for military destruction worldwide, the U.S. Department of Defense evidently thought it would be a good idea to look into atomic bullets. Troops could then wipe out an entire enemy installation with a single shot from the ground. The result was the M65 Atomic Cannon, which could fire an impressive eight-hundred-pound, 280 mm shell up to thirteen miles. The weapon, nicknamed "Atomic Annie," weighed eighty-five tons with its carriage and sported a barrel measuring an imposing forty feet in length.

It took two specialized tractors to move the howitzer, one tractor in front and the other in back, steered like a fireman's hook-and-ladder. It reached a maximum traveling speed of thirty-five miles per hour. It was the largest mobile artillery device ever built. The initial test shot traveled nearly eight miles, taking a nerve-racking nineteen seconds to detonate.

Twenty such guns were built in all, but by the time they were deployed, they were already obsolete thanks to the development of rocket-based weapons. The test at Frenchman's Flat was the only time the United States ever fired a live nuclear round of its kind. Only eight of the atomic cannons are known still to exist and are spread out across the country serving as museum pieces. The original, and the only one to ever deliver a nuclear payload, serves as a tourist attraction at Fort Sill in southwest Oklahoma.

ATOMIC ANNIE

King of the Hills

Who says size doesn't matter, especially when it comes to tourism? After all, who wants to drive hundreds of miles to see the world's second-largest shovel or take pictures of the nation's third-tallest stack of matchbooks? Visitors want the best, baby!

In Poteau, just a few miles from Oklahoma's eastern border, the matter of measures gets even trickier. A few extra inches and the local claim to fame would have been shot. Cavanal Hill, so they claim, is just twelve inches short of being a full-fledged mountain, which effectively qualifies it as the "world's highest hill."

The designation reportedly came about sometime prior to World War II when a local high school class engaged in a correspondence project with a class in England. The students across the pond, having read about Cavanal Hill, informed the Oklahoma students of the mound's honor, based on the British Geological Society's classification of a mountain as rising two thousand feet or more above the surrounding terrain.

To verify the claim, we wanted to find out just exactly what the difference is between a hill and a mountain. And to do that, we hit the library.

Webster's Third New International Dictionary calls a hill "higher than a rise and lower than a mountain." No help there. But mountains, it says, project above the surrounding land "1,000 feet or more." Not looking good so far.

The *American Heritage Dictionary*, on the other hand, says a hill is a "well-defined natural elevation smaller than a mountain," while a mountain has a height "greater than that of a hill." Terrific.

The *Encyclopaedia Britannica* refuses to say one way or the other, insisting that the terms have no "standardized geographic meaning." The *Oxford Companion to the Earth* is just as noncommittal, emphasizing disparate labeling of local land forms among various regions.

The *World Book Encyclopedia* is confusing. Hills, it says, "rise less than 1,000 feet above the surrounding area. Mountains always exceed that height." Yet, a mountain has to include two zones of climate and typically "must rise about 2,000 feet above its surroundings" to do so. That leaves us with a full thousand feet of wiggle room.

Finally, we come to what many consider to be the king of lexicons, the *Oxford English Dictionary*. It suggests that "heights under 2,000 feet are generally called hills." Finally, things start to look up. Unfortunately, its editors admit that this definition pertains generally to Great Britain, where the *OED* just happens to be published. So, we come full circle, like a dog chasing its tail.

Who, we ask, stands as the authority on such matters here in the good old US of A? Why, that would be the U.S. Geological Survey, the nation's leading organization in geological matters. Regrettably, the agency doesn't appear to make any authoritative distinction between a hill and a mountain, although it's probably worth noting that Cavanal Hill is officially listed in their database and on all topographic maps as "Cavanal Mountain." So there's that.

Where does this leave us? Well, seeing as Poteau has already installed a big plaque celebrating the town's point of pride, we may as well give them the benefit of the doubt. Besides, no other town, it seems, wants to challenge their claim. So, the World's Highest Hill it is.

One well-placed wheelbarrow full of dirt, though, and the whole issue is closed.

The Bulb

With all the talk in recent years about practical energy conservation, the traditional incandescent lightbulb has been dethroned as a proud symbol of invention and has been vilified almost universally as a gluttonous electricity hog. Not too long ago, it stood as an unmistakable icon of imagination and ingenuity, but in a swift, global serving of cold shoulder, it has been thrust aside in favor of replacement products with dispassionate acronyms like LED, CFL, and HID.

Proponents of the compact fluorescent light seem especially proud of the new technology's endurance. "You can go without changing a bulb for as many as five years!" they proclaim, raising a condescending eyebrow on what we like to imagine is a coldly lit and patronizing little face. "Ha! That's nothing," we reply. And then we smile and lift a finger toward Mangum.

Nestled in the southwest crook of the state, burning quietly in an upstairs corner of a modest old firehouse, is a small, incandescent globe. This fireball beat the new-fangled spiral bulb's endurance record even before 90 percent of rural America had electricity. Installed in 1927, "the Bulb," as Mangum firefighters affectionately refer to it, has outlasted almost every other lamp in history.

Only two other lightbulbs are known to have burned longer than Mangum's. The oldest, which also hangs in a firehouse, is in Livermore, California, and has burned since 1901. The runner-up, which was originally installed in an opera house in 1908, is now in a museum in Fort Worth, Texas. All three have glowed almost continuously, save for short interruptions during power outages and oh-so-careful relocations. A cantankerous hardware store owner in New York once claimed to hold third place with a bulb from 1912, but both he and his bulb vanished mysteriously several years ago, though we don't mean to imply any foul play.

Mangum's bulb has spent most, if not all, of its life on the second floor in the firemen's sleeping quarters. (It may have originally been installed in the engine bay, but the bulb has outlived anyone who would know for sure.) It continues to flake bits of paint from decades ago when it hung in the middle of the room and residents dabbed black dots on it for a better night's sleep. Since being moved sometime in the late 1960s or early 1970s to a fixture in the corner, firefighters apparently too macho or too light sensitive to sleep with any night-light at all covered it up with an opaque globe. The firemen on duty are more than happy to uncover it for any visitors who stop by for a peek.

We recommend you pay a visit and bask in the Bulb's welcoming radiance as soon as you can, because, at some point, it will have either burned out, or lobbyists will have successfully prohibited its warm, power-sucking glow by law.

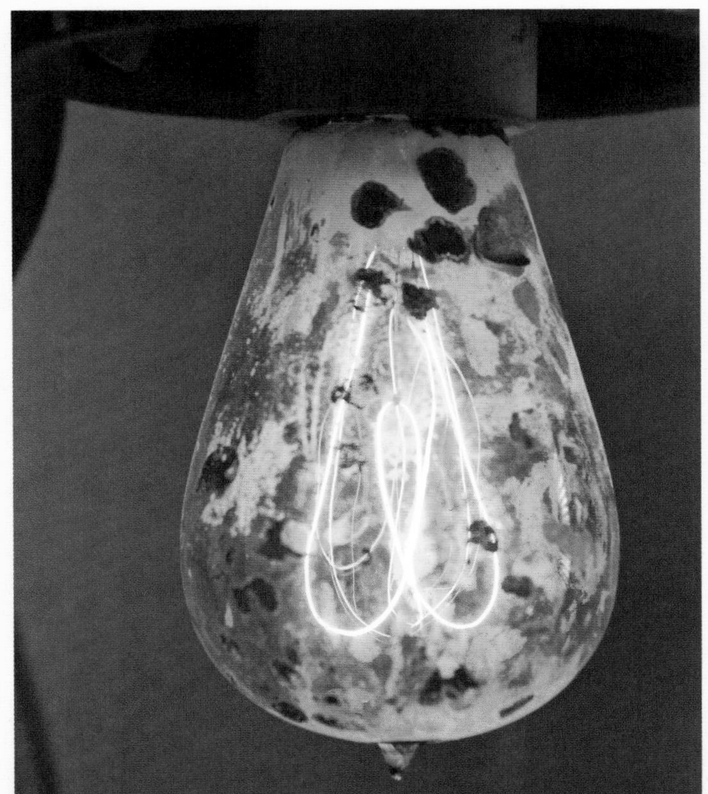

Hell's Angles Rule

Roads Less Traveled

What is it about the open road that draws us out onto those long stretches of pavement? Sure, we almost always have some destination in mind, some customary target offering familiar entertainment. But for many of us, something lures us down a less recognizable path to someplace we haven't been before. Perhaps it's the discovery of the unknown, or the potential for anything at all to happen just around that next corner.

There are some roads out there with more of that potential than others. Oklahoma's tangled web of asphalt consists of some unusual byways, some forks of which are cursed, haunted, or awash in inexplicable phenomena. Some don't even obey the laws of physics.

There's a whole network of paved possibilities out there. Are you intrepid enough to see what they might hold and to experience what could happen?

Crybaby Bridge

If there's one legend everyone's familiar with, it's Crybaby Bridge. The reason is because, it seems, nearly every town's got one. If you plot every alleged Crybaby Bridge on a map, you'll see they cover nearly the entire state, meaning that either this is one popular tale or bridges and infants just don't go very well together.

If you're not familiar with the story, it usually goes a little something like this: During a time long before seat belts or infant car seats became common equipment in automobiles, a woman and her baby were taking a leisurely drive through the country. The mother unexpectedly lost control while driving across a bridge. In the resulting accident, the child was fatally injured or drowned. In many versions, the woman loses her life, too, sometimes due to decapitation.

Sometimes, you can even hear the splash of a baby hitting the water.

In at least one version, the woman was actually trying to cross a bridge in high water when the vehicle was predictably washed into the river. Her child was swept away and never found. Occasionally, the story goes, the woman was drunk.

In a more ghastly variation, numerous children lost their lives at the bridge, all at the hands of their mother. This unhappy legend says that a young girl, repeatedly raped by her father, drowned each of the resulting offspring.

In yet another, less common version, both parents were involved. Instead of driving across the bridge, they were simply picnicking on the bank or rowing in a nearby pond when their child fell into the water and was lost in the weeds.

Whatever the cause, the result is that you can now go down to the bridge at night and hear the faint cries of the child, or children, wailing in the darkness. Sometimes, you can even hear the splash of a baby hitting the water. According to some, this has to be experienced at midnight. According to others, it only works on Fridays. If you drive there, you're supposed to stop in the middle of the bridge, turn off your ignition and your lights, and roll down the windows. If you're one of the unlucky few, your car might even fail to start when you're ready to get the heck out of there.

In some instances, if you're brave enough to get out of the car, you might see a ghostly image of the baby's mother, either hovering above the creek, walking the banks, or wandering beneath the bridge searching for her lost child. Or she may appear as a softly glowing blue light.

Whatever the case, Crybaby Bridge is a perfect place to take a car full of visiting relatives for a little local flavor, especially if you can load one or two of them in the open bed of a pickup. So, if you find yourself in Ada, Alderson, Catoosa, Checotah, Hontubby, Jenks, Kellyville, Kiefer, Moore, Newcastle, Pryor, Schulter, or Vinita some evening and you're looking for a scare, just ask any high-school kid where you can find Crybaby Bridge. He'll surely be able to point the way.

Gravity Hills

America loves its gravity hills. Every state's got 'em and everybody knows someone who's been there and insists, "Yeah, it really works!" Everyone has their own idea just what's going on there, too, causing cars to roll uphill, be it magnetic confluence, ley lines, or pushy little ghosts.

One thing is for sure, though. When it comes to these puzzling spots, Oklahoma will not be outdone. It has two gravity hills. And each one can compete in the best of class when it comes to legend and mystery.

Perhaps the most talked about of the two is Gravity Hill in Bartlesville. To get there, take W2400 Road west from US 75. After about two miles, you'll cross the Caney River, drive over some railroad tracks, then pass Gap Road. Another quarter mile later and you'll come to a sharp curve to the left. Turn the car around just before the curve, facing the way you came, and put it in neutral. (Be careful, though, because not everybody slows down around that curve like they should.) You should soon begin rolling—uphill, mind you—all the way back across those railroad tracks and onto the Caney River bridge.

Stories differ on what happened at this location to result in the anti-gravity phenomenon. One says that a busload of kids was hit by a train years ago and that the spirits of those who were killed are trying to draw you safely to the other side of the tracks. Another claims that a group of teenagers were on their way to a local football game when they stalled on the tracks and were killed. They, too, are trying to push you safely out of harm's way.

More impressive, perhaps, is Springer's Gravity Hill, often referred to as Magnetic Hill or Mystery Hill. Here, the apparent climb is long and relatively steep. Whether you're at the top or the bottom, it seems pretty obvious just which way you car should roll, even though it won't.

To reach it, take Exit 42 from Interstate 35 and head west along Highway 53. In about 1.4 miles, turn right on Pioneer Road and head to the end. Stop on the dark patch at the bottom of the hill and take your car out of gear. The uphill action on this one is unmistakable, and you can reach speeds as high as fifteen miles per hour under no power whatsoever. For a real thrill, some people do it backward.

Theories regarding this spot usually lean toward the scientific, involving anti-gravitational forces, magnetism, or optical illusion. However, some do share a legend involving a woman who was kidnapped, taken to this spot, and murdered. It's purportedly the victim's spirit who pushes visitors away from the area, protecting them from a similar fate. A few will tell you that if you sprinkle baby powder on the back of your car, you'll even end up with a pair of handprints on your trunk.

So, what do you think? Is it the supernatural? Alien energy? Natural electromagnetic attraction? We don't claim to have the answers, but there's one thing we do know: They're just plain weird and a lot of fun.

Green Eyes Bridge

Shine a flashlight into an animal's face in the dark of night, and its eyes, as everyone knows, will shine back, dilated and glowing like a creature possessed. When unexpected, the effect can be scary enough, but when the eyes continue to smolder after you've switched the flashlight off . . . well, that's a whole different terror.

Back in the woods northwest of Pawhuska, that very situation has frightened more than a handful of nighttime drivers who've dared cross Green Eyes Bridge with their headlights off. The span, which is more of a low-water crossing than a bridge, intersects Bird Creek along County Road 4070 just a couple of miles east of Bluestem Lake, and remains the site of the most infamous legend in Pawhuska.

According to Blanche, a Pawhuskan who's lived in the area for more than forty years and whose home overlooks the crossing, the tale of Green Eyes began sometime around 1965 when a man murdered his wife and did away with the body in Bird Creek. Having driven himself and the victim into the woods, he stopped at the top of the hill just above the bridge, put the station wagon in neutral, and steered it into the water.

Sadly, the couple's dog—a German shepherd, as Blanche recalls—was locked in the back. Trapped inside, the poor thing drowned.

When the authorities lifted the car from the water and recovered the bodies, they took the woman back to town for a proper burial but callously tossed the dog onto the bank and left him there. Blanche says she and her family had to pass the dog and smell his rotting corpse for days until they finally convinced the authorities to do something. Unfortunately, "something" consisted of simply dumping some dirt on his rotting carcass.

Not everyone in Pawhuska can tell you the back story in such detail, but they all know what's been happening down there ever since. Anyone unlucky enough to find himself crossing the creek late at night, they say, has a good chance of spotting that poor dog's restless eyes burning along the river, a pair of demonic, emerald-green orbs staring them down. Stop on the bridge and turn your headlights off, they say, and he's as good as summoned.

According to Blanche, "All the kids are just scared to death of that bridge." Apparently, with good reason.

Haunted Hallow

If you're ever traveling 289th East Avenue through Catoosa late at night, try to take it easy on the gas, else you may find yourself the guilty party in a hit-and-run case you'll never be able to explain.

About a half mile north of US 412 lies Timber Ridge Cemetery, on the edge of an area known as Haunted Hallow. This is where more than a handful of motorists have allegedly encountered a young boy kneeling next to his bicycle, positioned perilously in the path of oncoming traffic. Those who've crested the nearby hill at too high a speed have little time to swerve, resulting in a number of near-misses with the lad.

A Native American boy was struck by a car . . . in front of the cemetery gate.

Others, some of whom never see the boy, experience the worst. Multiple reports of collisions with the youngster have made the rounds, some of which reportedly result in actual damage to the drivers' vehicles. And despite the vehicles' passengers having distinctly heard the sound of an impact, no body and no bicycle are ever found following the accident.

The incidents may be some sort of spiritual afterimage resulting from an actual, traumatic event. Sometime in the late 1980s, a local Native American boy was reportedly struck by a car on that very spot, directly in front of the cemetery gate. The boy was later buried just yards away—some say in the first row, although his gravesite remains unmarked.

R RIDGE
KEEP
GATE
CLOSED

Skiatook's Cursed Avenue

North of Skiatook, between two sharp bends in the road, lies North Garrison Avenue, a stretch of narrow asphalt just a quarter mile long. It lies in a relaxed, rural area that, on a cool summer day, would probably make a great backdrop for a peaceful drive. But at night it turns more toward the uninviting. Save for the ramble of an occasional pickup truck making its way home, this moderately secluded spot carries a chilling quiet. The slowly undulating trees and the ethereal, green glow of nearby mercury-vapor lamps only add to the sinister feeling in the atmosphere.

The dread this place tends to inspire, however, may be justified. It's said that travelers passing this way occasionally come across a lost soul wandering the roadside. The figure, a teenage boy, is seen walking the grassy shoulders, seemingly stunned and disoriented. He appears only briefly, leaving any would-be Good Samaritans at a loss when stopping to offer assistance. As yet, no one's identified the boy, but he's presumed to be a young driver who perished in the 1970s while crossing a bridge over one of the nearby creeks.

Adding to the foreboding is an adjoining graveyard that dates well into the 1880s, a dark necropolis said to include a cursed burial plot. Many decades ago, a woman was reportedly executed vigilante-style and stuck in the ground in the hope that she would no longer subject the locals to her witchcraft. Unfortunately, the attempt to suppress the woman's activities was less than successful. Though everyone hoped she would be gone and forgotten, she has continued to haunt the area, terrifying passersby, even cursing those who dare to disturb her grave.

Three-Two Bridge

It's probably fair to say that, over in Hobart, there aren't a whole lot of places to hang out. So, when the kids decide to party, there's just one place to go. "Meet us at Three-Two," they'll say, and everyone knows where they mean.

They're talking about a bridge just outside of town, three miles south and nearly two miles west. Near the old dumping ground, it crosses Elk Creek on E1410 Road.

Sometimes kids go out there just to have a few beers, maybe spritz some new graffiti on the guardrails, or light a bonfire. More often than not, though, it's to get a glimpse of the inexplicable. Visitors report strange lights in the trees that line the creek, sometimes appearing like a string of bulbs that extinguish when the curious get too close. Unusual sounds and other unidentifiable glimmers emanate from along the banks.

Legend has it, if you're brave enough to stop your car in the middle of the bridge and flash your lights, the ghostly image of a woman will emerge from the creek. Try to drive away and your car won't budge until the ghost is gone.

According to an unnamed city official, who admits to going out there himself when he was younger, there's another bridge about a mile north, this one an older wooden structure, where similar things have occurred. He says he used to go camping out there just to see what would happen. On yet another bridge about two miles south, a man was killed when his truck flipped over, ejecting him halfway out the window and severing his arms and head on the metal railing. Witnesses told authorities they saw a pair of lights off in the trees shining in their direction, but disappearing before police arrived. The incident was never explained.

Broadway and Grand

The unluckiest intersection in all of Oklahoma lies in the center of downtown Enid, two hours west of Tulsa. It has nothing to do with faulty traffic lights, traffic congestion, or unsuccessful business ventures, mind you, but the fact that, over the span of forty years, a total of five men, four of them law officers, were killed at this very spot.

The first was in 1895 when Marshal E. C. Williams was shot to death trying to break up a fight. R. W. Patterson, a government official, was scuffling at Broadway and Grand with J. L. Isenberg, publisher of the *Enid Daily Wave*, over a series of venomous articles that had appeared in the newspaper. Patterson, who was a registrar with the U.S. Land Office, published his legal notices in a competing paper. In retaliation, Isenberg began publishing scurrilous opinions and accusations concerning Patterson. After Isenberg accused him of infidelity, Patterson decided he had had enough and punched Isenberg in the face.

About the time Marshal Williams arrived to break up the fight, Patterson pulled out a gun and starting shooting at Isenberg, who quickly ran into a nearby store. Williams pistol-whipped Patterson; Patterson shot the marshal just above his heart. Before the marshal collapsed, however, he took a shot at Patterson, striking him in the temple. Both Williams and Patterson died. Isenberg escaped and later moved to California.

Ten years later, in 1905, another Enid officer was killed at the same intersection. According to a newspaper report at the time, Deputy Sheriff Robert O. Beers received a message one evening alleged to be from the city attorney, which asked for a meeting in the Anheuser-Busch building at the corner of Broadway and Grand. When Beers arrived, he was met instead by two angry men, J. W. Walton and Jacob Erickson. When an argument ensued, Beers pulled his gun but was shot in the head by Erickson before he had a chance to fire. Few details regarding the argument were released, but the confrontation reportedly had something to do with Beers's involvement in an illicit relationship. (Did you get the irony of a man named Beers dying in the Anheuser-Busch building?)

In 1906, less than a year later, yet another lawman was fatally shot in the same building. Marshal Thomas Radford had been in office for only eight months, and just weeks before he had been declared by the chairman of the police committee to be the best marshal Enid ever had. Unfortunately, not everyone agreed, especially John Cannon, who ran a rooming house on East Broadway known for its pleasures of the flesh. Radford, determined to close down the rooming house, forced the business's tenants to move, then thwarted Cannon's attempt to set up shop across the street by warning the new building's owner not to rent to Cannon.

Furious, Cannon confronted Radford at the Tony Faust Saloon in the Anheuser-Busch building. Cannon walked up to the marshal, placed his gun to the officer's chest, and fired. As Radford tried to run, Cannon fired and struck the lawman a second time, in the torso. Radford continued staggering out the front door, where Cannon shot him again, this time in the head. The marshal fell to the street and died shortly thereafter.

Radford's funeral procession, which consisted of 115 carriages, measured nearly a mile long. John Cannon served twenty-five years in prison.

At the end of a hot July day in 1936, patrons were filling up the German Village Saloon to refresh themselves with a few mugs of beer. Owner Jim O'Neal, however, couldn't relax that evening, as he had been tipped off earlier in the day that someone was going to try to rob him.

O'Neal had been keeping an eye on one particular patron for some time, who seemed oddly familiar. When he realized he may have seen the man in some notorious photographs, he called Enid police officer Cal Palmer to come check the man out. Palmer, along with Officer Ralph Knarr, asked the man to come with them, who replied, "I think I know what you want me for," but kindly asked if he could first finish his beer. The officers agreed.

When the man set down his empty mug, however, he pulled out a revolver and shot Palmer three times, Knarr four times, and another man in the leg once. He then took off out the side door and up an alley, quickly pursued by five other officers. When the killer reached the street, he jumped into the backseat of a car occupied by two men and commanded them to drive.

After the driver hit the gas, he noticed the officers in pursuit, and both he and his passenger jumped out, leaving their hijacker behind. The driver directed the officers to the vehicle, who began firing. The fleeing man jumped out and hid behind the car, but was fatally struck in the head by one of the officers' bullets.

The man was later identified as Lawrence DeVol, a member of the infamous Karpis-Barker gang, which had recently broken up. As for the two officers shot in the saloon, Knarr recovered from his wounds, but Palmer died instantly when one of the bullets struck his heart.

Thankfully, Broadway and Grand, save for a few ghostly encounters reported in the surrounding buildings, has been quiet ever since. Probably the worst you'll encounter today is a few red-light runners and the resultant blasts of car horns. But, of course, history is still being written.

Tulsa's Time Cars

Here in Oklahoma, a handful of vehicles have taken a trip through time—a journey across decades that begins and ends in Tulsa.

The Buried Belvedere

In the summer of 2007, a vehicle appeared in downtown Tulsa, having driven down what was most definitely a road less traveled. It was, for all intents and purposes, a trip through time—a journey from the 1950s that began and ended on the courthouse lawn.

No, the vehicle was not a DeLorean, nor was it driven by a handsome young Michael J. Fox. Rather, the car was a gold and white 1957 Plymouth Belvedere hardtop coupe that had been entombed below ground as part of the city's celebration of Oklahoma's semicentennial.

It had been placed about a hundred feet from the intersection of Denver Avenue and Sixth Street beneath a bronze plaque marking the "Golden Jubilee, Inc. Time Capsule." Engineers built a steel-reinforced concrete vault, approximately twelve feet by twenty feet, into which the plastic-wrapped vehicle was lowered via crane. As part of

the burial ceremony, organizers also included a steel capsule containing various historical artifacts. At the last minute, someone decided to dump the contents of a woman's purse into the glove box, items that included bobby pins, combs, a compact, a tube of lipstick, a pack of cigarettes, matches, tissues, a plastic rain cap, a little over $2 in cash, gum, an unpaid parking ticket, and a bottle of tranquilizers. Somebody else donated a case of Schlitz beer.

Organizers also had the foresight to include with the car ten gallons of gasoline and several quarts of motor oil, just in case all the futurists were right and we had all moved on to nuclear-powered flying cars by the twenty-first century.

Finally, a package of microfilm was added to the time capsule, which contained the names and guesses of all the contestants who had participated in a contest held in tandem with the event. Entrants were invited to predict the population of Tulsa in 2007, and whoever came closest would win the Belvedere when it was unearthed.

When the day finally came, fifty years later, most people had forgotten about the car. But as news of the impending disinterment spread, excitement grew not only throughout Tulsa, but around the world. Visitors across the globe came

to see just what had become of the vehicle after all these years. Would it emerge pristine, a gleaming showroom-ready classic, or would it be a pile of rusted metal?

A sock hop was held in honor of the event. Car collectors brought in hundreds of classic vehicles for an auto show. The courthouse lawn was cordoned off and the Tulsa Convention Center was prepared with a special stage and a light show for the Belvedere's unveiling. When the vehicle was unearthed, it was kept under wraps; no one was allowed to see its condition until the big event.

Finally, before seven thousand spectators and a live television audience, the curtain was lifted and the special protective wrap was removed. Gasps filled the auditorium. The vehicle, which had taken on the endearing nickname

of Miss Belvedere, was a mud-covered and rusted hulk. A celebrity hot-rod builder, who had been invited to take part in the event, called her "a mess."

The car's vault had been built with advice from experts at the Atomic Energy Commission, who unfortunately were skilled in designing things more for protection against nuclear attack than from rain. As a result, when the seal was broken and the lid lifted away, Miss Belvedere was discovered sitting in about three feet of water. Evidence showed that the entire vault had, at one point, been filled with water. The upholstery had disintegrated, the frame had rusted, and most of the contents had dissolved away. Only the glass jars full of gas, a few dirty cans of Schlitz, and the steel time capsule had survived.

A week later, officials announced the winner of the rusty Plymouth. Raymond Humbertson, who had apparently just been passing through town in 1957 when the contest was held, came within less than 2,300 of the actual population. He had died in 1979, and so the car went to his sister.

The Planted Prowler

In 1998 a second car was entombed in Tulsa, this time to commemorate the city's centennial. The vice president of Chrysler Corporation had seen historic footage of the Belvedere being lowered into its time capsule and thought it would be a great idea, not to mention a terrific PR opportunity, to donate a vehicle and repeat the event.

Tulsa was given a handmade prototype of the new Plymouth Prowler, a retro-styled tribute to 1950s-era hot rods, that would serve as the centerpiece to an all-new capsule to be buried in Central Park. Citizens donated a collection of items to include with the car, such as a pair of inline skates, a cell phone, and a faceplate from an ATM. In the spirit of the former Schlitz donor, someone contributed a more politically correct case of root beer.

The lessons from the Belvedere's burial had yet to be learned, but organizers decided to be better safe than sorry and made more careful arrangements for the Prowler's interment. All fluids were drained or substituted with synthetics, the car was sealed in a specially designed plastic container, the air inside was replaced with an inert gas and the whole thing was closed up in a vault made from corrosion-resistant aluminum. And rather than being stuck below ground, the container was only halfway buried, then covered up to form a small hill. The keys were left in the ignition, and once again, a container of gasoline was included just in case. Finally, Central Park was renamed Centennial Park lest anyone forgot it was there.

No contest was held this time, however. When the Prowler is revealed in 2048, it will be given back to Chrysler.

The Inhumed Harley

When Miss Belvedere was unearthed in 2007, Tulsans decided to bury yet another vehicle. It would be a replacement for the semicentennial capsule, which would remain sealed for another fifty years in anticipation of the state's 150-year celebration.

However, coordinators decided this time to bury a motorcycle. A local dealer donated a 2007 Harley-Davidson Street Glide and organized the donation of items such as iPods, a DVD player, a Budweiser sign, and various personal artifacts, all to be entombed in Veterans Park.

Taking a cue from the small steel container buried alongside the Belvedere, organizers chose as their capsule a scaled-up version of the pressure vessel, five feet wide by fifteen feet long and made from half-inch-thick carbon steel.

Oddly, though, no one could decide exactly where in the park to place the capsule, so after it was sealed in November 2007, the big tank was hauled off to a storage facility to be buried unceremoniously at a date undetermined.

Oklahoma Ghosts

We've all heard bumps in the night, the lazy creaks of a slowly swinging door, or maybe the quiet thumps of what sound like footsteps. And whether or not we admit to a belief in ghosts, that's the first thing our minds tend to think of.

The idea of spirits, of life after death, is ingrained in our culture. For some it's a fundamental belief system. For others, it's a source of curiosity, the foundation for a pastime whose primary draw is a good old-fashioned scare.

Yet, no matter where one's interest in the hereafter lies, there are few among us who don't enjoy a good ghost story. Credence aside, a haunting tale is just plain alluring and, with enough detail and peculiarity, can stir the most stagnant imaginations.

Luckily, Oklahoma's buildings and back roads, packed with unexplained occurrences, provide more than enough material for otherworldly tales and, perhaps more important, plenty of opportunity to generate one's own stories.

AT
REST
CHARLES D
SAVAGE
OV. 13, 1881
OV. 4, 1918

The Constantine

When the city of Pawhuska decided to resurrect their historic Constantine Theater in the 1980s, they didn't realize what a can of worms they were about to open. Even before the crew started sweeping out the dust, the age-old structure released spirits, mysteries, hidden secrets, and even political controversy.

The Constantine is fraught with unexplained activity, the most common being the sound of footsteps made by someone with an obvious limp. At first, everyone assumed the footsteps were those of the late Charles Constantine, the man who bought the former hotel and renovated it into an opera house in the early 1900s, or even those of his daughter, Sappho. However, Constantine had a sister, the designer of the opera house. She was a psychic and, most interesting, limped due to a corrective brace worn on one leg.

Footsteps aren't the only sounds to emanate from the building, though. Visitors often report the murmur of a barroom crowd or the sounds of a fistfight, noises one would've heard back when the building was first erected and served as a hotel called the Pawhuska House.

Then there was the mysterious light that just wouldn't behave. During the building's renovation, all the wiring was torn out and the electricity was shut off, but one fixture, a blue light in Charles Constantine's old office, remained on. It was later discovered that it alone was wired into the building next door, but that never explained why it kept flickering by itself or why, when the light was turned off, it would come back on in the middle of the night all by itself.

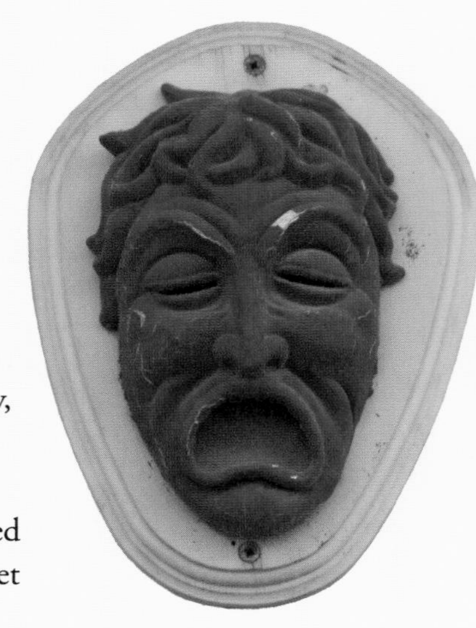

Far more puzzling was the magically regenerating wall. One Friday during reconstruction, volunteer students tore down one side of Constantine's office to make the room larger. Come Monday, however, the team returned to find the entire wall completely restored. After that, they decided the room was big enough and let it be.

Renovators even discovered a series of hidden tunnels running beneath the building. One leads across the street to a bank Constantine once owned. Another leads to an underground room about ten feet by twelve feet, where it's believed someone used to run a moonshine still. (A ventilation duct leads from the room to the building's main ventilation system, which would have hidden the telltale white smoke from the still amid the ordinary black smoke of the building's heating oil.) Additional rooms and doors were discovered throughout the building, as well.

Not everyone is so proud of the Constantine's arcane qualities. In 2005, several members of the theater's board of trustees let their feelings be known about the spiritual aspect of the building. When a paranormal group accepted an invitation by the chamber of commerce to tour the theater, the board held a vote on the building's haunted status with a result of 8–3 against. As the board's president put it, "we voted and decided that we don't have ghosts."

The chamber's director, astounded by the board's legislative power, responded by asking if they could also "decide that I'm skinny and rich."

CONSTANTINE CENTER

Ghost of Fort Reno

Historic Fort Reno is located just north of the highway in El Reno as well as on Historic Route 66. It was built to quell the unrest of the local Indian population in 1874. The name Fort Reno was bestowed in 1876 by Gen. Phil Sheridan, a dedication to his friend Maj. Gen. Jesse L. Reno. The fort at one time was one of the major military bases in the world that housed many military recruits and buffalo soldiers, as well as German and Italian prisoners of war. Over its history many people that came to fame later in life had visited and spent a good amount of time on the fort. The painter Frederic Remington spent three months on the fort and painted many depictions of buffalo soldiers, as well as the cavalry. Amelia Earhart flew her autogyro, which was the forerunner to the modern helicopter, onto the airstrip located on the grounds.

Today the fort is home to agricultural studies as well as many spirits. Every building located on the grounds has its own stories of ghostly events. The home known as the "Victorian" is perhaps one of the most haunted homes on the site. Over the years, reports of a little girl seen on the second story peering out of a window as well as running up

to the home from the sidewalk have been told by visitors both young and old.

I have had many experiences that have left me considering it to be one of the most haunted sites I have visited to date. During one investigation, I was on the second story where the little girl watching out the window was reported. I could hear a little girl singing and laughing coming from the next room. There were no little girls found in the investigation that evening. I started to dig into the history and found that the room that I had heard the singing from was actually an older gentleman's room, who was none too happy of having visitors coming into his home.

After an investigation one night we felt that it was time to leave and that we upset the man. One week later we returned to find torn wallpaper on the walls and scrape marks on the ceiling. When we asked the curator if anyone had entered the building, we were informed that no one had. The doors are actually screwed shut when there is no investigation happening.

There are theories about the "Victorian," one of which includes the older gentleman having murdered the little girl and buried her in the basement of the home. I have entered the basement a number of times only to leave just as soon as I went down. My last experience in the home was during a private tour that I was working on along with a research group I was a part of. I, along with one other member, had gone to the attic to see if we were able to bring any of the tour group up with us. We had watched a shadow at the corner of the window moving back and forth. We decided to shut off our flashlights and see what would happen. After a few moments, we started to talk to each other. The whole time I thought I was facing my colleague only to turn my flashlight on and watch the face in front of me retreat back into the chimney stack.

Some of the other claims on the grounds include playful shadow figures in the upper area of the commissary as well as buffalo soldiers walking the grounds, a general that hung himself in the upstairs bathroom of the visitors center playing with the lights, and many other voices. There is even a spirit that is said to stay in one building that enjoys his women and his whiskey. I have chased many out-of-place voices and yelled at many spirits that I mistook for tour members in a number of the buildings. All in all I would say that this is definitely one of the most haunted locations in the central Oklahoma area.

The property is government-owned, so to those seeking a good adventure be very careful before choosing this location for a night of ghost hunting. The fort does hold ghost tours to the public and there are many groups that hold private investigations. Those are the best ways to actually enter the grounds and the buildings.

—Charles Carter

Brown Springs

Topping the list of Oklahoma's most popular haunts is an unassuming natural spring located less than a half a mile north of the Red River. Luckily, it's also one of the most easily accessed, lying right along a dirt road just a mile off Interstate 35.

Its short distance from civilization, though, in no way negates the site's incredible foreboding. Surrounded by thick brush and woods, Brown Springs, and the path leading up to it, remain uninviting even in the daytime. Dust kicked up from the roadway creates an ominous miasma and, in the summer, the lagoon that lies just across the road can reek with the choking stench of death. And despite the clear, cool appearance of the spring water bubbling up among the green grass, it doesn't seem very palatable when you consider the cemetery that lies just yards away.

The site, infrequently referred to as Dripping Springs or Refuge Springs, has been known for generations as a place of misfortune. The aforementioned cemetery reputedly originated with the deaths of several outlaws in the 1800s. For a time, bandits and fugitives supposedly used the springs as a hideout—a secret discovered by Texas Rangers who laid in wait for the criminals, then picked them off one at a time and buried the bodies nearby in unmarked graves.

In addition, there's the story of a homicidal family from the 1860s, who mugged and murdered passing travelers, then dumped the bodies at Brown Springs. Little is known about the family, except that their stories may be connected with the Bender family. The Benders ran a store in Kansas, where they routinely robbed and killed patrons before their secret was discovered and they escaped to Indian Territory. They were eventually caught, and the mother, father, son, and daughter were all hanged. Some insist the father actually died in a more gruesome fashion—staked to the ground by a

would-be victim and sliced open so wild dogs could eat him alive.

It's difficult to say why Brown Springs would make such a good spot for discarding evidence, but apparently its usefulness continues today. In 1988, two men on a murder spree killed at least four people from Texas and Arkansas. The last known victim was shot three times and robbed of his car, which was found the next day partially submerged in a pond at Brown Springs. Several bodies have been found in the area over the years, as well, according to newspaper accounts quoting the Love County sheriff.

As for the cemetery, which lies up a sandy hill to the north, it provides its own share of chilling tales. Those brave enough to hike back into the woods, especially at night, have encountered unusual noises, lights, and visions. Over the years, the curious have reported spotting unearthed bones, discovering bloody knives stuck in trees, and having trouble starting their cars when trying to make a quick exit.

Even if the stories of murder aren't true, it would be no surprise Brown Springs would possess such restless spirits, given the cemetery's condition. At least twenty-six people are known to be buried there, but few graves remain marked. Nearly all the headstones have been vandalized, broken, and dumped in a scattered pile. The few that still stand are barely readable. Numerous areas, oddly, have been charred by fires. Some particularly strange delinquents, in what must be one of the most ill-conceived acts of vandalism one could imagine, have even carved their own names into upturned grave markers.

To get a look for yourself, just take Exit 1 north of the Oklahoma–Texas border, go east and turn right just past the convenience store/casino. About a mile later, you'll see a turnout on your left. A word to the wise, though: Don't drink the water.

Brady Theater

Though you might not think of Tulsa as a hotbed of high-class culture, T-Town has actually played host to many of history's most reputable entertainers, most of whom have played at the city's Brady Theater. In its nearly one-hundred-year history, the theater has featured performances by such unforgettable names as Katharine Hepburn, Benny Goodman, Helen Hayes, Duke Ellington, Buddy Holly, and the Marx Brothers. Sadly, most of us will never get the chance to bask in the charismatic presence of our favorite classic entertainers, as they've not only left the Brady's stage, but also this mortal plane. That is, of course, unless you like opera.

One of the most highly regarded performers to appear at the "Old Lady of Brady" was the "Golden Voice" himself, Italian tenor Enrico Caruso. On October 17, 1920, the man who is considered one of the most significant vocal artists in history made his first and only appearance in Tulsa. In the flesh, anyway. Those who've worked at the Brady, and many who've visited, are adamant that Caruso has been making curtain calls for years now.

Caruso died shortly after his visit to Oklahoma from an illness that was apparently exacerbated by the state's dreadful fall climate. The concert promoters who organized the tenor's visit wanted to share the local culture with the esteemed performer by showing him an oil field. They drove

Caruso out to Sepulpa in the wet and blustery weather that befell the day of his performance. Following what must have been an exceptionally stirring field trip for the cultured Italian, the group turned back for Tulsa, but all three of the vehicles in which they were traveling broke down on the way. As a result, Caruso was forced to hitchhike in the cold, wet weather.

Caruso made it back in time for his performance that night, but it would prove to be one of his last. Less than two months later, he suffered a throat hemorrhage during a concert in New York, after which he made only a handful of appearances as his health deteriorated, reportedly as a result of his ill-fated car trip in Tulsa. After months of suffering from a painful lung ailment, Caruso died in August 1921.

Caruso died shortly after his visit to Oklahoma . . .

Since it was evidently his visit to the Brady that was to blame, it's said that Caruso returned to the theater postmortem to rattle patrons' nerves in retribution. Stagehands regularly hear noises in the theater when no one else is around. Sometimes, curtains move on their own. A local radio station even once held a séance at the theater, and although they were unable to identify the source of an otherworldly presence, participants were sure they had detected one.

Still, Caruso may not be the only one roaming the theater's halls. A despondent stagehand is said to have hung himself up in the catwalks several years ago and reportedly attends every show. Plus, the Brady played a central role during the Tulsa Race Riots of 1921, in which the building was supposed to serve as a safe haven for black residents, although it purportedly turned into a makeshift detention center into which some six thousand people were herded and subsequently mistreated. As many as three hundred people were unaccounted for when everyone was released, many of whom are said to have been killed, their bodies either burned in the furnace or buried in the basement. So, even if Caruso himself isn't making repeat performances like they say he is, there are plenty of other spirits with reason to haunt the theater.

Skirvin Hotel

Built in 1910, the neo-Georgian Skirvin Hotel is one of Oklahoma City's most majestic buildings. It is also, they say, one of the most spiritually active.

Located at One Park Avenue (just a block away from where the world's first parking meters were installed—see Carlton Cole Magee in the Local Heroes and Villains chapter), the hotel was constructed by oil magnate William B. Skirvin and was considered one of the premier hotels in the Southwest, thanks especially to Skirvin's daughter Perle Skirvin Mesta. Perle, socialite and U.S. ambassador to Luxembourg, was celebrated as the "hostess with the mostest" and was well known for her extravagant parties and connections with celebrities and politicians. She even had a Broadway musical written about her starring Ethel Merman.

William Skirvin, however, is remembered with a less favorable narrative. Allegedly, he had an affair with one of the hotel's maids. Unfortunately for the both of them, the maid, known simply as Effie, became pregnant. Afraid that this scandalous fact might be discovered, Skirvin supposedly locked Effie in one of the rooms on the hotel's top floor, where she remained even after the birth of her child.

Suffering from depression and increasing madness as a result of her incarceration, Effie eventually lost all hope. She took her child in her arms and flung herself out the window to the street below.

However, Effie and her child never really left the Skirvin Hotel. For years thereafter, strange incidents occurred within the hotel's walls. Overnighters complained many times to hotel staff that a crying baby was keeping them awake, even when no one with a baby was staying there. People have seen maids' carts moving on their own. They've also reported the ghostly image of a woman inside one of the top floor's rooms, running for the window. Plus, men have been startled by the voice of a woman trying to seduce them in their rooms. More startling, some men have reported seeing a strange woman appear in the shower with them, or a phantom seductress trying to take advantage of them in their beds.

The stories subsided when the Skirvin Hotel was shut down in 1988 and remained vacant for nearly two decades. In recent years, however, developers have renovated it to its former grandeur and the hotel was reopened in 2007. No one's sure yet if Effie and her child left the premises in the interim, but time will tell. We'll be keeping our ears open for new reports.

The Gilcrease House

Though Tulsa's Gilcrease Museum prides itself on being home to the world's most comprehensive collection of art and artifacts of the American West, the most talked-about relic in its collection is none other than the museum's late founder.

No, Mr. Gilcrease isn't stuffed and preserved in a glass case, no matter how cool that might seem. Instead, he's a member of a small, more elusive division of the institution's permanent collection—a sort of roaming exhibition seen only by a segment of the museum's patrons. It's made up of all that's intangible of Gilcrease and about a half dozen unidentified children.

Thomas Gilcrease, the man who assembled the majority of the museum's collection, died in 1962. A wealthy oilman, he spent a large amount of time traveling on business, which provided him plenty of opportunity to discover Native American treasures and Western artwork, both subjects in which he had taken a great deal of interest. Eventually his collection grew so large that it made less and less sense to store it away, so he opened a museum. His first was in San Antonio, Texas, but he soon moved things onto his own estate in northwest Tulsa, next to his 1913 sandstone house, which still stands at North Gilcrease Museum Road and West Newton Street.

After Gilcrease suffered a fatal heart attack at the age of seventy-two, his museum passed into the hands of the city, and his spirit, apparently, passed into the museum. Though his remains were entombed in a mausoleum nearby, Mr. Gilcrease seems to enjoy spending most of his time amid the halls showcasing his collection. He has been seen and heard by visitors and employees alike, quietly enjoying the hundreds of thousands of items he acquired during his lifetime. Now and again, doors will open and close by themselves, temperatures will fluctuate, and items will occasionally turn up in places they shouldn't be, though for the most part, Gilcrease likes to keep to himself. He does reportedly make a point to appear as a solid apparition once to each employee who comes to work at the museum, as if to welcome them. Some employees don't appreciate the reception, though, which explains the allegedly high turnover rate of security guards.

Gilcrease occasionally likes to retire to his old sandstone house, as well. It's not uncommon to hear unusual sounds coming from other rooms or an unexplained banging from upstairs. Some of the incidents, however, are attributed to the spirits of several children who also roam the grounds. When Gilcrease lived in San Antonio, his home served for several years as an orphanage for Native American children. It's presumed that some of the kids who once lived there remember it fondly and have returned to play among the twenty-three acres of gardens that Gilcrease established there.

Overall, the supernatural incidents at the Gilcrease Museum remain fairly tame, though one incident did cause quite a stir. One Easter evening, well after the building had been cleared and locked down for the night, Tulsa police were called out to investigate an alarm that had been tripped. When they arrived with Baron, a large and well-trained police dog, the officers entered through the front and let their canine companion take the lead. Baron was undoubtedly excited by something, but when he reached the stairs, the dog recoiled, bristled his fur, and cowered on the floor. Eventually he had to be carried outside, at which point the frightened hound made a beeline to his patrol car.

Police never found anyone in the museum, never discovered anything missing, and never found an explanation for whatever had tripped the alarm.

Stone Lion Inn

Foul play is afoot, and guests at the Stone Lion Inn like it that way. They walk the halls, their inquisitive minds trained on finding a murderer. Of course, it's all a game, right? After all, they signed up for a murder-mystery weekend in an old historic inn. Tensions are high, but the stakes aren't real. But then, who was the little girl lurking on the third floor, one moment there and gone the next? Or the older gentleman in period dress in the basement? Employees say they've been residents of the inn since long before it started taking boarders. One steeped in tragedy, the other in pain, the two remain within, making their presence known and startling guests.

If there is one thing that paranormal investigators can agree on, it is this: The past is never truly past. If it were, there would be nothing to investigate. Within the walls of a stately inn, history is remembered not just by the staff, but by all those who played a part. Certain buildings retain their memories in the form of memorabilia, relics of the past that present-day owners may find quaint or fascinating. Others may take pride in that past. Still others find a different way to remember, as the souls of those who walked before dwell within, a reminder of days gone by.

The Stone Lion Inn was built in 1907 by F. E. Houghton as a home for his large family. He built the house right next door to the one they'd already outgrown.

When he and his wife moved in, they had twelve children, including a daughter named Augusta. She was a very playful child, her games and toys confined to the third floor. Tragedy struck the Houghton family, however, when the little girl was just eight years old. She contracted whooping cough that left her bedridden. Because medicines of the day were often laced with opium and codeine, the child died of an accidental overdose. Houghton was devastated by the loss of his little girl.

The Houghtons lived in the home for many more years before moving on some time in the 1920s, when it was leased out as a funeral home. In 1986 it was purchased by Becky Luker. With the help of her sons, she was determined to fix the place up and turn it into Guthrie's first bed-and-breakfast. However, things took a strange turn when she began renovations.

During the night, she could hear the sounds of someone walking around upstairs and up and down the back staircase. On several occasions, Luker called the police, but no intruders were ever found. The large third-floor closet, where her son stored his toys, was routinely ransacked by an unseen presence. There were other events that the Lukers found strange, until a visit from Houghton's children cleared up some of the mystery. They told her of their sister, Augusta, and identified the chest in the third-floor closet as one they'd used in their youth to store toys. They also related that, after

their parents had fallen asleep, they would often creep along the back staircase for some late-night entertainment.

There appear to be several restless souls in this stately mansion, but the best known is the little girl named Augusta. Though rarely seen, she might be found tucking the Luker family into bed at night, or touching their faces to wake them up in the morning. Some guests have complained that the child played on their bed while they were trying to sleep. The most common manifestations of Augusta, however, come in the form of footsteps up and down the back stairs, the sound of giggling, and the sound of a wooden ball being rolled across the third floor.

Many people claim that Houghton himself haunts the basement. Many have seen him, but more have sensed his presence in other ways. The sudden scent of pipe tobacco, for example, is one of his common methods of announcing himself. Though the Stone Lion Inn is a nonsmoking establishment, the scent still pops up from time to time, with seemingly no source. Phantom voices are also reported, such as a laughing woman. While some guests find the phenomena fascinating, others are frightened to the point of leaving.

Several paranormal investigative groups, including the Oklahoma Paranormal and Research Investigations team and GHOULI (Ghost Haunts of Oklahoma and Urban Legend Investigations), have investigated the house with

interesting results. Among the findings: electronic voice phenomena (EVPs) of a young girl's voice, as well as that of an older man. Electromagnetic field meters have gone off in places with no discernible source, and cold spots have been felt throughout the inn.

Restless souls notwithstanding, the Stone Lion Inn has become famous for other reasons: Murder Mystery Weekend. During this time, guests can partake in a whodunit-style party in which one of the guests is more than they seem. Guests can stay in one of six rooms that feature private baths and sitting rooms, claw-footed tubs for two, and a full gourmet breakfast.

If you're looking for a first-class mystery weekend, book well in advance. Although there is never a bad time to stay at the Stone Lion Inn, Augusta is most often found sneaking up and down the back staircase between the hours of 10 P.M. and 12 A.M. The laughing woman is heard around 4 A.M. Mr. Houghton, however, seems to appear at random, keeping to no schedule but his own.

—Scott A. Johnson

The Shortgrass Playhouse

The Shortgrass Playhouse, Hobart's much-loved community theater, may boast all the usual unexplained footsteps and slamming doors, but the noises' presumed source is rather unusual. In fact, said poltergeist remains one of the most enigmatic specters to ever grace the dusty hallways of any building.

It seems that, even though the people who work in the building know the spirit's full name, and even the dates of both his birth and death, nobody has any idea who he really is, where he came from, or what on earth he's doing roaming the halls of Hobart's theater. Charlie, as they call him, just showed up, and in a most puzzling way.

After the building had served several decades as an auditorium, a city hall, a Works Progress Administration headquarters, and finally a youth center known as Teen Town, the old 1912 structure had been left vacant for several years before locals finally decided in 1978 to restore it and turn it once again into an entertainment venue. That's when volunteers working upstairs discovered an abandoned tombstone inscribed with the name Charles D. Savage, who had evidently died in 1918. No one had any idea how long the stone had been there, let alone how it came to rest on the second floor of a disused downtown building.

The weathered old marker sparked a genuine mystery. Despite extensive research, nobody could uncover a single fact about the man. There were no records of anyone by the name of Charles Savage having lived or died anywhere in the area, and no cemetery seemed to be missing a headstone. Not a single person even remembers having seen the memorial before it was discovered laying upstairs. To this day, no one has a clue who Charles Savage really is. And, so, his headstone has remained at the playhouse, standing unceremoniously at the bottom of a stairwell.

Charlie has made the Shortgrass his personal playground. Even though his epitaph insists he's "at rest," anyone who's spent time in the building will attest that he's quite active in these halls. Footsteps are very common, as are a variety of other noises. A door chime inside one of the building's entrances used to go off repeatedly even though no one was there. In one instance, a visitor to the green room was startled by a drinking glass that mysteriously fell from the ceiling, as though it had just materialized. Arlene Millermon, the theater's director, insists Charlie isn't malicious, but he has been known to flick small objects at her while she's been vacuuming. Apparently, he just doesn't like being disturbed, which is why he's most active following a show.

Charlie, as they call him, just showed up, and in a most puzzling way.

Charlie's most unusual lark, however, occurred several years ago when a painter was refinishing a wall along one of the theater's interior staircases. A man, presumed to be Charlie, appeared at the top of the stairway and insisted the painter stop making so much noise. The painter apologized, but said he had to finish the job. When Charlie left, the painter turned back to his work and spotted the faint image of a person above the doorway. Despite reported attempts to paint over it, the image has endured ever since.

Cemetery Safari

"*Gone, but not forgotten." That's what we like to say.* While everyone will someday pass on from this plane, we prefer to think that none among us will pass from memory. That's why we erect markers to commemorate our dead—to solidify their names in history, to leave some sort of record of their existence.

Unfortunately, the adage doesn't always hold true. Stones fall, engravings fade, and entropy reclaims entire boneyards beneath a veil of flora. Untold numbers, once laid to rest with all due reverence and ceremony, have slipped beyond remembrance, their names and achievements unrecoverable.

Thankfully, there are those burial sites that have been spared such a fate, due to the extraordinary legends with which they've become entwined or due simply to the memorability of their inhabitants' monuments. In this chapter, we explore some of these locations and hopefully, in the process, ensure their continued remembrance for at least a little while longer.

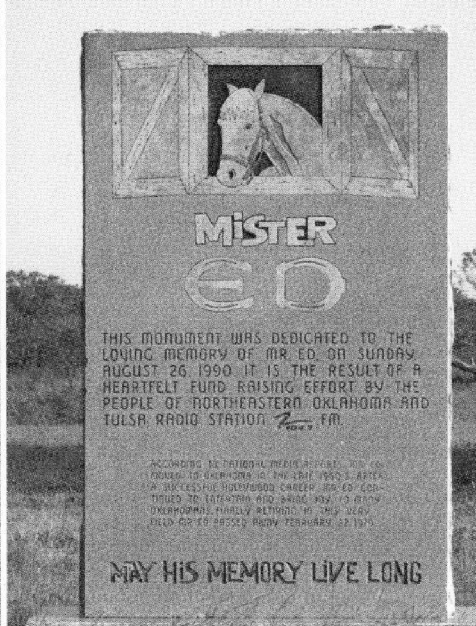

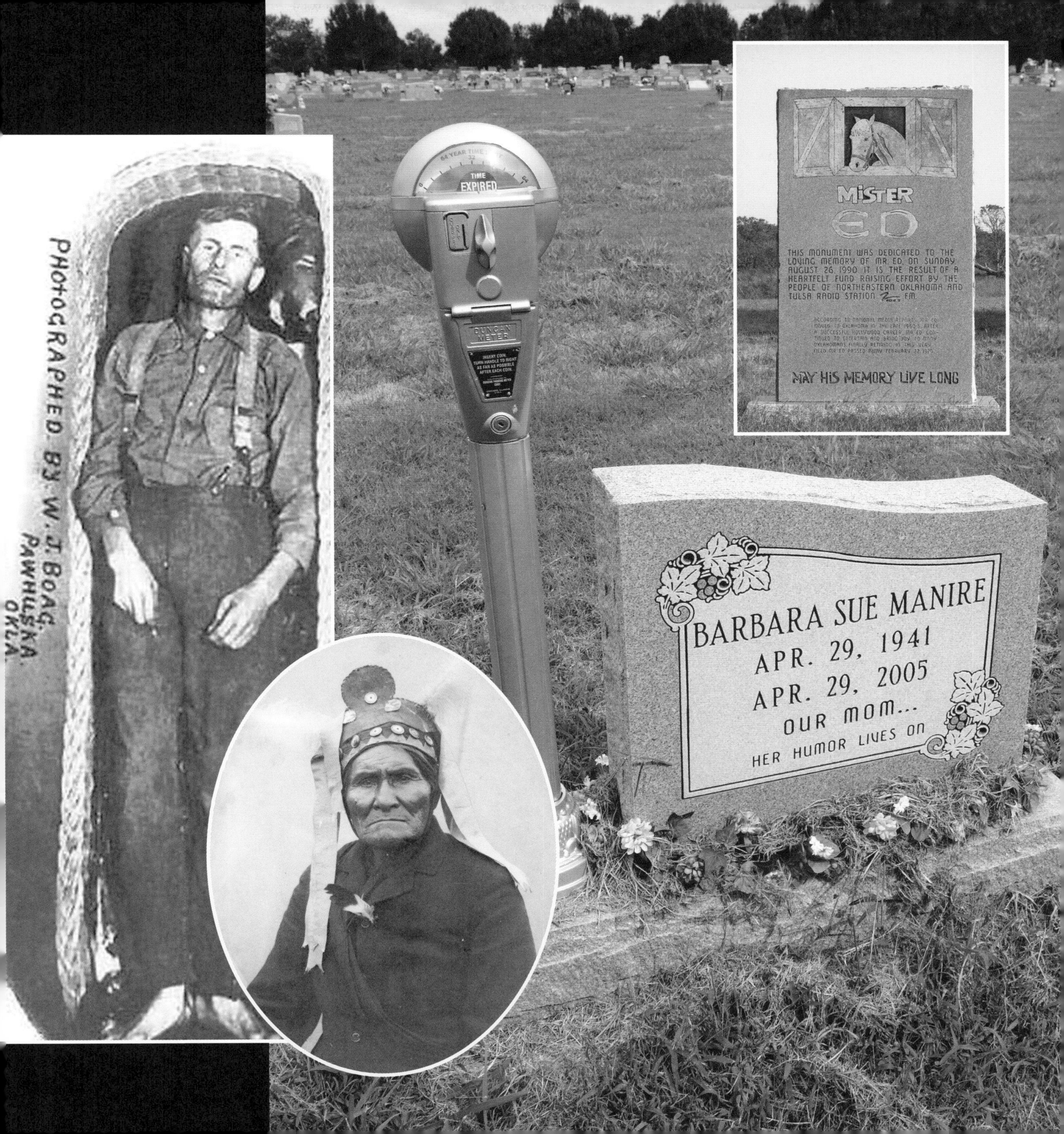
PHOTOGRAPHED BY W. J. BOAG,
PAWHUSKA,
OKLA.
TIME
EXPIRED
DUNCAN METER
MISTER
ED
THIS MONUMENT WAS DEDICATED TO THE LOVING MEMORY OF MR. ED, ON SUNDAY AUGUST 26, 1990 IT IS THE RESULT OF A HEARTFELT FUND RAISING EFFORT BY THE PEOPLE OF NORTHEASTERN OKLAHOMA AND TULSA RADIO STATION FM.
MAY HIS MEMORY LIVE LONG
BARBARA SUE MANIRE
APR. 29, 1941
APR. 29, 2005
OUR MOM...
HER HUMOR LIVES ON

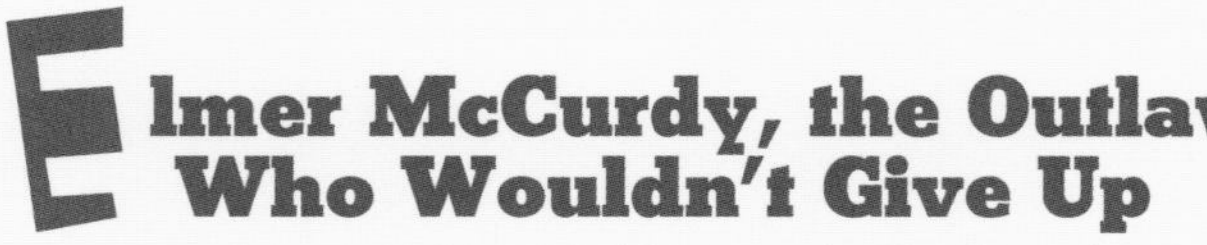

Elmer McCurdy, the Outlaw Who Wouldn't Give Up

Gather 'round my children, and I'll tell a tale of woe
About a famous cowboy outlaw who lived a hundred years ago . . .
A hundred hears have come and gone since he spoke his final words.
I'm not afraid to die and leave behind this rotten world.
So go and pull the lever hangman, now my race on Earth is run.
And he thought his life was ended but it had only just begun.

—*Brian Dewan, The Cowboy Outlaw*

Imagine this: It's 1973 and Steve Austin, a fictional astronaut, is a man barely alive. Now it's 1911: Elmer J. McCurdy, an outlaw—very, very dead! Who would have thought that these two show biz personalities would ever meet up?

In 1976, while Lee Majors played the role of astronaut Steve Austin on television's *Six Million Dollar Man,* the show's film crew found the mummified body of outlaw Elmer McCurdy as they were setting up for a shoot.

The crew was filming in Long Beach, California, at a funhouse called Laugh in the Dark. The place contained the regular spook-show decor, including wax figures, ghosts, and fake skeletons. While setting up at the location, the producer noticed a neon orange wax figure hanging from a makeshift gallows and asked one of the crew to take it down. He didn't like the way it looked in the scene.

The stagehand grabbed at the wax dummy's left arm, only to have it come off, revealing a human bone sticking out from its shoulder. Medical examiners and forensic investigators determined that the wax figure was actually a mummified body—and that it had been shot by a .32 caliber bullet manufactured between 1830 and 1920. Upon further examination, investigators found in the mummy's mouth a 1924 penny and a ticket from the Museum of Crime in Los Angeles. The ticket helped police identify the body as that of outlaw Elmer McCurdy, and the many roads he had taken in life—and afterward—that had led him to that Long Beach funhouse.

McCurdy had joined a few outlaw gangs and killed a few people, then he planned on robbing a Missouri Pacific train that supposedly was carrying a safe containing more than $1,000. On October 6, 1911, he robbed the train in Oklahoma, but when he opened the safe, he discovered it was the wrong train. Only $46 was inside. But he did manage to find a shipment of whiskey instead.

Heading into the Oklahoma farmlands a few days later, drunk and tired, McCurdy stopped at a farmhouse and fell asleep in the hayloft. A three-man posse that was tracking

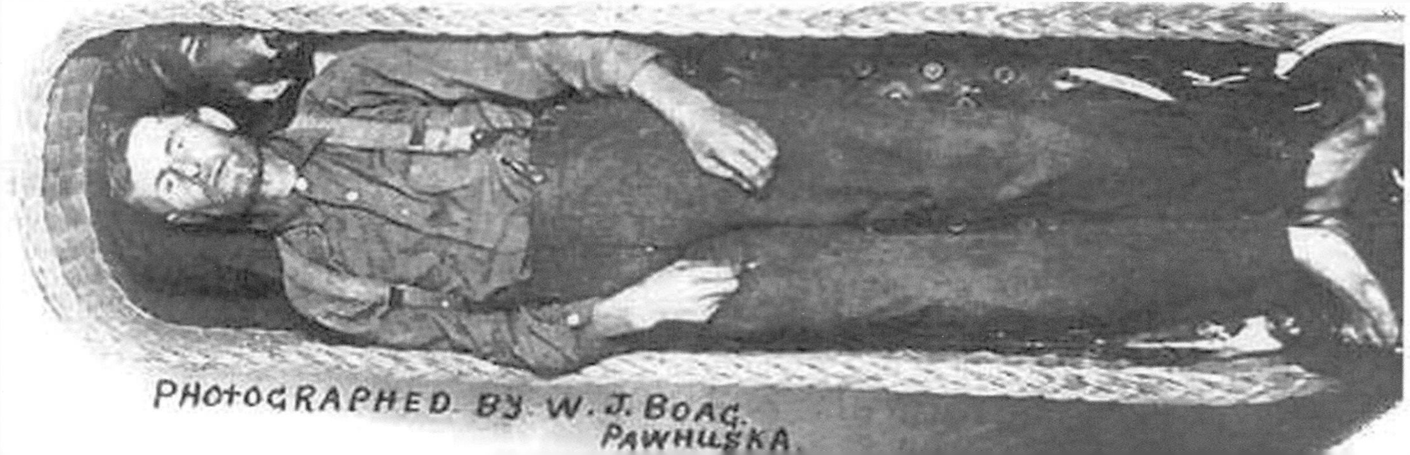

the outlaw trapped McCurdy and began firing. After an hour, a farmhand was asked to go into the barn and tell McCurdy to surrender. The outlaw refused, telling the farmhand, "They can go to the devil." The barn was shot up, and McCurdy was discovered dead soon afterward.

His body was taken to a funeral home in Pawhuska, Oklahoma, but he was never identified, and no one claimed the corpse. The undertaker embalmed him with arsenic, (a dose *seven hundred* times greater than was used in Egyptian mummies) and came up with a very entrepreneurial idea: Since the deceased looked very well preserved, and very stiff all dressed up in his last gun fightin' suit, he named the corpse "The Bandit That Wouldn't Give Up," and for a nickel, he would let the citizens of Pawhuska view it. The nickels were dropped into the mummy's mouth, later to be retrieved by the undertaker.

The mummy was on view for more than five years, and the undertaker refused many offers from carnivals and sideshows for his bandit corpse to use in their traveling freak shows. The nickel-swallowing mummy became a regular attraction for the funeral home in Pawhuska.

One day two men showed up at the funeral home claiming to be cousins of the mummy, and the undertaker had no choice but to give up the stiff to his next of kin for a proper burial. The two men turned out to be sideshow promoters who traveled around Texas, using McCurdy as, you guessed it, The Bandit That Wouldn't Give Up.

After Texas, the McCurdy mummy traveled around the country, often showing up at amusement parks, lying around in an open coffin in an L.A. wax museum, and—believe it or not—being used as a prop in low-budget films. He was known sometimes as "The Thousand Year Old Man." After a while, his body was coated with wax to help preserve it during his many road trips. His greatest tour was in the 1930s with Louis S. Sonney, a sheriff who acquired McCurdy for his traveling Wild West show.

Elmer was shuffled as collateral from one sideshow to another and eventually faded into obscurity. No one knows exactly how Elmer ended up at the defunct Laugh in the Dark funhouse in Long Beach, but when he was identified as McCurdy, medical examiners used a little-known method called "medical superimposition." Known photos of McCurdy were overlaid with x-rays of the mummy's face. From this they made a positive ID.

McCurdy was given a proper funeral in Summit View Cemetery in Guthrie, Oklahoma, in 1977 and was buried in the same cemetery as such notorious figures as Wild Bill Doolin (of the Doolin–Dalton Gang) and Tom Capers, in Oklahoma's only Boot Hill (a.k.a. gunslinger cemetery). The town residents gave old Elmer the full treatment: a parade ride to the cemetery in Wild West gear.

With his California show-biz days now behind him, McCurdy was certain to never again be a "ramblin' man": The Oklahoma state coroner ordered two cubic yards of cement to be poured into McCurdy's grave.

Geronimo's Bones

Geronimo, leader of the Chiricahua Apache and one of the most recognizable Native Americans in history, was a fearless and determined warrior. Many believe he may also have possessed abilities reaching well beyond the average Joe.

Legend says that Geronimo, who grew up a powerful medicine man, received protection from harm following the murder of his family by Mexican soldiers. As he grieved, a voice spoke to him and told him that no gun could ever harm him, that he would never be killed by any weapon. It was a divination that seemingly held true, as demonstrated by the warrior in later years when he revealed the astounding number of bullet wounds in his body and exclaimed, "Bullets cannot kill me!"

Some say Geronimo could walk without leaving footprints, and some of his pursuers claimed he could vanish altogether, talents that would come in handy as he defied the U.S. government. In an effort to avoid relocation, Geronimo took nearly forty of his people and fled across Arizona Territory. For more than five months neither five thousand U.S. troops nor four thousand Mexican soldiers were able to capture or kill a single Apache under Geronimo's protection.

Sadly, the warrior's skills could not protect him and his people forever. In the end, he was forced to surrender to the U.S. Cavalry in 1886 and was later imprisoned at Fort Sill, Oklahoma. There, he lived out the rest of his life, never to return to his homeland. He died of pneumonia in 1909 and was buried in Fort Sill's Apache Prisoner of War Cemetery.

In the mid-1980s, Ned Anderson, chairman of the San Carlos Apache tribe in Arizona, initiated a campaign to have Geronimo's remains removed from Fort Sill and given a proper burial on Apache land in Arizona. But his crusade quickly hit a speed bump. In the midst of his efforts, he received an anonymous letter from someone claiming to be a member of the infamous Skull and Bones secret society at Yale University. The writer alleged that the organization was in possession of Geronimo's skull and even provided a photograph of the alleged object in a glass display case, which was kept at the society's headquarters, known as "the Tomb."

The claim was supported by a 1930s historical account of the organization. That historical account quoted a Skull and Bones logbook entry that detailed the supposed robbery of Geronimo's grave in 1918 by six members of the society. They considered it their greatest "crook," or prank theft.

> *From the war days also sprang the mad expedition from the School of Fire at Fort Sill, Oklahoma, that brought to the T[omb] its most spectacular "crook," the skull of Geronimo the terrible. . . . The stirring climax was recorded by Hellbender in the Black Book of D.117: ". . . The ring of pick on stone and thud of earth on earth alone disturbs the peace of the prairie. An axe pried open the iron door of the tomb, and Pat[riarch] Bush entered and started to dig. We dug in turn, each on relief taking a turn on the road as guards. . . . Finally Pat[riarch] Ellery James turned up a bridle, soon a saddle horn and rotten*

leathers followed, then wood and then, at the exact bottom of the small round hole, Pat[riarch] James dug deep and pried out the trophy itself. . . . The skull was fairly clean, having only some flesh inside and a little hair."

Along with the skull, the thieves purportedly made off with Geronimo's leg bones, as well as his prized horse bridle, which had been buried with him. According to details leaked by society insiders, the items have been used in Skull and Bones rituals ever since, including an initiation rite in which inductees are compelled to kiss the skull. Interestingly, one of the six members named in the grave robbery was Prescott Bush, father to George H.W. Bush and grandfather to George W. Bush.

Ned Anderson, in an attempt to recover the items, contacted Skull and Bones, as well as the FBI and the Bush family, but ultimately got nowhere. Skull and Bones representatives did produce a case that was identical to the one in the photograph Anderson received, but the skull inside it was that of a child, leading Anderson to believe the organization was trying to pull a fast one. The society has since claimed that the above-mentioned logbook was a hoax and, although they admittedly have a skull that they refer to as Geronimo, the cranium is not actually that of the legendary Apache warrior.

In the years that followed Anderson's investigation, the matter subsided, and it remained little more than a quirky legend until 2006 when new evidence cropped up in Yale's library archives. While researching a book about World War I aviators from Yale, a writer discovered personal correspondence between two Skull and Bones members that mentioned Geronimo's bones explicitly. The letter, written on June 7, 1918, assured its recipient that the bones had been safely stored in the society's tomb.

The skull of the worthy Geronimo the Terrible, exhumed from its tomb at Fort Sill by your club & the [Knight] Haffner, is now safe inside the [Tomb] together with his well worn femurs, bit & saddle horn.

It was one of many letters in the archive discussing society affairs and, given its date, is very likely to be true, say experts. The writer of the letter was never at Fort Sill himself, so it's not proof of the bones' origin, but it shows that Skull and Bones members, who were compelled to be truthful to one another regarding society matters, indeed believed the bones to be those of Geronimo from the very beginning.

This new evidence has instigated a fresh effort to recover the bones, this time led by Geronimo's great-grandson Harlyn Geronimo. Like Anderson, he seems to have gotten nowhere. In 2006, the younger Geronimo wrote to President George W. Bush asking for help, but no one from the White House ever responded.

That shouldn't come as a surprise, though, since Skull and Bones members are sworn to secrecy, and George W. is himself a confirmed Bonesman.

Murdered by Human Wolves

One of the most mysterious gravestones in Oklahoma lies in Konawa Cemetery, a little more than an hour's drive southwest of Oklahoma City. Bearing the name Katherine Cross, the grave sits near the intersection of Highway 39 and N3500 Road, just a few feet from the U.S. flag that softly breaks the otherwise calm silence filling the graveyard.

Oddly, it's not the woman buried there who is the origin of the mystery, but the cryptic inscription on her stone, which has made her a sort of postmortem oddity. According to the epitaph, young Katherine was "murdered by human wolves."

Naturally, one wonders exactly what is meant by "human wolves." Could it mean shape-shifting skinwalkers in the form of wolves? Feral children raised by wolves? Half-human, half-wolf inbreeds? A hockey team?

The most common rumors that surround the death of eighteen-year-old however, Katherine Cross revolve around werewolves wearing cut-off pants, feasting on the blood of unsuspecting women at every full moon. A writer by the name of Steven E. Wedel has even written a novella titled "Murdered by Human Wolves" that suggests werewolf activity plagued the Konawa area at the time of Katherine's death.

According to researchers who've dug into *Seminole County News* archives, however, Katherine Cross died at the hands of Dr. A. H. Yates due to complications from a "criminal operation." Yates was arrested for performing what historians assume to have been an abortion. It was the second time he was charged with the crime, the first being two months earlier after performing another "criminal operation" on eighteen-year-old Elise Stone, who also died.

Reports indicate that a local schoolteacher, Fred O'Neal, was also arrested in connection with the botched abortion, presumably making him the plural of the "human wolves," although the extent of his involvement remains unclear.

Regardless, young Katherine's gravestone continues to be a curiosity, standing not so much as a memorial to the deceased as it does an emotionally charged grievance against those responsible for her death.

The Kiowa Cemetery Rider

The entire area surrounding the town of Hammon, located about thirty-five miles from Oklahoma's western border, is said to be a hot spot for spectral activity. It's hard to say why this particular region would be so active, but ghostly figures have reportedly been spotted frequently in this area, roaming around not only at night, but sometimes in the light of day.

No image, however, has been as prevalent as the one that appears within Kiowa Cemetery, found southwest of Hammon at the corner of E0090 Road and N2000 Road. Known as the Kiowa Cemetery Rider, he turns up just inside the graveyard's gate, beneath a lonesome shade tree. Witnesses describe him as a Native American dressed in a simple breechcloth, sitting idly on his horse.

Determining who he is or where he may come from has proven to be a difficult task. The cemetery is named for the Big and Little Kiowa creeks that flow on either side, which are themselves named for a tribe of American Indians that settled in southwestern Oklahoma in the late 1800s. However, the cemetery is not known to be a burial site for members of the Kiowa tribe.

The cemetery was established in 1899 as a free place of burial for local homesteaders. The land's owners made it available to the community after their neighbors lost their one-month-old son Tommy Hill and needed a place to lay him to rest. Since then, approximately two hundred burials have taken place here, many marked only by a simple field stone, and others not marked at all.

Oddly, one name that doesn't appear in the cemetery's register is that of William Bossa, even though his grave is clearly marked with an unusual blue stone and is not at all hard to locate. In fact, it lies just inside the cemetery gate, beneath the adjacent shade tree. Could Bossa be connected in some way to the apparition on horseback? It's possible the name has simply escaped the latest update of the register, his headstone being installed very recently, after old records of him turned up. It may not even mark his exact burial place. So, at this point, it's all conjecture.

The question remains: who is the Kiowa Cemetery Rider?

A Glow in Imo

Oklahoma is peppered with an abundance of small, out-of-the-way cemeteries. Communities that appeared and vanished in the early days of settlement left behind meager plots of a few headstones. Some lie neglected among a sea of weeds. Others are better maintained, yet still mostly forgotten.

Just a few miles southwest of Enid, along N2800 Road south of E0470 Road, lies one such burial ground, the last resting place of a long-gone community known as Imo. Its deceased took up residence here roughly between the years of 1897 and 1910.

With fewer than three dozen headstones, the unkempt cemetery isn't much to look at. Yet, like many back-road cemeteries, it has its secrets. According to a number of nighttime visitors, an otherworldly beacon shines in this dark and secluded graveyard in the form of a glowing grave marker. If you catch it at the right time, you can see the luminescent tombstone as you approach the cemetery gate. It smolders among the smattering of trees that dot this corner of rural land, enticing the curious and the intrepid to investigate its mystifying radiance. Try to get closer, though, and the stone will mysteriously extinguish.

Skeptics insist that the glow must be from lights across the street reflecting off a polished headstone, which seems like a clear-cut and perfectly valid explanation. At least it would be, if only there were any lights anywhere in the vicinity.

The Many Legends of Tucker Cemetery

No greater number of legends have ever been connected with a single graveyard. Ghost lights, spectral horsemen, even Bigfoot have, according to local stories, frequented this burial ground south of Duncan.

Tucker Cemetery sits just off N2850 Road, between Sunray and Oliver, hidden at the end of a particularly creepy gravel driveway. According to recorded epitaphs, it dates to at least 1889, back before the community in Tucker pulled up and reestablished itself at nearby Comanche to be closer to the railroad.

It's not a rich man's graveyard. The cenotaphs are humble, some improvised from aluminum mailbox letters or drawn in wet cement. Some graves are marked only with local rocks, many others with plastic pipes filled with artificial flowers. A visitor's pebble left atop one headstone reminds us that someone was here. A mysteriously charred section of ground suggests that others may have visited for nefarious purposes.

Local legend states that a headstone, now broken by vandals, once glowed just inside the gates at every full moon. On occasion, a headless horseman appears, the ghost of a local cowboy who was supposedly scalped and decapitated by Indians. He was buried in the cemetery without his head and infrequently shows up on horseback looking for his missing noggin. An old newspaper article tells about a group of boys whose car broke down by the cemetery and, as believers in the legend, were frightened off by a stray white horse, prompting them to run all the way back to Duncan.

Some visitors have told of red lights that move among the trees, chasing off unwanted guests. Others report having seen Bigfoot in the area, although in one instance, investigators discovered the hairy beast to be a cow that had wandered through the graveyard fence.

There's also the story of Old Man Tucker, who murdered his wife and children in a nearby house and buried them in his cellar. Visitors can find the ruins of said house just off the gravel driveway, which are now reportedly used as a site for pagan rituals.

In truth, however, there was never any Old Man Tucker, and the "house" was actually a school that was closed in 1957, sold to a rancher, and used to store cattle feed until it was burned by vandals in the 1970s. The cellar in question is a storm shelter that was added in 1937.

Unfortunately, this and other legends appear to be fabrications concocted several years ago by a couple of sheriff's deputies who decided to drive a group of kids out to the property around Halloween and give them a good scare. Of course, the gag backfired, turning the cemetery into a hot spot for vandals and thieves, two of whom stole entire headstones as "gifts" for their girlfriends.

However, according to stories told by those who once attended Tucker's school, there is yet another legend attached to the property, this one apparently based in truth. A previous schoolhouse, which once stood not too far away from the current ruins, was torn down after a man died on its doorstep. Around 1920, some sort of antagonism had grown between the man and a local rancher who had warned the fellow to stay off his property lest he meet the wrong end of a shotgun. The man ignored the rancher's warning and subsequently bled to death, permanently staining the schoolhouse steps. Apparently, the children needed a new school anyway, so the locals razed the whole thing and just built a new one.

Showmen's Rest

Ah, the majestic days of yore. The people who grew up in the first half of the twentieth century enjoyed simpler, more pure forms of entertainment, didn't they? Instead of iPods, they relaxed to the dulcet tones of megaphone crooners. No Xbox? No problem, as long as there was a hoop to hit with a stick. And long before NASCAR became the nation's most popular spectator event, people attended what was called the greatest show on earth.

There was a time when the country supported dozens of traveling circuses. A circus could roll into the outskirts of town in a caravan of ramshackle pickups and trailers on a Saturday morning, do a show that evening, and leave town before Sunday-morning church services. It's hard to imagine how a three-ring big top could be erected so quickly, but an efficient team of roustabouts could put up a tent or break it down in a matter of hours. Circus folk were a hardscrabble people, spending most of the year on the road. Their

only respite came when the weather was too cold in more northerly climes, when they would hunker down for the winter in Hugo, Oklahoma.

Hugo was the perfect southern home for the country's circuses. The local cotton and timber industries provoked rail service that was rather robust for such a small town, running seven passenger and freight trains in and out of Oklahoma each day. Also, the milder winter climate allowed acrobats to train and animals to thrive. From December to March every year, Hugo was where the circus folk lived, loved, and sometimes died. When a performer went to the center ring in the sky, his earthly remains stayed in Showmen's Rest.

Oklahoma's version of Showmen's Rest (the original is in Forest Park, IL at the site of the tragic Hammond Circus train wreck of 1918) occupies a section of Hugo's Mount Olivet Cemetery, and is reverently maintained. The graves are marked with some of the most visually interesting headstones the state has to offer. The body of ringmaster John Strong lies under a large granite marker with a life-size portrait of Strong in top hat and tails. The headstone of Jack B. Moore is a carved replica of a big top. A stone image of The Great Huberto depicts the deceased aerialist traipsing across a tightwire, a parasol his only means of balance.

The epitaphs of Showmen's Rest provide great insight into the psyches of the hardworking men and women of the circus. Ted Bowman's grave marker, which is shaped like a wagon wheel, proclaims, "Nothing Left but Empty Popcorn Sacks and Wagon Tracks." The headstones of concessionaires Donnie and Ione McIntosh declare, "We have had the good life, but the season ended." Perhaps the most apropos summation of the weary circus life can be found on D. R. Miller's headstone: "Dun Rovin."

Hugo still serves as the winter home for three circuses. If you make an appointment by calling (580) 326–3173 and head north of Hugo on Highway 93 toward Kirk Road, you can visit the animals, and if you're lucky, you can see a trapeze artist practicing a death-defying stunt. Who knows, maybe they'll even ask you to run away with them. *—Craig Robertson*

Parking Meter Tombstone: Time's Up!

Nobody lives forever. We all know that. Some people even say we each have our own predetermined time limit. An expiration date, if you will. Somewhere, in some existential kitchen, there's a personal egg timer counting away the minutes of your life . . . *tick tick tick tick* . . . until one day that little bell goes off and you're back to ashes and dust.

Okemah resident Barbara Sue Manire was fully aware of this fact, except she didn't go for egg timers. She chose something a little more industrial. If you drive by the front row of the Highland Cemetery in Okemah, you'll see it. About midway across the graveyard, you'll happen by her headstone, ornamented by that most bothersome and ubiquitous of regulatory devices (and, incidentally, an Oklahoma invention), the parking meter.

According to her daughter, Sherri Ann Weeks, that's what Barbara always wanted: a meter at her grave that displayed the words "time expired." So Sherri's brother Terry Heiskill located a meter on eBay, then had it restored, customized and mounted to their mother's headstone.

Appropriately, the epitaph reads, HER HUMOR LIVES ON.

As indicated by the meter's display, Barbara had precisely sixty-four years here on this earth. The little red flag went up on her birthday, April 29, 2005. If you add that up at a typical downtown Oklahoma City rate of 25¢ for every fifteen minutes, that's a total of $478,776 (excluding Sundays and holidays).

Dan Landers, the cemetery's caretaker, says the headstone has been a sightseer's destination ever since it was installed. People even try to plug the meter. No coins will fit, though; the slot's sealed up.

Strip-Mall Graveyard

There's always plenty of parking at Sand Springs' Indian cemetery. Plus, you can pick up some batteries, rent a TV, and renew your insurance policy while you're there. It's all conveniently located at Atwoods Plaza, your one-stop shopping and Native American burial center.

Though only half of the graves are marked, there are about forty known burials here, comprising a quarter-acre of the only patch of grass in sight. The rest is unadulterated progress. In every direction lay asphalt and commerce, a free-market paradise held back by a short, white fence.

How did a single swatch of sacred ground become locked in the middle of a parking lot? Well, at one time the land was home to the Creek Indians, who buried their people here between 1883 and 1912. Philanthropist Charles Page purchased the land in 1906, where he then established the town of Sand Springs as a refuge for orphans and widows. From there, Sand Springs rapidly developed as a center of commerce, becoming the industrial capital of the Southwest. So, sometime in the 1960s, what had previously been grassland and pecan groves was bulldozed and paved to make way for a strip mall, with the proviso that the cemetery be preserved. About one hundred square feet was cordoned off and spared from the cover of blacktop.

When you park, though, just keep in mind that the cemetery wasn't thoroughly surveyed before it was blocked off, so although you're outside the fence, you're still more than likely parking right on top of somebody's great-great-grandpa.

Sand Springs' Sacred Shopping Ground

There was nothing really spooky about this place, other than the fact that, well, how weird is it to have a cemetery in a parking lot?

I spoke with a few people in the area who were shopping, but surprisingly enough, most of them didn't know a lot about the cemetery. I was told by one couple that it was the family who actually started the town of Sand Springs (most of the headstones I looked at bore Indian names). Another man told me that the cemetery had been there longer than the state of Oklahoma. Imagine how foolish I felt when I walked around front and saw the sign, which clearly stated that the cemetery was established in 1883, a full twenty-four years before statehood.

The cemetery is located just off of Charles Page Boulevard and I-244. —*Colby Weaver*

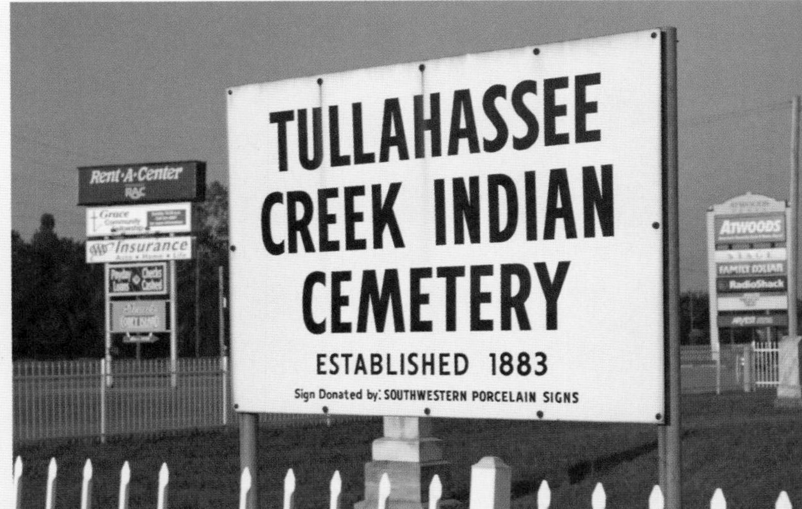

The Lucky Coffin

A restaurant might be the last place you'd expect to see a casket, but there it is. And believe it or not, it's actually a bit of a draw. People visit Waurika's Red River Cantina (at 209 N. Main Street) not only for the food, but also for a look at the famous box. More than that, they want to touch it.

You see, people believe it's lucky. Sure, a dead man's box is not something typically associated with luck—at least not good luck—but that doesn't stop people from putting their hands all over it. A quick rub and a quiet wish, and everyone feels a little more fortuitous.

It all started somewhere around 2004, give or take. According to the building's owner, Billie Porter, the previous owners uncovered the antique coffin in an old barn, cleaned it up, and propped it against the wall for ambience. Then, one day, a patron jokingly rubbed it for good luck and subsequently won the lottery. Ever since, people have been coming by to stroke it for their own helping of providence.

One of the coffin's most recent beneficiaries is a local woman who for years had trouble conceiving a child. As of this writing, she's seven months pregnant.

Billie says some people try to rub the coffin surreptitiously, hoping no one will notice. Others proudly announce their intentions. As far as results go, it doesn't seem to matter either way. Regardless, Billie's advice is to walk right up, rub it just below the window, and quietly make your desires known. Oh, and your request has to be realistic. No wishing for extended space missions with a crew of amorous supermodels or anything.

By the way, if talk of stroking an old corpse carton isn't enough to creep you out, Billie offers another story. One evening, a family was dining at the table right next to the box when their little boy asked about the man inside. Billie explained that he's Lucky Joe and is just an old dummy, not an actual person. But the little boy kept insisting he was real. When Billie asked what made the boy think Joe was a real person, he replied, "Because he told me he is."

Every visit since, the family has sat on the other side of the restaurant.

A Horse Is a Corpse, of Course, of Course

The five-foot grave marker depicts the television star in his trademark pose, sticking his head out of a barn door. No, it's not Roy Clark. Born with the name Bamboo Harvester, it's the famous Mister Ed who now rests amid a grassy Oklahoma field.

After the 143-episode TV series ended in 1966, horse trainer Clarence Tharp purchased Mister Ed at auction in California. Tharp retired to Tahlequah, with his Mister Ed entertaining local children with his Tinseltown tricks. The horse died in 1979 at the age of 33, which is equivalent to 140 for a human.

To celebrate the famous equine, the fine people of Tahlequah once held Edstock, an event that raised the funds for the large tombstone that stands today. Not long after, the rural community was rocked by the news that the Tahlequah grave might not contain the "real" Mister Ed.

Some said that thirty-three is simply too old for a horse, even though Roy Rogers's trusty Trigger, another palomino, died at that age. But then Alan Young, the actor who played Mister Ed's longtime TV companion, Wilbur Post, told a radio interviewer that the horse had died in 1970 of an accidental tranquilizer overdose.

According to a regional conspiracy theory, the Hollywood studio bosses kept the death of Mister Ed a secret for years because the show had become a hit in reruns. Apparently, CBS used a different palomino as a Mister Ed doppelganger for advertising and publicity photos in the early 1970s, and it's possible that Tharp purchased this second horse. The once-peaceful town of Tahlequah is now composed of two bitter factions: one consisting of those who believe Mister Ed rests locally, and a second consisting of those who believe the town merely contains the grave of an impostor.

Either way, we at *Weird Oklahoma* see it this way: Multiple dogs have played Lassie, and none of them are considered "false" Lassies. Therefore, we say Tahlequah is indeed the final resting place of everyone's favorite talking horse. So we encourage you to stop by and leave a sugar cube or two. *—Craig Robertson*

You can find the grave of Mister Ed on land now owned by the Carroll family. It's located in a field behind the Carrolls' house on the north side of Moody's Curve, a sharp turn in Highway 82 five miles north of Tahlequah. The Carrolls welcome visitors to pay tribute to America's most beloved horse but ask that you keep the hours reasonable and let them know you're there before wandering around.

Russell Carroll believes the horse was a second Mister Ed that took over the role after the first one became too old to continue acting. *—Wesley Treat*

Abandoned Oklahoma

The growing phenomenon known as urban exploration—or "urbex" as the cool kids call it—offers an exciting adventure through modern ruins, remnants of failed businesses, or a whole community gone belly-up. Such locations present a fascinating journey into the recent past, an adventure in urban archaeology that conjures nostalgic thoughts of life in a time not so distant, yet wholly disconnected from our own.

Aged only a few years, or entire decades, these vestiges of civilization left to the elements show us just how quickly one's legacy can fade. Yet, for those in the know, the few deteriorating relics that remain present a reminder of the stories left behind, too—stories of tragedy, of ghosts, and of people who were once very much like us.

Concho Indian School

One of the most extensive urban abandonments in the state lies just a few miles west of Oklahoma City, along Black Kettle Boulevard in Concho. The former Concho Indian School consists of a dense cluster of school rooms, administration buildings, dormitories, dining and exercise facilities, and outbuildings, all completely deserted and falling to pieces.

The school had served its final decade in these buildings before it suddenly lost funding and shut down in 1983. Before that, Concho Indian School had been a place of learning for nearly a century, educating local Arapaho and Cheyenne children.

Although a number were glad for the opportunities the school provided, many, especially the Cheyenne, initially viewed the school with disdain. In their early days, boarding schools like this one were used to "civilize" Native American children, encouraging or forcing them to put their culture behind them and to shed their spiritual beliefs in favor of Christianity. Discipline tended to be very strict. Children were often forbidden from speaking their native tongues and were guaranteed punishment if they defied the rule.

In more recent decades, however, the Concho school had become a valuable asset to the Arapaho and Cheyenne tribes, who vehemently fought its closure. Unfortunately, there was simply no money available to continue operations. Hoping to make the best of things, the Arapaho-Cheyenne Nation retained ownership of the site with plans to repurpose the buildings for business ventures, but after nearly thirty years, the structures remain vacant, their walls covered in mold or charred from fire damage.

The site has since become a popular destination among ghost hunters. Paranormal researchers and psychic investigators both have said Concho Indian School is one of the most spiritually active locations they've experienced in Oklahoma. Visitors have witnessed strange shadows darting among the

already darkened hallways, as well as unusual lights and luminescent apparitions. In the gym, some hear the sound of a bouncing basketball, even though no equipment remains. People have also described disembodied growls and footsteps, and several visitors have reported speaking with the spirit of a bygone caretaker who is generally upset with those who've dared trespass.

There are rumors of many children dying of disease here after being denied proper care in the school's early days, allegedly the reason for so much unusual activity. Some say there's also a burial ground right next to one of the site's water towers. Sounds of children talking and laughing are common, heard from other rooms, or from just feet away, as if coming from some youngster tagging along beside investigators. Sometimes, a child is seen as clear as day, running from one room to another, only to disappear when followed.

Even without a supernatural encounter, though, the old buildings still impart an acute spookiness. Having been vacated with such apparent haste, relics of everyday life fill the deserted spaces. Filing cabinets full of old records stand waiting to be used. Chairs line the walls and obsolete computer equipment remains stacked in the corner. In the kitchen, industrial appliances gather dust while five-foot stacks of cafeteria trays fend off ivy that has somehow found its way inside. A net still clings to one of the gymnasium's basketball hoops.

It's as if the inhabitants had just stepped away for a moment and then forgot to come back. That, or some nightmarish event had spontaneously eradicated humankind. Stay too long and you might start to think that every horror movie you've ever seen had suddenly come true.

The Island

The Island is like a post-apocalyptic nightmare. Cut off from the rest of the world, it's an easy reminder of what life will be like once the human race has eradicated itself and the earth is starting over from scratch. Only traces of civilization remain and even the most durable of structures are quickly succumbing to the deceptively powerful tenacity of foliage.

Often referred to by the locals as simply "the ghost town," this enormous patch of land lies just west of Guthrie's downtown district, entirely isolated by a cutoff of Cottonwood Creek. Although many otherwise up-to-date maps will hoodwink you into thinking you can still get there via Perkins Avenue or Ninth Street, access to the old neighborhood, at least by car, has long been impossible thanks to the scrubbing power of floodwaters. The bridges are gone. Only by crossing a ruddy, and often dangerous, tributary on foot can one penetrate the Island's borders.

It's hard to believe the place was once inhabited, and very recently. The streets have now been virtually swallowed up by nature. Only short, random patches of asphalt remain visible, bleeding up through the soil. To find the roadways, you have to pay attention to the tree line. If you're lucky, you might spot part of an old fence or maybe a fire hydrant for orientation.

The Island has been populated at various times in recent history, but without exhaustive research, it's hard to tell just when and for how long. Due to its geography, Guthrie is highly susceptible to flooding, which often divides the town in two, sometimes multiple times in a single year. It's this tendency toward deluge that's wiped out civilization on the Island on more than one occasion.

According to some locals, the last exodus was in the mid-1990s. Unrelenting rains drove the Cottonwood far above flood stage, damaging roads and bridges, and destroying homes along the flood zone. Ever since, this area of southwestern Guthrie has remained conspicuously desolate.

TVs and refrigerators lie everywhere. Kitchen appliances poke out through buckled walls. Bottles, furniture, and toys cover the ground. Here an old mailbox, there a child's wading pool.

To the east, majestic stone ruins tower above the trees. Although it's most likely a former church, the local youth now refer to it as the Castle, a place where pagans supposedly practice clandestine rituals, leaving behind occult symbols on the walls and foundation.

Farther into the Island's interior, residential buildings barely remain standing. One house, its floor verging on collapse, is strewn with shoes. Scattered sheds lean in Burtonesque fashion, their corrugated roofs slowly

corroding. Back in the street, the odd manhole threatens to swallow adventurers in a single gulp.

Sadly, this isn't the first time the area has looked like this. The remains that lie here today are a fresh reminder of an event that occurred a hundred years earlier, when a devastating swell overtook the Cottonwood valley in 1897. According to reports, a mile-wide wall of water six to eight feet high swept through Guthrie, destroying about 650 homes, damaging farms, bridges, and railways, and leaving some two thousand residents homeless. The *New York Times* reported on many of those who lost their lives:

> *A woman with a babe in her arms desperately tried to steady herself in a treetop, calling the while for help. She grew weak and the baby slipped into the water and was drowned. . . . A woman wading from home with a baby on her head was seen to go under, and a man swimming the channel to reach four women and a baby in a tree was carried down stream. Two women and a child were carried away on a bridge further down stream, and one man and two women, in plain sight of shore, were on a house roof when it went to pieces. They all perished.*

Though today's ruins are a feeble testament to the 1897 disaster, one can't help but be reminded of the disturbing aftermath that must have resulted a century ago. The homes, the clothes, and the myriad personal items that litter the ground tell a patchy story of those who once lived here. Standing in the isolation of the Island, between the horn blasts of the nearby train line, you can almost hear them.

My Little Haunted Hospital on the Prairie

There used to be this old, abandoned hospital here in Oklahoma City. It was built in the late 1800s, and it was the original Mercy Hospital. It was abandoned in the 1960s and a new Mercy was built. The old building was very frightening. All the windows were knocked out, and even in the daytime the inside was pitch-black. All one had to do was walk past it to get a whiff of its musty, hospitally, old-building smell. Anyway, last summer me and my friend Jeff were out wandering the streets like good little delinquents, and we ended up near the hospital. We had the brilliant idea to go inside and explore. We crawled through a one-square-foot hole in the fence, and got in the actual building through the incinerator room.

The whole time we were in there, we kept hearing sounds, like someone on another floor or something.

The moment we got inside, I nearly crapped my pants. The place was full of debris, and the smell sent chills up my spine. It smelled like the doctor's office from hell. Old, musty, and SCARY. Just being inside the place gave me this weird threatening feeling and I wanted to scream. I felt like I was going insane the whole time we were in there. I think maybe they kept some mental patients in there when it was still in use.

We started out in the basement, where we found this underground room that was flooded with this white water, and I swear I saw shapes moving around in it. While we were down there staring at the water, this icy-cold breeze started blowing on us. It was strange because it was the middle of summer, and it had been hot down there just a second ago, and this place, having been abandoned for over thirty years, had no air-conditioning. It felt like we were sitting in front of an open freezer!

We got the hell out of the basement. We made our way up, and there were these endless corridors with rooms on either side. We went in some of the rooms, and the old, smashed-up toilets all had shit in them. We wandered around for at least an hour, trying to find the X-ray room and the morgue. We didn't find either, though I think that flooded room was probably the morgue. We found the cafeteria and the old triage and medicine dispensing area. By the way, the whole time we were in there, we kept hearing sounds, like someone on another floor or something. There were these geometric paintings on the walls. I swear the whole damn place was something out of a horror movie. I was waiting for a crazy, syringe-wielding dead doctor to jump out at me.

There was all kinds of graffiti all over the place. We eventually wandered into a room where we found a bunch of unopened cans of food. We decided to get out of there then, since the bum who owned those cans would probably be back soon, and would not be too happy to find a couple of kids messing with his dinner. Anyway, we crawled back out and went home for the night. I've been back there a couple times, once last Thanksgiving, and around February they tore it down, all except the parking garage and the incinerator's chimney. That place was scary as all hell, and I'm gonna miss it. —*Kristy Cox*

Logan County Memorial Hospital

Located just north of Oklahoma City in Guthrie is the Logan County Memorial Hospital. Construction began in 1927 under the name of the Methodist Episcopal Church of Oklahoma. In 1931 the hospital was sold, initiating a series of name changes and owners. In 1972, the doors to the hospital closed and was soon overrun with local teenagers looking for a place to party. Soon after, reports of paranormal activity started to surface. Included were apparitions on the third floor, strange sounds, and a feeling of doom that looms over any visitor, which becomes stronger when anyone dares take a picture.

In the fall of 2007, I visited the hospital along with fellow team members of a local paranormal group to investigate the premises. We entered the hospital in the lunchroom area of the old hospital. Upon adjusting to my surroundings, I went from floor to floor. While walking through the hallway of the third floor, I watched what appeared to be a form move from a door and into a room. Upon entering the room, I noticed that it was an odd bathroom with what seemed to be a cot shoved in one stall. The room, I discovered, was once used for doctors to rest when not treating patients.

I felt my head being drawn to a window which had only a little of the original glass left in the wood. I soon felt my shirt being pulled—and not lightly. It felt as if I were being yanked towards the window. When I got close, I felt a cold wind start to swirl around my body. The pulling ceased, but a very warm sensation started up my arm. Oddly, the hotter my arm became the colder the wind would feel around the rest of my body. When it all seemed to stop, I escaped back into the hall.

There, I spotted a shadowy figure looming around a wall, and it watched me until I shined my flashlight in its direction. Dropping the light, I gave chase, thinking that someone had entered the hospital without permission and

LOGAN COUNT
MEMORIAL
HOSPITAL

was trying to scare me or harm me in some way. When I reached the area where the figure was standing, I rounded a curve only to run into a wall.

A few days after the investigation I spoke with the building's caretakers and discovered that the feeling I experienced of wind wrapping my body is not uncommon. It's actually associated in some way with a little boy that supposedly died there choking on a piece of wood.

The third floor does seem to be the hottest spot as far as activity is concerned. Observers from the outside have seen figures moving between the windows on that floor on more than one occasion, although they sometimes point to the second floor, as well, where other team members have themselves heard footsteps with no apparent source.

Unfortunately, access to the hospital is highly restricted, and it's pretty well sealed up. However, investigators have rigged the building with video cameras and microphones, and keep the property under continuous surveillance in an effort to capture any activity as it happens. Plus, they've made the video feed accessible live on the Web at www.researchwebcam.net, where the curious can investigate from the safety of their own homes.

—Charles Carter

All Aboard the Train to Nowhere

Whistling in the wind and acquiring a lovely orange patina sits a unique abandonment out behind Guthrie's old Santa Fe depot. Formerly part of the Dodge City Ford and Bucklin Railroad, three train cars, which date to around the 1930s, sit forsaken and forlorn.

The cars were originally part of a plan to establish an excursion train between Guthrie and Fairmont, and possibly as far as Enid, but since the cars found their way to Guthrie around the year 2000, they've just been sitting there, growing more and more dilapidated.

The adjacent depot itself, which was completed in 1903, has seen better luck. It had been sitting vacant since 1979, but has since been completely refurbished and now houses a model-train museum, as well as a diner that serves some of the best burgers in the region. It was one of three historic depots to receive state funds in the hope of creating the longest excursion-train route in the United States.

Due to unending difficulties, however, the rail tour has yet to materialize. The Oklahoma Transportation Department deeded the necessary line for the project, but some $600,000 was still needed to restore it and the four flood-damaged bridges along the way. Additionally, there was mass disagreement on how far the train should go, not to mention the problem of where the engine would come from and who exactly would operate the thing.

And then there are those cars, which themselves have become part of an FBI fraud investigation. In 2007, the *Oklahoman* reported that a state senator acquired the $300,000 necessary to purchase a train, shortly after which he announced that—lucky day!—he had found one to buy. After the sale was complete, evidence surfaced that the train belonged to a company in which the senator was a silent partner. In other words, the senator had used taxpayer money to sell off his own train.

So, more than fifteen years after the idea was originally floated, the plan has come to a screeching halt. A passenger coach, one of the reported seven cars that were originally acquired, has since been sold to a museum in Oklahoma City for restoration, but three—a lounge car, a dining car, and a power-generating car—remain next to the Guthrie depot.

DODGE CITY FORD AND BUCKLIN RAILROAD
DINING CAR
138

Camp Scott

Just off State Road 82, southeast of Locust Grove, a locked and rusted gate marks the threshold to a dark patch of woods that, though long neglected, has never been forgotten. It's the former site of Camp Scott, a several-hundred-acre forest that, for nearly fifty years, served as a summer campsite for young Girl Scouts looking to meet new friends and maybe share a few tips on how to read a compass or start a campfire.

Then, on a rain-soaked morning in 1977, camp counselors discovered the bodies of three of their scouts lying together beneath a large tree. The girls had been dragged for more than a hundred yards from their tent, gagged and bound with electrical tape, sexually assaulted, and beaten to death. As law enforcement officers descended on the scene, the surviving campers were immediately evacuated and the camp sealed up.

More than thirty years later, remnants of Camp Scott still stand. Various buildings, though suffering from weather and age, remain almost completely intact. Screen fabric still clings to the former picnic area, now swallowed by weeds and saplings. A large swimming pool, now empty of anything but the occasional rainwater, reflects the sun with a blinding glare. Down a tangential path sits a large red barn, once a spot for preteen girls to play hide-and-seek.

Largest among Camp Scott's ruins is the main hall, its resilient brick

shell standing out among the trees. Little remains there, save for corroded appliances, a rotten couch, and a couple of old wagons that years ago may have carried a scout or two on a midnight hayride. Although the walls show virtually no age, the building's doors have recently suffered enough decay to provide little resistance against the elements, exposing the hall's interior to the slow destructive forces of wind and rain. Smaller, yet more poignant, a wooden kiosk just yards away marks what was probably the camp's bulletin board, which once displayed the hand-typed leaflets announcing meal times and a list of the day's activities, a meeting place for scouts to convene each morning to plan their day and trade stories.

And this is how the campsite has remained for more than three decades, shut down since the day Lori Lee Farmer, age eight, Michele Guse, age nine, and Doris Denise Milner, age ten, were found dead. A dark atmosphere yet looms over the site, an unsettling mood that has never been lifted by justice. To this day, the slayings remain mysteries.

Though one man was tried for the murders—a convicted rapist and escaped convict named Gene Leroy Hart—he was acquitted of the crimes. Many believe he was indeed the girls' killer, but despite several increasingly sophisticated DNA tests over the years, nothing has ever been proven. Moreover, Hart died years ago of an apparent heart attack while completing a previous sentence, leaving us with unanswered questions. As far as anyone knows, the guilty party may still be out there. And so, the murders continue to weigh heavily on the slain girls' families and upon the residents of Mayes County.

As for the Camp Scott property itself, it now lies in private hands and is leased to both resident caretakers who enthusiastically guard against trespassers as well as to hunters who take advantage of the overgrowth in their search for game. So, although it appears Camp Scott will remain a tangible record of this disturbing tragedy for some time to come, it's a decidedly treacherous place for any would-be explorers looking to witness the scene for themselves.

Clay Hall

Looking like some sort of flat-pack, self-assembled building for a do-it-yourself university, the defunct Clay Hall on Enid's Lakeview Drive appears almost as if it's never been used. Even though it's been vacant for decades, the structure's drab brick walls are surprisingly devoid of graffiti and its windows remain meticulously sealed with cream-painted plywood, giving it a look of soulless catatonia.

Despite the stale odor of lifelessness wafting up from the grated cellar windows, many visitors have reported figures deftly moving about the building's corners, sometimes motioning witnesses to follow. Others describe unusual sounds coming from the basement. The rattle of keys, the reverberations of unidentified objects crashing to the floor, and a strange sound like that of metal being twisted all emanate from below, despite there being no apparent point of access. Some have even heard the sound of a piano playing, occasionally accompanied by singing.

Formerly part of Phillips University, Clay Hall served as a women's dormitory until it was closed around the 1980s. Shortly thereafter, thanks to continuing financial trouble, the entire school suffered the same fate. The property was then bought up by Northern Oklahoma College, and although it now serves as a satellite campus for NOC, sources report that mold, lead paint, and asbestos prevent the old dorm from being utilized along with the rest of the property grounds.

A security guard we found patrolling the area said he hadn't witnessed much of anything around Clay Hall, but he's "seen some pretty weird stuff" nonetheless. Although he had been working there only a few months, he'd encountered the same mysterious figure on more than one occasion skulking around in some of the building's old fallout shelters. He described the figure as an older man, maybe in his sixties, with short, gray hair, sporting a beard and glasses. At first, the guard thought he might be a vagrant, but he didn't appear down on his luck. "It was weird," he told me. "He always had [the same] gray suit on."

The mysterious gentleman was usually seen in the basement of the old science building where, according to the guard, they used to keep cadavers for teaching purposes. "It was basically a morgue down there. They had a freezer area for them. . . . You go down there and you get a weird feeling. It's just someplace you don't want to be in." Oddly, the whole place is locked up, so there's no reason the guard should have seen anyone else moving about down there at all.

Still, the old man appears to get around. A maintenance worker once reported seeing the same gray-haired chap in the darkened basement of a neighboring building. The men both turned a corner at the same time, startling the handyman so badly he fell to the ground. When he looked up, the old man had vanished.

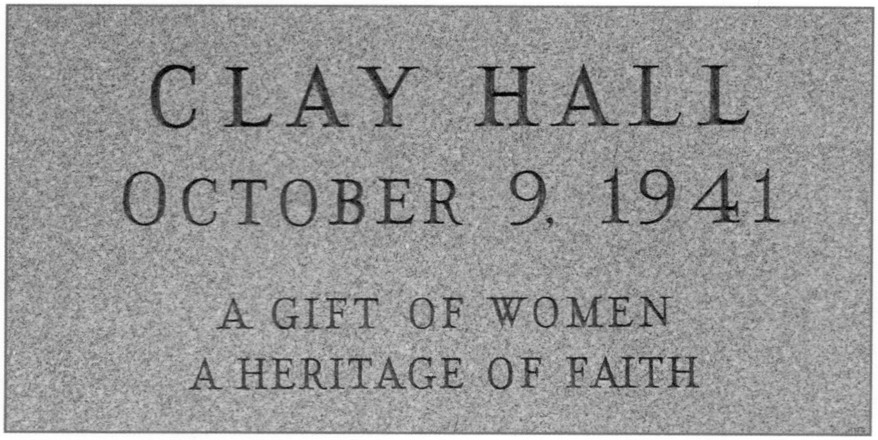

CLAY HALL
OCTOBER 9, 1941

A GIFT OF WOMEN
A HERITAGE OF FAITH

Wheelock Mission and Academy

In 1832, Reverend Alfred Wright and his wife Harriet, missionaries to Native Americans in Mississippi, followed the Choctaws on the Trail of Tears in their forced migration to the Oklahoma Territory. When they arrived, they set up a new missionary operation in what is now Millerton, in the southeast corner of the state.

Reverend Wright held services under an oak tree, preaching from behind a wooden barrel until he could construct a proper church. Meanwhile, Harriet Wright

established a small day school for the Choctaw children, which eventually grew into a boarding school for girls. The boys were moved to their own academy at Clear Creek.

After suffering a fire in 1869, Wheelock Academy was rebuilt in 1882, but eventually shut down in 1955. Since then, the buildings have been allowed to deteriorate despite several endeavors to save them.

Today, efforts to resuscitate the Wheelock structures continue, but caretakers have made little progress. Pushmataha Hall, the academy's dormitory and centerpiece, is a sad version of what it once was, its wooden facade warped, peeling, and covered with dead ivy. The Art and Domestic Science cottages, where girls learned crafts and homemaking skills, had deteriorated so badly by 1980 that they had to be demolished, leaving only their stone chimneys, which now stick up from the ground like triple sore thumbs. The laundry building is gone, as well, save for its foundation and a conspicuous row of rusting, open-air washbasins. What's left has been declared one of the eleven most endangered historical sites in the United States.

Most of the properties are fenced off, but they are not without their appeal, not only for photographers, but especially for myth hounds. Storytellers relay tales of mistreatment of students by academy instructors, beating them for misconduct, sometimes so brutally that the thrashings proved fatal. Many girls, they say, were buried secretly on school grounds. At one point, an unidentified man allegedly forced his way into the dormitory and brutally slaughtered several girls.

Visitors claim to have witnessed apparitions among the buildings, notably those of former students peeking out from windows and dancing in the moonlight. Phantom adults have reportedly appeared as well, and have been assumed to be former teachers and groundskeepers, who sometime run off unwanted trespassers.

Down a dirt road to the west stands Reverend Wright's former Rock Church, completed in 1846. It's fared better over the years, having been restored in the 1970s, and stands today as one of the oldest church buildings in Oklahoma. It, too, has its stories. Legend says one of the former preachers hanged himself from the enormous tree behind the church and can be seen at night still swinging from one of the branches. (Some say it's Reverend Wright himself, who's buried in the adjacent cemetery, but history says he died of failing health due to bursitis and a chronic heart condition.) Plus, once a year—on Halloween, according to many—the surrounding trees ooze blood.

If you're an aspiring ghost chaser or urban explorer, Wheelock Academy would be a good place to start. With a museum onsite, curators are available to provide information and personal tours.

Picher, Oklahoma: Poison City

The West is littered with ghost towns. Formerly bustling communities went belly-up when the local industry, usually mining or drilling, dried up, leaving no money and no reason for anyone to stay. In Oklahoma, places like Ingalls, Boggy Depot, and Provine, among dozens of others, offer little more than a few scattered buildings, perhaps a cemetery, and a handful of fading memories.

A tour through these old communities can be an exciting and enjoyable adventure into urban exploration. It's an entirely different experience, however, to see a ghost town in the making. Picher (pronounced "pisher"), tucked away in the northeastern corner of the state, is a community in the spasmodic throes of death, just a few rattled breaths from the end. A town that just a few decades ago buzzed with the activity of twenty thousand Oklahomans now houses just a few hundred. Its main street is lined with vacant businesses,

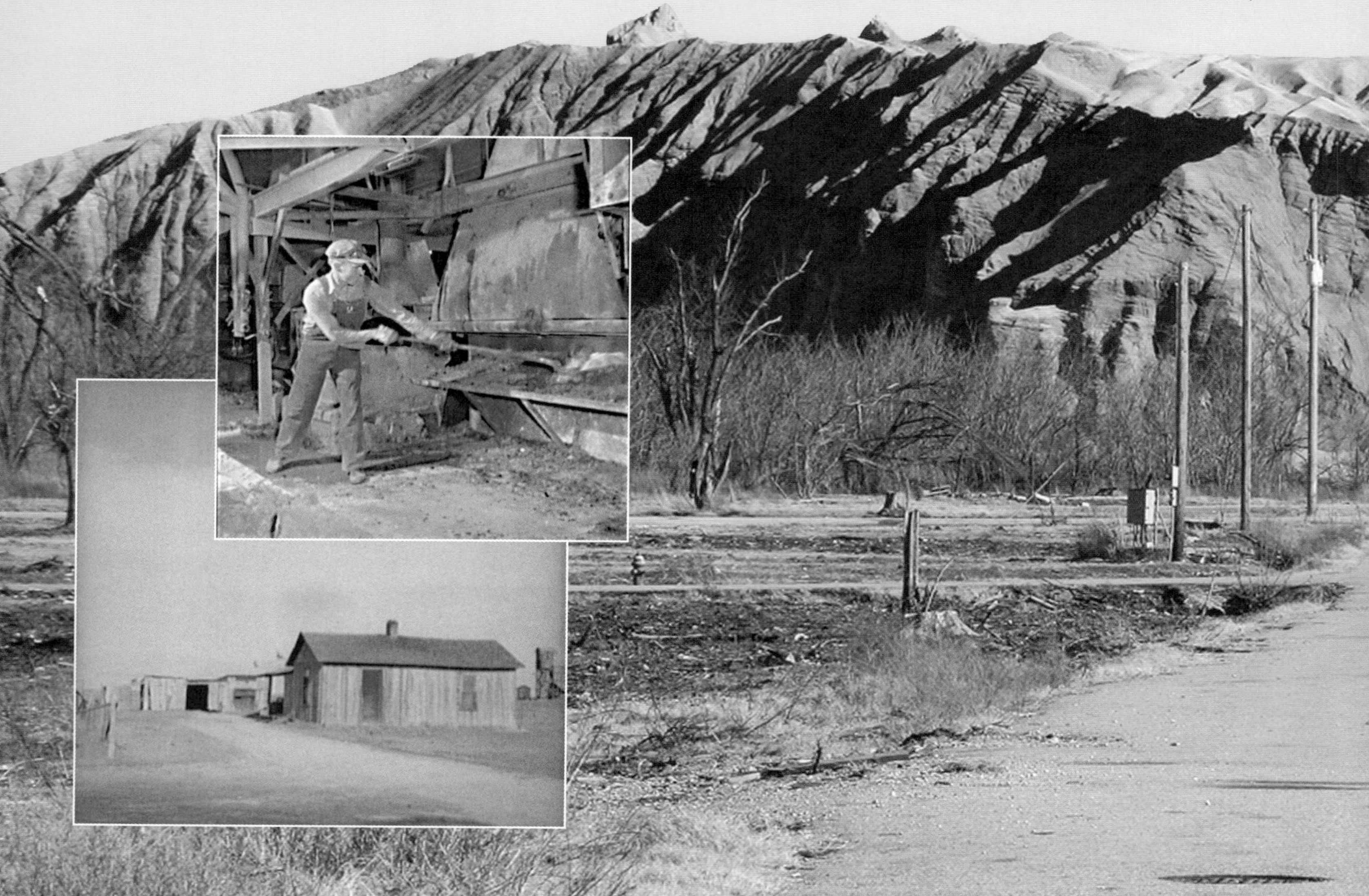

and the outer walls of unoccupied buildings display notices marking them as "condemned."

A pass through its tranquil streets reveals the reason why. Picher is a town literally poisoned by its own success. What might appear at first to be gravelly hills are actually massive piles of contaminated chat, the polluted remains from years of lead and zinc mining. The tainted mounds, some measuring as much as a hundred feet high, fill nearly every available space between homes and businesses.

And where there aren't piles, there are sinkholes. The abandoned tunnels that crisscross just feet beneath Picher's sod are collapsing, opening up cavities large enough to ingest entire houses. In 1967, a single collapse swallowed nine homes in a single gulp. A hundred more, according to a study performed in 2006, are in eminent danger of the same fate. Residents report a daily rumbling beneath the earth. Cave-ins have become such a hazard that the highway into town has been closed to heavy trucks and the city park

has been fenced off lest the ground consume Picher's few remaining children.

Lead-contaminated dust blows through town, breathed in by the residents who have yet to move away. Nearby Tar Creek runs orange with acidic water seeping from the mines. The ponds that dot the landscape glimmer with a strange, blue-green hue. Before anyone knew better, the enormous chat piles were used for sledding, biking, and picnicking. In the 1990s, a frightening study revealed elevated levels of lead in the blood of Picher's schoolchildren. It's been called "one of the worst environmental nightmares in the country."

The mines closed in the 1970s, and soon thereafter Picher and about forty surrounding acres were recognized by the U.S. government as a toxic hazard. The area, cleanup of which has proceeded at the pace of a nauseated snail, remains one of the oldest and largest Superfund sites in the nation. Recent property buyouts, however, have helped in moving many of the remaining residents out of harm's way.

As if to drive another nail into Picher's coffin, a devastating tornado tore through the town on May 10, 2008. There were six confirmed deaths and at least 150 injured. Twenty blocks of the town suffered extensive damage with houses and businesses destroyed or flattened. The twister continued eastward, passing just north of Quapaw and Peoria before crossing Interstate 44 into Missouri. This was the deadliest tornado in Oklahoma

since the South Oklahoma City tornado of May 3, 1999, which killed thirty-six. The federal government determined that there would be no aid given to rebuild homes, but the buyouts would continue as previously scheduled and people would be assisted in relocation.

When Picher held a parade in the spring of 2008 in honor of the town's ninetieth birthday, only about eight hundred people were left. Save for the few predictable holdouts who refuse to leave their homes on account of a little "harmless" tangerine-colored drinking water, that number is destined to reach zero before long.

INDEX

ACKNOWLEDGMENTS

As always, thanks first and foremost to Mom and Dad for their support. And, of course, thanks to the Marks for another fantastic opportunity to add to the Weird series and for their seemingly endless patience in my getting the job done. Thanks also to all my fans and friends for their perpetual help and interest, especially to Christian, Stephanie, Craig and Colleen for constantly asking, "So, how's the book coming?" even though the question was usually filled with subtle ridicule.

Finally, I'd like to thank all the hospitable Sooners who overlooked my place of origin long enough to share with me all their fantastic stories and creations, and help advance my cause to finally bring Texas and Oklahoma together.

PICTURE CREDITS

All photos and illustrations by the author or public domain except as indicated below:
Page 7 George Sozio; 28 Peggy Davis/Creative Commons; 26 Eironymous Rowe/Creative Commons; 39 bottom © *The Oklahoman* 1969; 45 istockphoto.com/DNY59; 48–49 background istockphoto.com/billnoll; 50 © *The Oklahoman* 1969; 53 istockphoto.com/Immortal-Bliss; 54 istockphoto.com/Rebekkah_ann; 58 background illustration Mark Moran, bottom inset © Jill Reed; 59 left © istockphoto.com/MDK Graphics; 61 Ryan Doan/www.RyanDoan.com; 65–66 © istockphoto.com/MDK Graphics; 70–71 © istockphoto.com/Clint Spencer; 75 Mark Moran; 77 © Jill Reed; 78 right Ryan Doan; 79 background Ryan Doan, inset © Cathy Wilkins; 80 Ryan Doan; 83 Mark Moran; 84 © Cathy Wilkins; 85 Ryan Doan; 86–87 Ryan Doan; 90–91 Ryan Doan; 96 istockphoto.com/davidf; 100 © Colby Weaver; 103 istockphoto.com/deanmillar; 109 © istockphoto.com/Dan Leap; 154 top © Henry Jewell; 167–168 © Henry Jewell; 171 background © Robyn Meade; 174–175 © Robyn Meade; 178 © David Stapleton/Creative Commons; 182–185 © James Mazza, courtesy Becky Luker/stonelioninnphotoalbum.com; 203 bottom right © Johanna Jacky-Brinkman/moonlightcocktailjohanna.blogspot.com; 228–229 background © Johanna Jacky-Brinkman; 230–231 © Johanna Jacky-Brinkman.

SHOW US YOUR WEIRD!

Do you know of a weird site found somewhere in the United States, or can you tell us about a strange experience you've had? If so, we'd like to hear about it! We believe that every town has at least one great tale to tell, and we're listening. It could be a cursed road, haunted abandoned site, odd local character, or bizarre historic event. In most cases these tales are told only in the towns in which they originated. But why keep them to yourself when you could share them with all of America? So come on and fill us in on all the weirdness that's lurking in your backyard!

You can e-mail us at: Editor@WeirdUS.com,
or write to us at:
Weird U.S., P.O. Box 1346, Bloomfield, NJ 07003.

www.weirdus.com